ALSO BY LIZ CARPENTER

Ruffles and Flourishes

GETTING

BETTER ALL THE TIME

Liz Carpenter

SIMON AND SCHUSTER · NEW YORK

Published by Simon and Schuster
A Division of Simon & Schuster, Inc.
Simon & Schuster Building
Rockefeller Center
1230 Avenue of the Americas
New York, New York 10020
SIMON AND SCHUSTER and colophon are
registered trademarks of Simon & Schuster, Inc.
Designed by Edith Fowler
Manufactured in the United States of America

10 9 8 7 6 5 4 3 2 1

Library of Congress Cataloging-in-Publication Data

Carpenter, Liz.
* Getting better all the time.*

1. Carpenter, Liz.   2. Journalists—United States—
Biography.   3. Feminists—United States—Biogra-
phy. I. Title.
PN4874.C253A3 1987   070'.92'4 [B] 87-4802
ISBN: 0-671-61157-7

Title page photo: The Grand Rapids Press
Page 11 bottom photo: Tennessee State Museum,
Tennessee Historical Society Collection

Acknowledgments and Thanks

THERE ARE many ingredients that make a book: idea, agent, publisher, editor, and a variety of people who believe in you, shove you, encourage you, and make themselves available to help.

I am forever grateful to a mother who inspired me to love words; to the droll Dickensian agent, Aaron Priest, who called one day and said, "Erma Bombeck says you have a book in you and I must come to Austin and extract it from you. I will be there Thursday at the Driskill Hotel, and you will have an outline awaiting me. Then we'll go to lunch and talk it over." He did and I did, and before you could say Simon and Schuster, their talented executive editor, Alice Mayhew was on the phone to start the process.

My children, Scott and Christy, grown up and living in Seattle and New York, were ecstatic: "Go for it, Mom!" So began the process— word process, a new word in my dictionary. After a turbulent introduction, a strong sense of guilt in saying good-bye to my lifelong friend, my upright manual Underwood, which has served me so well for fifty years, I married Big Mac, who, as promised, increased my productivity. Oh, he lost a few things for me but finally taught me—when in doubt, punch Save.

So many special friends believed in me and helped:

• The irreverent *Texas Monthly*, which published and received a warm response to an article about growing old with grace and humor. A perceptive young editor, Dominique Browning, said words I was to hear over and over during the next few months: "My mother needs to read this." So did publisher Mike Levy and editor-in-chief Gregory Curtis, who made me feel that I had said something very special to their readers.

7

• A battery of understanding new friends and old ones, whose judgment I treasured while reserving the right to discard it in favor of my own.

• My neighbor and ally, Henrietta Jacobsen, a believer in dictionaries. She also has an antenna that detected when I needed cheering up, and, having once been an executive at the University of Texas, she executed whatever I lacked: groceries or grammar. And laughter.

• Christie Bourgeois, a history and graduate student who is hell on wheels at the word processor and can patiently master its idiosyncrasies as well as mine. Her willingness to rise eagerly and smilingly was invaluable, as she deciphered my imperfect disks at yet a second word processor set up in the solarium.

• A lovely and ever-polite assistant, Julie Hale, and a delightful young artist from Arkansas, Jayme Huff, both breezed through my life in the early writing and brought their talented hands to my telephone, word processor, and kitchen. I wore them out too soon. One became a travel agent and headed for Peru, the other turned home to Arkansas and meditation.

• Betty Sue Flowers, a blithe literary spirit who lives in the nearby woods, and Anita Brewer Howard, a longtime newspaper friend who shared my generation, romance of reporting, and the heartbreak of widowhood. Both stood by with advice and encouragement. Sally Muehlberger sorted out what I laughingly call "my papers." Two cousins, Becky and Charles McCarthy, waded through tons of letters to separate wheat from chaff.

• My friend and off-and-on assistant over the years, Shirley James, who deserves and prefers other careers to helping me, spunkily came when called. She knows my past and my present, my friends, my files, and my weaknesses as well as anyone, and she makes it all work for me. Shirley juggled the phone calls and demands of my various lives while jumping in to learn the word processor as the manuscript grew.

• Sue Drake, whom I have known for fifty-two years, since we met as second-graders, helped revive my memory with childhood pictures as well as gathering together our old crowd to, as the song goes, *try* to remember.

• And in the final countdown, it was my "little sister" from Alpha Phi, Jean Begeman Bergmark, who came from Atlanta to prod all of our battered crew and whip the final product into the best possible shape for the publisher. She gave me two weeks of her life, a large gift for a sixty-two-year-old newlywed.

My bounty was a family that saved letters, bills—paid and un-paid—and old contracts, recipes, personal accounts of their lives dating before the Texas Revolution. When Alice Mayhew decided they were part of the story, I found a treasure trove at the great University of Texas collections. Five feet of Sutherland papers at the Eugene Barker Collection, an entire room of Sterling Clack Robertson papers at the University of Texas at Arlington, and the Texas Woman's History Collection at Texas Woman's University all provided solid and invaluable information. And thank God for Aunt Florence, Mrs. C. E. Hudson, who devoted the last days of her life to compiling and publishing the genealogy of the Sutherlands in Texas: "We Cousins."

Innumerable relatives with expertise in family stories and geneal-ogy stepped in: my brother George and his wife, Jean Sutherland, who gave me their love, support, anecdotes, calculator, and swimming pool, as needed; my aunt Mable at Westminster Manor Retirement Home; my cousins Dr. and Mrs. Malcolm McLean, distinguished archivists of the Robertson papers; my aunt Lucile Robertson, director of the Cen-tral Texas Area Museum in Salado; my cousin Laurann Gipson, who combed her attic for invaluable letters; my cousin Mary Lucille Am-brose in Nashville, Tennessee, who searched the family archives in that city founded by kinsmen; my questioning niece Carol Hatfield. And, of course, my allies and devoted friends at the LBJ Library: Lady Bird Johnson, inspiration of the living monument to her husband; Harry Middleton, its lovable and quixotic director; and Michael Gillette, the knowledgeable oral historian with an infallible memory.

Kindliest of all throughout the whole year was Tommy, my sev-enty-five-year-old brother, gifted poet and philosopher, who disdains all rules, reveres Mark Twain as the greatest American writer, is available any hour, day or night, for soul searching on any subject, life and death, and who, like me, wakes each morning at five and needs to talk to some-one. Our early morning phone calls replaced my husband, who cared deeply about my first book, *Ruffles and Flourishes,* and is no longer at my side. Tommy was, even across town, at my side every word of the way. He never wearied of my talking about "the Book." His presence was invaluable to me personally and to the continuity of family. We bounced ideas back and forth like Ping-Pong balls.

I cannot forget Minnie Vasquez, who came each week, always cheerful, to vacuum around my writing chair while I stayed at the assignment. Nor Bettina Welch, masseuse, artist, and comforter, who massaged aching joints back into action.

What would I have done without them?

Dedicated to this marvelous country of ours, with these words spoken across two centuries and eight generations by the men and women of my family:

"All you have to do is believe in yourself and things start happening."

> —My grandson,
> Leslie Scott Carpenter,
> age six, 1986

"Remember who you are . . . . Make something of yourself."

> —My mother,
> Mary Elizabeth Robertson Sutherland,
> at Salado, 1926

"After the Battle of San Jacinto, we were coming home almost naked for want of clothing when we spied our old milk cow. . . . I learned however dark the clouds that overshadow our paths, there is a silver lining."

> —My great-grandfather,
> Samuel C. A. Rogers,
> describing Texas of April 1836,
> in recollections written in 1891

"We are the advance guard of civilization and our way is across the continent."

> —My ancestor,
> James Robertson,
> on the founding of
> Nashville, Tennessee, 1779

CONTENTS

OVERVIEW

TODAY I AM sixty-five years old. That seems like a lot to my grandchildren. The youngest is six, and he looks at my white hair and wrinkles and thinks "old." Maybe everyone does. But for me, it seems like nothing at all. I am still the same person I have always been, the child wading in Salado Creek, writing school songs in Austin, attending the University of Texas, going to

Washington as a cub reporter, working in the White House, coming home to live a new kind of life as a widow.

Life has always led me where things were happening, where people were exhilarating, where actions and laughter came quickly.

Sixty-five years! I'm a third as old as our country.

"There is a certain vigor, a certain zest, a certain desire to accomplish, in this still very young country," a friend was saying the other day. "This is a country that has reached its frontier physically but not spiritually." That goes for me, too. So we're both young and healthy, me and the United States of America!

Oh, there are signs of aging, an ache here, a nagging pain there, a brief lapse of memory. What is this paper doing in my typewriter? Oh, yes, a book to describe what I've seen and learned in living. I want to tell it myself, what it has been like walking around this planet for sixty-five years. Sixty-five years on God's green acres. That may seem like a billion minutes to my grandchildren, but to me, well, life just whizzed by.

Aging is becoming stylish, though, not just for antique furniture but for antique people, too. After all, I'm ten years younger than President Reagan. And more good news—that sex symbol Paul Newman is sixty-two. Greta Garbo is eighty. George Burns, the godfather of us all, is headed toward one hundred. Yesterday I got a birthday card from Sargent Shriver saying, "Welcome to discount movies!" Cary Grant, my longtime movie idol, eighty-one and silver-haired, was here to visit the other day. He brings to mind a toast.

> *Here's to the ability*
> *To have the agility*
> *To take your virility*
> *To your senility.*

I woke up this morning eager to begin my book. Even though it is still dark, the deer are out in my yard nudging the empty pans, summoning me to the corn bin. In the cool dawn the river rolls below my shelf on the hill; in the distance Austin's lights twinkle at me, alive, awake, old friends welcoming me to the day. My day! This day, in which I begin sorting out my thoughts about what the accumulation of my years means. I feel so close to that little boy Les, my grandson, and to my granddaughter, Bonnie, now becoming, even at sixteen, a beautiful woman. I ache because they are a continent away in Seattle. Yet they are so close to my thoughts, right now I feel close to them and to God.

What do I mean in the infinite scheme of things? And what am I doing at this hour of the morning with demanding deer who eat $42.75 worth of corn each month? Why am I out here in my rainbow nightgown and airline slippers tiptoeing around my front yard to fill six deer pans? It's not at all like the rest of my life.

Okay, hold it, Dasher and Dancer, I'm hurrying. The lame one—the really nervy one (that's what got her into trouble in the first place; she ran into a car)—is staring at me, mutely threatening me if I don't hurry up. What is a loving, sexy, sophisticated, wonderful woman like me doing catering to the whims of deer? I'm preventing warfare here on this hill, that's what I am doing. I have to spread out the feed so the bucks don't shove the females out of the way and the little spotted fawns don't get left out altogether. Here is the oldest story in the world occurring right in my front yard.

Sixty-five years! My Medicare birthday! The day I have marked to begin writing an account of my life and the wisdoms I have learned.

The newspaper sent over a photographer to take a picture of me yesterday. He spent four hours on close-ups. That's so he wouldn't miss a single wrinkle. And he didn't. A reporter interviewed me about aging. I recounted the story of the one-hundred-fifteen-year-old woman asked by some interviewer, "How did you live to be so old, Aunt Minnie?" Through her toothless grin, she replied, "Well, Buddy, I was born one hundred and fifteen years ago and I ain't daid yet."

He asked me to tell him of my proudest accomplishments in these sixty-five years. I don't think of the different things I've done in life as accomplishments so much as milestones, happenings, adventures. I pulled out some of my scrapbooks for him and thumbed through them. Me, behind the editor's desk at the Austin High School Maroon—my first identity as a writer. Me, the first girl in the history of the University of Texas to be elected vice-president of the student body. My mother's serene face—she was supportive through it all, urging me, after college, away from the altar to wartime Washington, where opportunity lay. And me again, on my first job as girl reporter in that heady city of action and power. I remember walking up to the White House clutching a press pass to Eleanor Roosevelt's press conferences, and yes, I had another one, a gold-embossed one to FDR's. But when I married Les Carpenter, my best friend through college, through life, now gone from me and missed every moment, that day topped it all. Being married to Les was life at its best, and he made it so easy. We worked side by side, as equals, covering Washington through our own Carpenter News Bureau for eighteen newspapers in the southwest. I worked through two pregnancies, and yes, God, I had it all, as mother of two darling, healthy children, Scott and Christy, now grown and doing so well. In 1960 I accepted Senator Lyndon B. Johnson's invitation to join "Lady Bird and me in the great adventure of our lives"— his race for vice-president on the Kennedy-Johnson ticket. I was swept up in the victory as LBJ's executive assistant and later became press secretary and staff director to Lady Bird. My scrapbook is jammed with the White House years—I survived two White House weddings, five White House dogs, and raft rides down the Snake River with cabinet members. I danced in the East Room with two presidents, a king or two, and innumerable prime ministers and ambassadors. Heady stuff for a girl from Salado. But there it all is, dining on the Sequoia with Speaker Sam Rayburn, invited to all the glamorous parties, sharing moments with young friends and colleagues—Bill Moyers, Art Buchwald, Shana Alexander, Helen Thomas, Tom Wicker—and old newspaper lions, Drew Pearson, Walter Lippmann, Eric Sevareid.

I served my country proudly and to the best of my ability

(they make you swear to do that, and for me, I felt it in every pore) under three presidents—for President Johnson, of course, the longest and most exciting stint, for President Ford on his International Women's Year Commission, and for President Carter as the assistant secretary of education for public affairs. I have hundreds of photos and clippings in my scrapbook from my fight for the Equal Rights Amendment, hammering out a new organization, the National Women's Political Caucus, with Bella Abzug, Betty Friedan, and Gloria Steinem, and campaigning on the back roads for ratification with columnist Erma Bombeck, President Carter's daughter-in-law Judy, and then-Governor Ronald Reagan's daughter Maureen.

But perhaps it's the present that counts more. Perhaps my most challenging accomplishment is not losing faith and not losing steam when so many tell me to slow down. Perhaps it's getting up at the crack of dawn to feed the deer and admire the sunrise, or staying up late planning a party to help fill in the empty gaps, molding each day to my liking and finding new joys at a slower pace. Perhaps it's taking each day and making it useful to me, or someone, and adjusting to this new condition (aging) with grace and humor.

Which reminds me, I've got to do a really long memo about my funeral. None of this "don't mention the bereaved" stuff—no high Episcopalian ceremonies for me. I want low Methodist, with hymns you sing and go away whistling. I want the church full, and I want open sobbing, not just a few wet eyes. Hold it in a phone booth if everyone I know died first, but after all the political meetings I've advanced and pew-packed for politicians, presidents-to-be, and presidents that were, I deserve a good funeral. I want good press and glorious obituaries with some irreverent anecdotes about my life. And I want laughter along with tears. I want friend and foe alike to know I had a whale of a time walking about God's earth. I want them to know it was mostly sunshine, along with a few shadows: my husband died too young, and I've missed him terribly. I've missed marriage with its loving, holding, talking, arguing, laughing, fighting, making up, sharing ideas, its vulnerabilities, and its joy. I heard a line in a song the other day: "We didn't know what happiness was." That was us—living so fast that we didn't stop and say, "Hey, hold everything, this is happiness."

Meanwhile, back to my funeral. I want a duet of "How Great Thou Art," even though I know my friends will twitter that it's my favorite song because I think it's about me. I want Marijane Maricle and Ruben Johnson to sing it because they are the two people I know best who can hit the high notes in the line, "Then sings my soul, my father God to Thee."

I am hoping that my grandson will be about thirty then. I wouldn't mind his being forty. I hope he will know enough about me to do a eulogy. That's one of the reasons for this book. I don't want him to be caught short of material. Besides, I can't bear to die and not have him hear all the things I've learned in this good life, meet some of the people I've known, and share what they have taught me.

I've spent a lifetime looking for wisdoms wherever I go. Just this last summer, the summer of '85, I decided to have one more go at Europe before one of us failed. I ran into Eric Sevareid, an old friend from Washington days, standing in front of the Hyde Park Hotel in London looking absolutely elegant. He was wearing a black bowler hat over his silver hair, leaning on a walking cane, and it appeared he had just been fitted for his suit by a British tailor. I walked up to him and said, "Behind every successful broadcaster stands a woman, and behind her stands his wife." It was an old line that I used once in a speech to TV broadcasters, and he had liked it.

We decided to go inside and talk over a cup of tea. Tea was *his* idea. I could have gone for a martini with Bombay gin; so would Eric, ten years ago. I complimented him on how elegant he looked. He told me he was trying to do his part for elegance because he worries about how sloppy the rest of the world looks.

"Their purses have increased faster than their tastes," he said. "People aren't stylish anymore. They don't look as good as they used to. The older I get, the more vulgar things upset me." I didn't pursue the conversation because I was sitting there with loose stockings and was in no position to straighten them. So we turned to words, writing, and I asked him why he wasn't doing it.

"Clare Luce asked me once if I kept diaries," he said. "I never have. What's important is what you remember." And at that moment he remembered Eric Hoffer, the marvelous old labor leader and philosopher.

"I went to see him in the hospital," Eric said, "and when I walked in he was propped up on one arm. He looked at me and said, 'Sevareid, old age ain't a rumor.' I loved that old man. The older you get, the more you know that old friendships mean the most. Nothing else means a damn."

Well, maybe good conversation does if you can find it. Eric quoted Max Beerbohm: "True happiness can be found in three ways: dining with old friends, writing something you care about, and traveling south with someone your conscience permits you to love." Eric told me that I should do the latter and not mind my conscience. I'll work on it. Eric knew my husband, Les, and he knows I am lonely now—not always, but often.

Being in London is like roaming around your grandmother's attic. You are in a black hansom cab, you look out, and there is "Wimpole Street" or "Baker Street" jumping out of the books you have read. On this occasion in London I was searching for a poet I've quoted a hundred times but never met—Jenny Joseph. I discovered her poetry through a young British girl who rented my guest house one year and revived my interest in English verse, first introduced to me by my mother before I could walk.

As a result we spent that year holding literary salons and pulling in all the writers around Austin, good and bad, to read their own poetry. The salons got long; hearing the sound of your own voice reading your own words is irresistible.

Jenny Joseph is the author of a poem called "Warning," which captures a gypsy spirit I recognize as my own. Apparently it touches others as well. Once I recited the poem when Bill

Moyers was interviewing me on TV for CBS, and afterward, I received numerous requests for a copy of it.

When I am an old lady I shall wear purple,
With a red hat which doesn't go and doesn't suit me,
And I shall spend my pension on brandy and summer
  gloves
And satin sandals, and say we have no money for butter
I shall sit down on the pavement when I am tired
And gobble up samples in shops and press alarm bells
And run my stick along the public railings
And make up for the sobriety of my youth
I shall go out in my slippers in the rain
And pick the flowers in other people's gardens
And learn to spit
But maybe I ought to practice a little now
So people who know me are not too shocked and sur-
  prised
When suddenly I am old and start to wear purple.

My whole wardrobe has changed since I started quoting Jenny. People give me red hats and purple dresses, and on good days even brandy and summer gloves. *Purple* gloves, can you believe it? So I had long wanted to meet Jenny. Finally I did that day in London. She is a shy, gentle, bookish darling, about forty, who carries her manuscripts down to Oxford and back to the poetry sessions in London.

How did she happen to write about the old lady who wore purple?

"One's writing comes from walking around one's own parish, don't you think?" she began. "And one day I was doing that, and saw in the park this old lady, and the verse began to form. My verses have to be experienced awhile and finally it was right."

I asked her what she is doing now.

"Oh, dear," she said, "you make me think of Athene Seyler, who was a great British actress and lived to be ninety or so. A reporter interviewed her and asked, 'What have you done, Miss Seyler?' 'You mean, since breakfast?' she replied."

So I learned something important from Jenny Joseph, as I have from so many. Thinking back on that day, and this one (my sixty-fifth birthday), I feel like Miss Seyler. I have been riding my train of thought. But it is *my* day and, for me, the beginning of a journey backward into my life. I will be more disciplined in the future. But not too disciplined, because mainly I want to reenjoy my life, savor some of the moments that I rushed past, and share them with the world. I am the sum total of the places I have seen and the people who have loved me, challenged me, taught me, questioned me, and angered me. I, Liz Sutherland Carpenter, being of sound mind and generous heart, do hereby bequeath my collectible thoughts to my family and friends. I won't feel right if I just take them with me.

There are wisdoms you learn from family and roots, wisdoms from work and experiences with people, with travel, with friends. I have learned so much from living through the early days of the women's movement, lobbying state legislatures in our desperate effort to gain admittance into the Constitution of our own country with the Equal Rights Amendment. I have learned wisdom from men and about men, how much they have missed because of traditional attitudes. I believe men are taught to fight for themselves, and women to be calm and avoid confrontation. That is frustrating for both sexes.

I have learned that a sense of humor is essential. I wonder if humor isn't born in us and then life sometimes erodes it or takes it away altogether. I learned that from my grandson, Leslie Scott Carpenter, who is named for my husband. When he was two or three months old he laughed out loud every time his little cousins came into the room. They were closer to his size than the others. He identified with them. He was joyous about them. I hope he never loses that laughter. We are born without the strain of inhibitions. The year President Carter called me back to Washington to be assistant secretary of education, Scott and my daughter-in-law, Jean, brought Les up to see me sworn in. I held him in one arm and put my hand on the Bible with the other. The judge wasn't crazy about the idea, but he went along with it. So did my grandson, who jabbered the oath of office along with me. We still don't know which of us was legally sworn in.

Laughter has always been part of my life. I had a mother who admonished her five children not to take ourselves so seriously. "Remember," she would tell us when we got too earnest or uptight, "as Martha Washington always said, 'There is nothing in this world really worth worrying about.' " I have often wondered through the years, Where did Martha say this—Valley Forge? But the thought has served me well throughout life.

You pick up wisdoms from taking risks, too. There isn't anything very wild and wicked in what I do, but I made up my mind five years ago on my sixtieth birthday that I was never going to say "no." That decision has made life more interesting—busier, of course, too packed with happenings—but why say "no" when "yes" might lead to a new open door, a new wisdom, a new friend?

IN THIS REFLECTION on my life, I want to describe the houses I have lived in and how they have influenced the type of person I am. Houses shape everyone. Ella Grasso, once governor of Connecticut, told me that she was shaped by living in the same neighborhood and the same house for forty-five years. Barbara Jordan, the former congresswoman from Texas famed for her role in the Watergate impeachment hearings, said she grew up in her grandfather's brick house in downtown Houston, and every morning at breakfast he thanked President Roosevelt and the Home Owners Loan Agency for lending him the money to buy it. That shaping marks you for life.

What is home? Roots, trappings, family, work, love. I ask myself, Where is home for me? Five houses take shape, walls come alive, the porches and rooms reach out to touch me. There were more than five, of course, but these five are the ones that framed my life and those I knew and loved. They surround me, echoing another time, another me.

My houses were in Texas and Washington. I almost forgot one—the White House—but it was mine along with two hundred million other Americans. I just had the chance to know it from the inside when I worked there for five years. Houses embody spans of time in my life and in the life of the country and the events that were upon us. These houses are personal friends that comforted me and satisfied my needs at certain times in my life. Four houses altogether, all part of me.

My roots are firmly anchored in a big white plantation house with a red tin roof, twenty-four rooms, and no bathrooms, the house of my childhood in Salado, Texas. I come from pioneer stock, tough men and women who challenged life's odds and won. My male ancestors were in the front ranks of the battle to free Texas from the dominance of Mexico, and my female ancestors manned the rifles against the enemy alongside their husbands, raised scores of children, and still had stamina left over to fight for better education and women's suffrage. When I read stories of their lives, I become more and more convinced that I had the courage to face some of the difficult things in my life because their blood runs through my veins. That house in Salado is still standing, is still in my family, and still in my heart and soul.

When I was seven, my family moved down the road to Austin and rented another big house near the University of Texas on West Avenue so we could all go through college. "All" was not just my family. So long as there was space, any kinfolk with $25 could move in, if they would sleep on the porch or in the attic on an army cot. And they did. It was a marvelously noisy, unlocked house, a homey "think tank," now that I know what "think tanks" are. My mother was the scholar-in-residence, both cook and wordsmith, who always had just the right quotation, without looking it up, when someone needed one for a theme, and who made meatloaf and biscuits taste good throughout the Depression.

When I graduated I took myself and my journalism degree to Washington, D.C., where I later moved into my "married and raising children" house. For twenty-five years, it was our dream house, that two-story cottage of rock and white wood tucked away at the end of Woodway Lane. It was a place for children—ours

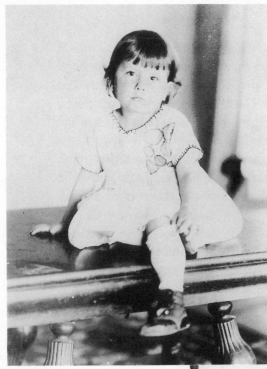

I was all of three, but holidays and summertime found me at my Grandmother Robertson's house in the village of Salado, where I was born. Its walls, its ghosts, its marvelous trees and springs, even the family cemetery where I played as a child around the tombstones of kinfolks, enveloped my life, shaped my sense of belonging, and gave me a sense of purpose and reverence for those who have gone before.

STATE HISTORICAL SURVEY COMMITTEE

TEXAS

OFFICIAL HISTORICAL MEDALLION

ROBERTSON HOME
BUILT BY COL. E.S.C. ROBERTSON AND WIFE, MARY ELIZABETH (DICKEY). RARE ANTE-BELLUM PLANTATION COMPLEX, COMPRISING HOME, SERVANTS QUARTERS, LAND, FAMILY CEMETERY, STABLES. STILL A WORKING RANCH. THE HOUSE, OCCUPIED BY FIFTH GENERATION OF ROBERTSONS, IS AN EXAMPLE OF CLASSICAL REVIVAL STYLE, SHOWS PALLADIAN INFLUENCE IN ITS RECESSED PORCHES, AND GALLERY ROOMS FORMING TERMINAL PAVILIONS, BALANCING A CENTRAL GABLED PORTICO.
RECORDED TEXAS HISTORIC LANDMARK — 1967

BIRTHPLACE OF WHITE HOUSE AIDE
MARY ELIZABETH CARPENTER
GREAT-GRANDDAUGHTER OF BUILDERS, DAUGHTER OF THOMAS S. AND MARY ELIZABETH (ROBERTSON) SUTHERLAND. FIRST WOMAN VICE PRESIDENT OF STUDENT BODY, UNIVERSITY OF TEXAS. MARRIED LESLIE CARPENTER; HAS 2 CHILDREN. IN 1954 WAS PRESIDENT WOMEN'S NATIONAL PRESS CLUB. FIRST WOMAN EVER TO SERVE AS EXECUTIVE ASSISTANT TO THE VICE PRESIDENT OF THE UNITED STATES, 1961. FIRST NEWSWOMAN TO BE STAFF DIRECTOR AND PRESS SECRETARY TO A FIRST LADY, MRS. LYNDON B. JOHNSON.
OUTSTANDING WOMEN OF TEXAS SERIES — 1967

After my stint in the White House, the State of Texas placed a marker on our great old family house, which deserved it far more than I did. For 130 years, it has been sending its sons and daughters forth to "make something of yourself. Remember who you are."

and neighbor kids—who raced from yard to yard in summer, wheeled doll carriages and wagons, or, when the heavy snows came, sledded down from our house to the foot of the hill.

Life revolved around our garden of dogwood trees and azaleas by summer, our fireplace by winter, with two big chairs that held all four of us. Phones rang, of course, interrupting day and night, for we earned our living reporting. And newsmakers came to our backyard. There we lazed on Sundays, newspapers spread around, children racing through the house even when the guest was the speaker of the House, a congressman or a senator.

That house saw so many come, talk politics, talk issues—in the garden or around the fireplace. I wouldn't have missed for the world knowing Speaker of the House Sam Rayburn or President Lyndon Johnson at the height of their power, or having my children know they were important men in our country. It seemed the whole Congress came, too. For twenty-five years our family lived with the actions and passions of our times, the deadlines, the sense of urgency, the behind-the-palms intelligence, the majesty, and the . . . well, hysterical happenstance that a democracy allows. When I go back now I can't drive up that street. It tears at my heart, because that phase of life is over.

Then there was the White House, not because I lived there, but because its walls and great rooms and history thunder through time at me. I worked there night and day for five years. The East Room, where Abigail hung her wash, was our place for big bill signings. I stood in the back of that room when LBJ launched the War on Poverty and thrilled to hear him say, "When I was a boy, there was so much poverty around, we didn't know it had a name." Well, he gave it one, and a program. The library, the room where once milk cows were kept, was where I held my press briefings. The State Dining Room, with the brooding portrait of Lincoln, was the scene for candlelit state dinners. And by day every room hosted a meeting of some sort to handle the nation's business. Once, when Calvin Coolidge was walking with a friend outside the grounds, he was asked in whimsy, "Who lives there?" Coolidge replied, "No one." But in truth we all do.

My last house is here in Texas, where I married a word processor after a turbulent courtship. This one sits on a green bowered shelf looking down the Colorado River. I've named it "Grass Roots" because it symbolizes my returning to where I came from, the earth of Texas. From here each morning I watch the sun rise and welcome a new day. I have refashioned its walls and rooms around my needs and my life. I can't afford a swimming pool, so I built a spa made of rock like a wishing well. I can sit outside and bubble under the sun or stars, which hang low here. (You can almost reach up and touch them.) The spa accommodates eight friends or six enemies and a champagne bucket. The heated waters and soft music, played over speakers given to me as a homecoming gift by my son, have made it a natural gathering place. I've had committee meetings in it and commiserated with friends who have lost a job, a boyfriend, or a husband. It's a conversation place and a magnet for young and old. My brother's children and my grandchildren delight in splashing in the bubbles. My daughter says it is "Mom's favorite decadence." I think it's my fountain of youth. Whatever else, it is a perennial source of health and pleasure, for in it I can relax, think, and maybe wash my sins away.

Texas is strong country. It's optimistic country with blue skies, white fleecy clouds, warm sunshine. Today it is friendly country, though when my ancestors came it was hard enemy land. You're not crowded here in Texas. You can look out and see a lot of the world. I like looking to the farthest horizons.

By doing so, maybe I can provide some guideposts, save my grandchildren some bumps, help give others the riches from an historical perspective. Bill Moyers, my longtime friend, says that young people today don't look in the rearview mirror. "They even ask, 'Who is this fellow Churchill you keep quoting?' " Our past does make a difference. Most things that happen, nationally and otherwise, are the consequences of events often unremembered but always inescapable. "No story I cover began today," he says.

So young people miss a great deal by being determined to make all the mistakes over again without taking advantage of accumulated wisdom. I am no wizard, but I have a talent for writing and talking things through. I want to put this legacy on paper. I want to be used up when I depart this life, giving back everything I got. I want to say "Thank you, God, for living."

My young friend Cheryl Darnell sent me a poem she wrote:

I have this fear
of waking up one day
and finding I've worked too hard
on all the wrong things,
and all the things
I've said I'd do
when I had time
are still undone.

Today, with this book, and with the rearview mirror fixed in place, I begin to banish that fear.

COMING HOME

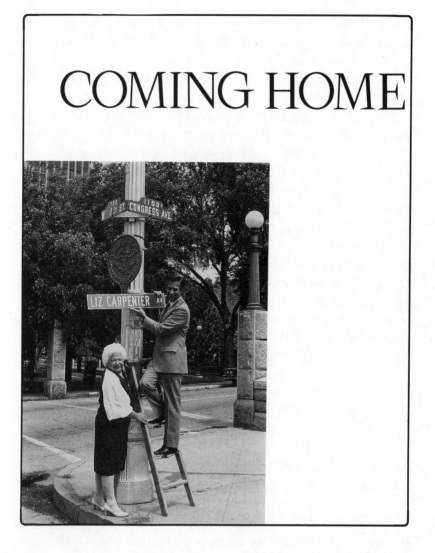

IT HAPPENED, that moment all couples fear the most, dread the most. Suddenly one of you is gone. Such a simple thing as a phone call in the night, and your whole life is changed. For a while you think it is lost forever, but as the numbness wears off, and if you are whole enough, wise enough, to heed the question "What shall I do with the rest of my life?"—you can find new trails. How can I bear it? How do I end this awful feeling inside me? How do I cope with everything around me? Will I ever, dear God, be happy again?

I hurt again as I sit here looking out at the sun slowly rising above the horizon. At first there is just a touch of light, and then steadily, slowly, the bright glow of orange and red emerges, and finally it is day again. It is not a cloudless sky. That will come later. But the darkness is gone, and you look around and there is life. You go back to the church where you said the funeral good-bye, and you hope there is someone there who knows you, beckons you to come sit by them, helps you reenter. If you are really lucky, you have a friend who calls and says, "Let me know when you are ready to talk. I'm here, night and day." And she presses a phone number in your hand to put by your bedside table. If you are unlucky, you have to go it alone or even walk away from those well-meaning but negative people who just want to wail with you and tell you how bad it was for them. But the days do break with the welcoming sunrise, and you must find a way to reach out, to welcome each day.

The death of someone you love can shelve you if you let it. I have seen that happen. Some people react that way even at the death of a lifelong friend.

"I wake up each day thinking I will feel better, and I never do," Kenny O'Donnell, appointment secretary to JFK, said months after the president's assassination. He sat in his office in the White House, almost in a trance, wishing that one godawful moment in Dallas could be erased. He was never able to resume his life afterward, and he became a tragic figure, disintegrating in body and spirit for the next ten years until finally he was gone from the world. He never let the sun rise again.

"The death of Jack Kennedy was Kenny's own death," said Pierre Salinger. Pierre served as press secretary to JFK and for a time to LBJ and was my comrade-in-arms in the White House; recently we talked over lunch, reliving our lives and the tragedies and triumphs of the sixties. Back then Pierre's job was to worry about the news from the president, Kosygin, Vietnam, and De

Gaulle; mine was to worry about women, dogs, old brocades, Luci changing the spelling of her name, Luci becoming Catholic, Luci having her ears pierced, Luci getting engaged, Luci getting married, Lynda getting married, a hot-tempered French chef, and forty of Lady Bird's trips covering two hundred thousand miles.

Remembering Kenny, Pierre became sad. "Most of us still hurt, but we have managed to assimilate our own lives and live on. Look what I've gone through during my own lifetime. Two of my best friends were killed. A son committed suicide. All important. I lost a Senate race; not so important. Each of these things is something you have to live through to understand. I never write it off—the past. I never will, but at the same time, you have to go forward. I have learned you can't understand winning until you have lost."

I agreed with him. I have sipped champagne by moonlight at the Acropolis. I have thrilled to the beauty of the Taj Mahal. I have watched two White House brides come down the aisle on the arm of the president of the United States. I have danced under the crystal chandeliers in the East Room beside Princess Margaret, Lord Snowdon, and the shah of Iran. Only now do I know that I could not have enjoyed those experiences half as much if Les had not been there to share them with me. And now that he is gone, going forward alone seems nearly impossible.

Building a new life is a challenge. I ache for a thousand widows who have called me or written me to talk about *it* . . . grief, anger, guilt, hurt. "How do you go through airports alone, travel alone, ride across town alone?" "Little things make me feel so alone, like putting up the storm windows and checking out the car." "I've never done the bookkeeping." "I feel lost in a crowd."

Dolly Levi in the musical comedy *Hello, Dolly!* kept asking for a sign:"Ephraim, give me a sign to go on with life." And he did. If you are alert, you do receive guidance—some inner voice, your own or someone else's, moving you out of grief and into acceptance.

Can it be fourteen years now since the night the long-distance phone call brought the heartbreak?

"This is the hardest thing I've ever had to do, Mom." It was our son, Scott, speaking.

His voice broke. "Dad died an hour ago of a heart attack. Instantly. I don't believe he suffered any pain. I am so sorry, and I wish I were there with you now. But I'll meet you in Washington in the morning. I have made you a reservation on a plane leaving in two hours." We talked on a little longer before hanging up. Then I rushed to pack, tears streaming.

My son had reached me in Houston, Texas, where I had given a speech earlier that evening for a national convention, one of the ways I contributed to our income. Les had put me on the plane early that morning. He usually saw me off when I went on a business trip. He had called twice after I arrived to bring me up to date on what was happening in Washington. Maybe it would be interesting to the audience to know the latest bit of information on the Watergate story, maybe it would provide material for humor. That was the kind of partnership we'd had. We had tasted the excitement and champagne of life together, shared the successes and disappointments of pursuing careers and raising a family. Now, at fifty-two, my husband was dead. And the champagne was flat.

Les was gone, I had to keep reminding myself. I was alone. After the first numbing shock came other stages of grief. I went through them all in the days, months, and years that followed.

Guilt is the second stage, after the shock wears off. Why hadn't I sensed that Les wasn't feeling well? I didn't have to go out and make speeches. Why hadn't we treasured each moment more, traveled more together, relaxed more? Our whole life had been one of deadlines, and while we had shared them and lived them fully, we had rushed through the moments. I even found myself thinking back twenty years before to a trip we had taken through Italy, when Les had wanted to buy an expensive oil painting. I had not been interested, so we hadn't bought it. Damn!

"Look," my doctor finally told me, "I've never known of any death when someone didn't punish himself by feeling guilty.

Aunt Nellie may be ninety-five, but there will always be someone who will say, 'Why didn't I play dominoes with her? Why didn't I take her driving?' Guilt is normal, but you have to put it aside."

Anger is another part of grief. Why should this happen to me when life could have been so lovely for another twenty years? We had been blessed with interesting jobs, and now, with the children educated, we had more money to enjoy. Our children were getting established in their own professions: news reporting for Scott, law for our daughter, Christy, now married. We had all begun to indulge ourselves with family holiday vacations taken together in Mexico or Hawaii.

Funny, I remembered it was Barry Goldwater, the Republican senator, who had suggested that. Once when we were dancing at an embassy function, Senator Goldwater said, "Time will come, Liz, when your children will be grown and there won't be anything left to give them. Well, give them a plane ticket, rent a house somewhere different each year. Peggy and I do that, and then everyone has a holiday together."

So we had begun this pattern and planned many more trips. I was angry that the good years, all the good times you look forward to having "when we have time," had been cut short.

A friend told me, "You had an enviable life; you couldn't ask for more." But you do, of course. I suppose the price of a long and happy marriage—thirty years, in my case—is that one must go first, leaving the other a deep void to fill.

Then comes the last and longest-lasting stage of grief—the enveloping sadness that sets in when you face the glaring fact that there is no one in the world who loves you more than he loves anyone else. And chances are there never will be.

Your children love you, of course. Your family and friends love you and call and offer comfort. But there is now no one to whom you are first.

"That's egotistical," you tell yourself. But the feeling is there, ego or not. The bed you shared so long, where you reached out to touch each other, now is empty—a constant, gaping reminder that you are unalterably alone.

Sex? Of course you miss sex. Any woman who has had a happy marriage is going to miss that ingredient.

"Have an affair!" a friend advised.

But if you grew up in the Bible Belt, were a virgin at the altar and faithful in your marriage, this is not easy. And it isn't just sex you miss. It's love, companionship, commitment.

I began to sort out my emotions and think about the future. Everyone tells you not to make any changes for a year—yet you have to make some. I had a compulsion to redecorate our bedroom and build it around one instead of two. There is therapy in repainting, redoing, creating something different from the scene of sadness. It allows you to be selfish and good to yourself. I did that. It wasn't enough.

Weekends were unbearable. That was the time Les and I used to relax and share so many good talks. We liked to go out and shop at the farmers' markets, cook good food, maybe have friends in.

Now I found myself "racing" to get out of town for weekends. I jumped at invitations, speaking dates—anything to keep me out of the house.

Once when I was in Aspen, Colorado, during one of those get-away weeks, a wise woman, whose husband had been dead for several years, gave me the words that were to save me; they live with me still. I asked her simply, "How did you emerge from grief? I can't stand being a widow. I flinch at the word."

"You must think of it as a second life," she said firmly. "God has given you a chance at a second life."

Still, two years after Les's death I didn't feel any better. I was still racing, still not "at home" in my own home. I was restless, nervous, lonely, miserable. One friend finally said, firmly but kindly, "What is going to pull you out of this blue funk?"

Nothing, I thought, as long as I stay in Washington. Les and I had discovered the great, pulsating capital city of Washington, D.C., together as newlyweds and reporters shortly after World War II. For over twenty years we had shared a news bureau together, shared seats in the Capitol press galleries, shared insider political stories. We had our children in Washington, saw them grow up, graduate, and marry, and were beginning to enjoy them as adults. I realized as I thought about it that Washington had been "our" town, not "my" town. I knew that if I were ever going to start my "second life," I was first going to have to leave Washington. There were just too many ghosts there.

I knew I had to change my environment completely. I thought about going home to Texas. But first I had to deal actively with my loneliness. I began to count up my own pluses and minuses. After all, I had a lot going for me, and I knew I was luckier than many widows who had no work experience and had never dealt with the world on their own. I had mentioned this occasionally in speeches, and I felt a surge of empathy with so many women who began asking me for advice. What could they do? How could they occupy their time?

On the minus side, I missed being needed. I am maternal by nature, and with no demands on me from children or a husband anymore, I felt left out.

I began thinking of a cause that might need me, one that was important. Certainly the Equal Rights Amendment needed me, I concluded. I had been helping out on ERA long before my husband died. He had been encouraging and supportive of my efforts in the women's movement. Now I intensified my work. There was more time to travel and fight for ERA, and it fed my soul. It was something I felt deeply passionate about, and I needed to feel deeply passionate about something. It was also my way to pay my tithe for the blessings of life. Besides, ever since the women's movement began, I'd wanted to be part of it. I'm not one to enjoy sitting on the sidelines when a whole piece of history is being written for my own sex, for me, for my daughter, for all the women of this country.

ERA was the cause for me. I think this is good advice for any widow: find a cause, whether it is saving sick kittens or imperiled whales; find an endeavor that is close to your heart and fling yourself into it. "Who brings his neighbor's barque to land will find his own has reached the shore."

In Washington, we lived at the end of Woodway Lane for twenty-five glorious years of raising children and working at the National Press Building. Our children, Scott and Christy, grew up fishing with Speaker Sam Rayburn and listening to the political talk that was the only conversation. Nighttime frequently included a sail down the Potomac on the *Sequoia* with the big political names of the day: Senators Stuart Symington and Mike Monroney, former Governor William P. Hobby, Senator and Mrs. Price Daniel, and Mrs. Lloyd Bentsen and Senator Lyndon B. Johnson. Columnist Betty Beale and Scooter Miller are among those pictured, as is Cabinet member Robert B. Anderson.

I found myself thinking of Frances Perkins, the little lady with the tricorn hat, the first woman to hold a cabinet position, who proved what one person, maybe one woman, can do; for when you look at the New Deal legislation, the reforms in working conditions, most of it came from a crumpled list of national needs she had in her purse the day she took the appointment from an ambivalent FDR. He had been reluctant to name her to the post of secretary of labor because it would mean trouble with the labor leaders who wanted one of their own appointed. I learned later that it was Molly Dewson, the Democratic party official and warhorse so important to FDR's campaign, who insisted that Frances get the job.

Frances Perkins epitomized how one event can shape a person's fate. One afternoon in 1911 she was having tea with a friend in downtown New York when suddenly they heard fire bells clanging. They rushed outside to see what was happening. The top floors of a ten-story building of lofts across Washington Square were ablaze. It was the Triangle Shirtwaist Factory, and the girls were working overtime to turn out the famous shirtwaists that were the fashion of the day. As Frances and her friend drew closer, they saw frail young girls, aflame, hurl themselves out of the high windows, screaming as they crashed to their deaths. When the smoke cleared, 146 young women were dead. For Frances Perkins, the flame never went out. It burned like a torch within her until her death at eighty-five.

I knew I could work for ERA from Texas just as well as from Washington. In fact, Texas was even closer to the unratified states of the deep South.

I also asked myself, If I am going to live this second life, what do I want in it? What have I missed in my first life that I would enjoy doing now?

Growing up, I always enjoyed being around my big family. In Washington, I was twelve hundred miles from relatives. Les hadn't been as bothered by this as I had; his family was smaller and not as close as mine. Now I felt the distance even more. I wanted to know my nieces and nephews, to be near them, to see my brothers and sister more frequently. I could do that if I lived in Texas. And my son, Scott, was also living there.

Christy was wrapped up in her Washington job and a husband. She had been a comfort when I called on her, making an appointment for me with a psychiatrist when she saw I needed counsel and relief from grief.

"I'm afraid that if you move, Mom," Christy said, "you'll do just fine for a year while you are fixing up a house, but then you'll regret leaving Washington."

But I ignored her advice and went on racing to get away. Perhaps, in some childish way, I was really looking for a mother's lap or a strong shoulder.

Of course, my moving hinged on making arrangements for another job, not to mention selling my old house and finding another one. I let friends in Texas know that I was trying to come home and was looking for a way to do it. Since I wanted to write, I sought assignments. The South was beginning to be very much in the news again, as we passed the milestones and anniversaries of civil rights actions. I needed some permanent income besides the chancy freelancing, so I turned to my old friends at the LBJ Library, and they welcomed me as a consultant to their programs, symposiums, ideas. It bridged my old and new lives.

Once in Austin, I was self-indulgent about house hunting; I wanted to find exactly the right place. This would be my last move, my "last lap" house. Maybe I could make it my happy-hour house.

"You're crazy," a Washington friend told me. "If you have to move—and I think you are going to miss this place terribly— why not buy a condominium? You just lock the door and have no worries."

A condominium may be right for some, but I wanted what I had always had, a home, a setting, my own ambience, my own identity. I need people and am good at gathering them together and extracting interesting talk. This last house would be built around one fifty-seven-year-old writer who hoped that if she took good care of her health and could stop racing to forget, she might just live another third of her life.

One of my nieces, Carol, decided to help. During a visit to Austin, we drove along the river, the winding Colorado. From one side we looked at the city and from the other the green hills, already scarred with new developments. As the car rose along the Edwards Plateau, we saw the city and the river in the distance.

"I want a view," I suddenly told her. "Find me a house with a view of the city. I want to see water—the lake or the river." Those were my guidelines.

Finally, she called with the news I had been waiting to hear: "Liz, I've found your dream house. It looks out over the city, which sparkles at night. It has gorgeous live oak trees. It's the right size, not too big. And there's a separate small guest house that is perfect for a study where you can write. Get down here this weekend." I tried to find excuses. I couldn't spend $400 to fly down to Austin just to look at a house. Couldn't it wait?

"This is it," she said, "and it will be gone by Monday, so come on."

I went. We drove up the winding road, halfway up the hill. From the moment I stood in front of the house and looked down to see the Colorado River, the Capitol dome, and the University of Texas tower framed in the distance, I knew this was going to be home for me.

I put down a deposit and in another two weeks had signed the contract and had a buyer for my Washington home. In three months I was leaving my house on Woodway Lane to drive home to Texas. I wanted to come home slowly by car this time, to travel through the South and sense all that had happened since I first went north thirty-four years ago. Washington seemed north to me then, yet I know now it is neither north nor south, but where the power of both meet.

I circled the round, graceful Jefferson Memorial, and the shrinelike Lincoln, then crossed the Potomac into Virginia. I passed the LBJ Grove, the towering stand of white pines in memory of a man who changed both my life and the South forever.

"Ol' Lyndon carried this country a long way farther than many Americans thought they could go. When they finally did change, it was because he convinced them it was the right thing to do," a southerner once told me.

It had been a great thirty-four years in that exhilarating capital city, but it was time to leave. Now I know, despite the Washington cliché, that you *can* go back to Pocatello. It isn't as though you go empty-handed. Crammed into your brain are experiences, new talents, ideas, and perceptions. You would be a dunce if you didn't take back more than you arrived with.

Down past Charlottesville, Thomas Jefferson's town, into Tennessee, where the soft hills open wide in welcome. I wondered if there would be some awful grip of regret, some spell of sadness, that would settle over me on that last drive home. A new life lay before me, and at the end of the twelve-hundred-mile ride would be the Texas hillside, home again.

My companion on the drive home was an old friend, Betty Talmadge (former wife of Senator Herman Talmadge of Georgia), whom I had known since we were young and neighbors in Washington. She didn't really trust my driving and volunteered to lend a hand and, yes, sell some of her Talmadge Farm hams along the way. Betty went into the ham business during her mid-life passage, as writer Gail Sheehy calls it. So we were on our way, her order book on the backseat.

We were well into Tennessee when the car stopped—just stopped dead still—and we had to ease it to the gravel shoulder. We opened the hood and stared helplessly at the motor.

In no time at all we had company. Two husky young men from a large moving van.

"See," I murmured to Betty, "that's what makes me really know I'm in the South. People stop for you."

"Where you boys from?" Betty asked.

"Massachusetts, ma'am," they replied, and started poking around the motor.

•

AFTER A NUMBER of stops, we were in Alabama to visit old political friends and allies. That state has experienced a kaleidoscope of change in human relations within my own memory: Bull Connor's dogs; the march from Selma; and now today, five black councilmen, duly elected by the voters. In Selma, that lovely old town with the ugly name and the spectacular array of antebellum homes, I was shown the church where Martin Luther King rallied his followers to start their march to Montgomery. I saw the old Confederate cemetery and the campground where thousands of civil rights activists had gathered. What a confused and dismayed town it must have been in those traumatic days! But here, a dozen years later, there was a civility I did not believe possible from the town leaders. The city council of Selma, they said proudly, now had six whites and five blacks on it. They were busy transforming the downtown area into a place of today instead of yesterday, and black and white citizens alike showed off Selma to curious, disbelieving tourists like myself—both sides of it, Confederate statues as well as the road to Montgomery. They knew each spot where the march had been stopped by troopers, each place where confrontations had been photographed by cameramen.

Years later I discussed this with Barbara Jordan. "You see, Liz, we whites and blacks had a lid on our friendship, we in the South for so long. But we knew each other, and when the lid was lifted, we could take it from there. We didn't have to meet each other at lunch counters. We weren't strangers."

I felt close to the civil rights battles, not because I was out front marching, but because my Methodist upbringing had prepared me for it. I knew it was right. I also had a front-row seat for the signing of the great civil rights legislation of the 1960s. Bill after bill was signed in the East Room of the Johnson White House, and every milestone was familiar to me. This was what I was seeing now as I traveled south, the translation of legislation into people and places. It should have happened long ago, but at least it finally happened.

Next door was Mississippi, a state that speaks to me of old

battles and brave people: the Hodding Carters of *The Delta Democrat Times*, gallant knights of the Mississippi delta who had joined forces in the 1960s with Aaron Henry, the indomitable leader of the old NAACP. I once listened to him make the most passionate speech I have ever heard from a podium. It was 1972. The Democrats who would show their faces at a "George McGovern for President" rally were one of three types: blacks, hippies, or "yaller dog" Democrats, plus a handful of aristocrats who will never desert the party of FDR. I had been part of a lost cause to help hold the South in the election of '72. Now, driving home, I was retracing the steps of that campaign. Faces came to me, and memories.

Myrlie Evers, widow of slain civil rights leader Medgar Evers, had been there the night of that speech. She has that inner calm that seems to settle on the spirit of someone who has experienced the worst but made peace with the sacrifice. Aaron had embraced her and moved to the podium to introduce her to the audience. When Aaron talks, he's half Aristotle and half Brer Rabbit; he melds humor and poignancy like the Old Masters mixed oils—folksy one minute, compelling as Moses the next.

In that stifling hot room, his voice had lowered to an impassioned whisper. He had brought the audience into his confidence, his inner soul. "I was with Medgar Evers the night he was shot," he had said, glaring in anger, "shot—in the back." He'd paused and then begun again slowly. "But he fell forward! All six feet three inches of him."

The South fell forward, too, the night Medgar Evers was shot in the back. It didn't even need to be said.

Here, years later, had been his widow, without open bitterness, traveling in her own Mississippi again—a seventh-generation Mississippian, as Hodding Carter was, together with a small band of us trying to rally votes for the Democratic ticket. Here had been Aaron Henry, once excluded because he was black, now part of "the system" as duly elected national committeeman. Thank God for all of them and all the strong and gentle people who didn't give up on Dixie.

"Yes, I'm a seventh-generation Mississippian," Myrlie Evers had told me quite proudly. "My family has lived here through all of its phases. There's a gold ring handed down in my family— given to my great-great-grandmother by the white overseer. Yes, we have lived through it all."

Strong woman, Myrlie. How did she pick up her life from that hideous night and go on? I needed to see and talk with women like her for my own recovery.

Weaving our way through this multicolored patchwork quilt that is now the South called forth all my reporter's instincts to ask, write, and absorb passions that still layered our lives.

Now Betty and I were almost to our night's stop in Montgomery, where Scottie Smith, Zelda and F. Scott Fitzgerald's daughter, lived. The old Sayre house is gone from Montgomery. There Scott, the World War I soldier, fell in love with Zelda on a southern verandah. We found our way through the twilight down the oak-lined street to Scottie's house, also with a wide verandah and a porch swing. Scottie was at the door welcoming us in and laughing as she pointed to the bright blue welcome mat she had placed there for a joke: "Smile, you're in Wallace country!"

She had arranged a dinner party. The open fire and book-lined rooms were cheerful and contained a handful of liberal southerners and civil rights lawyers. There was lots of talk among those stoic young lawyers, editors, and writers who live in the capital of the old Confederacy. They have known economic punishment for their beliefs and have taken it with good humor and grace. Belief in a nonbigoted South is the bond that ties them together. Among them were a couple of good-looking young men from Harvard Law School who were interning for Judge Frank Johnson, the federal official who made civil rights history when he ruled against his white southern brethren and Governor George Wallace.

Montgomery, Alabama, was an unfamiliar setting for these bright easterners, a backwater town under the magnolia blossoms. "How do you like it here?" I asked them.

"It's a new world for us. The women! One minute they're

Tallulah Bankhead, the next Miss Melanie. We can't figure them out."

What would the new peace in the South between blacks and whites mean? Would it be—at last—the end of the Civil War? I liked the pride they took in telling me of all the good changes that had taken place in Alabama. George Wallace was no ogre, they told me. They looked on him as an enemy who had mellowed with age, and who had sadly missed out on a moment of history when he could have been a hero instead of a hindrance.

It was after midnight when we went upstairs to bed. I turned out the light and gazed at the moon-flooded garden and the sweetgum and magnolias. What a lot of ghosts haunt Alabama. The strains of "Dixie" and "We Shall Overcome" all blend now. I went to sleep half thinking of Myrlie Evers—and the night her husband fell forward—and then of a South when Zelda and F. Scott Fitzgerald could sit in a verandah swing or dance the night away . . . she in yards and yards of chiffon. Sleep came easily. Something good has been happening to the South of my past.

IT WAS TWILIGHT when we crossed the long, low causeway of Lake Pontchartrain into Louisiana. A crescent moon hung over the confetti city of New Orleans. There it was—delicate, breathtaking, wicked, and enticing. It seemed fitting that the last stop on my way home be New Orleans, for it had been the first stop on my way to Washington in 1942. Then, everything I saw had thrilled me. I had written a letter to my mother describing it all:

> This place is quaint and filled with antique shops that are bulging with many relics of the old Southern plantations: bed warmers, snuff boxes, whatnots, beautiful chinaware and candelabra. When I build a home, I want to come to New Orleans and outfit it completely from the old French Quarter. I was tempted to purchase the desk of one of the Czars of Russia until I found out the price. Of course, it could be a fake, but I hardly think so. No one would have anything that ornate but a Czar. Tomorrow I will have my fortune read in tea leaves by Madame Jean. You drink a cup of tea and she

can foretell your future from the leaves in the bottom of the cup.

This afternoon I went on a boat trip up the Mississippi. It had a real whistle like the one in Tom Sawyer and a large "chunk paddle" at the back. We passed by Baretaria, where Lafitte and his men lived, and by the site of the Battle of New Orleans. However, the guide was more interested in the industrial plants, so he skimmed over historic points. You could smell molasses from the factory all up and down the muddy Mississippi. And I saw little children playing on the levees. Between the levee and the river there is a deposit called a *batture*, or squatter's land, which belongs to no one. Many poor people have built shacks there on stilts and live all their lives depending on the river for both shelter and sustenance. This city certainly has everything to remind you of the grace and charm it once had. You must see it soon, for I fear new wars will crowd out the relics of the old ones. I leave now for Washington. Every minute I marvel at how lucky I am to get to enjoy all this, and without your enthusiasm and insistence I wouldn't have.

Thirty-four years later the city was still just as exciting. Like the river it embraces, New Orleans just keeps rolling on. The same antique shops are here, yet another czar's desk being offered, and the grace and charm intact. I hope I can keep on rolling along, too, despite the trauma of death, change, and a major move to a second life.

I felt that I was finally seeing the real New Orleans. Our destination was Bourbon Street, heart of the French Quarter, where Congresswoman Lindy Boggs lives in a home willed to her by an aunt who must have guessed that one day she would be the toast of that lovely bit of Paris on the Mississippi.

The French Quarter was already blocked off for the nightly revelers. We parked and walked the last two blocks, lugging suitcases and checking the door numbers on the narrow street, past the jigsaw of restaurants, street performers, bars, and wrought-iron lacework grill balconies. Could it be this big, barren, barnlike double-door front that looked like a warehouse? We rang the bell, and after a long wait the door was opened by the hospitable

Gloria Lifton, kerchiefed Creole housekeeper, whom Lindy had described as "the best politician in New Orleans." Gloria led us down the cobblestone carriage path into the most beautiful court-yard I had ever seen, a garden enclosed with tropical plants, vine-covered walls, a lighted fountain, and a persistent camellia bush. Enveloping it was the three-story house, there since 1795 when a Spaniard with an eye for beauty settled on this site a few blocks from the cathedral on Jackson Square and near the levees of the Mississippi River. Inside, the house was all red velvet and pale blue damask, crystal-chandeliered drawing rooms, stairways slanted by time. We pulled back the heavy draperies to watch the life of Bourbon Street over the lace ironwork window balconies. Below was the pathway of Mardi Gras parades since 1827.

In the corner of one room was the congressional desk and mementos of Hale Boggs, the handsome congressman who swept up Corinne Claiborne, known as Lindy, the prettiest girl in Loui-siana, married her, and took her off to Washington, where they opened their hearts and home to everyone in New Orleans style.

Now, in the parlor of his widow's home, the wheels of all the old campaign trains we had shared together started turning again in my mind. Hale, Lindy, and I had seen Dixie from the back platform of the JFK-LBJ whistle-stop train in 1960 and the *Lady Bird Special* in 1964—Lindy welcoming the riders and Hale in-troducing the dignitaries. Hale was great at warming up the crowd, "his moon-face split wide open in a hush-puppy grin," wrote one reporter. He'd say, "On the train this mornin' we started servin' grits; about noontime we're gonna serve turnip greens and black-eyed peas. Later on, we're gonna have some crawfish bisque, some red beans and rice, and some creole gumbo."

In the wake of the civil rights legislation of 1964, maybe the way to the southern voter's heart was through his stomach!

Then Lady Bird, softspoken, gentler: "I am fond of the old southern customs of keeping up with your kinfolks—all your uncles and aunts and cousins—of long Sunday dinners after church, of summertime filled with watermelon cuttings and

On the Washington Merry-Go-Round: with Queen Elizabeth of England and Paul Wooten at a Washington press gathering; with President and Mrs. Eisenhower showing my children the "David handshake" on my big night as president of the Women's National Press Club; with President and Mrs. Jimmy Carter; with Vice President Walter Mondale; and with my cochampion of ERA, First Lady Betty Ford.

The White House, "built for the ages," was my workplace for five action-packed years. As I had been at his swearing in on *Air Force I* in November 1963, I was upfront again to watch President Johnson sworn into office that January 1965 with his Secret Service agent, Bill Livingood, my husband, Leslie Carpenter, and Bess Abell. The LBJs (opposite) made it a people place with gatherings for staff, family—Lynda and Chuck Robb—and assorted Americans. My job running trips for Lady Bird and the press took me all across America, answering family questions. Right, a press briefing about Luci's wedding on the steps of the church.

swimming in the creek, and visiting for weeks," followed by the firm reminder that "the hard duty of assuring equal rights for all Americans falls, not only on the president, but upon all who love this land. I have always believed that there is, in this southland, more love than hate."

My job on these train trips was to make sure the First Lady's needs were taken care of and the reporters covering the event were kept happy so that we got lots of press. The former was usually a breeze, the latter earned me a prize for endurance and a place in heaven. The *Lady Bird Special* had nineteen cars filled to capacity with 225 reporters from all over the country. For the press, the whole trip was physically brutal. I accused Dr. Janet Travell, the train physician, of dispensing more medicine than I did press releases. There seemed to be an epidemic of laryngitis and sprained ankles. But the reporters seemed to thrive on the pace. As the train stopped, they would jump off the cars, race down the side of the track to the back platform, record the happenings—and, if they were on a deadline, grab one of the phones I hooked up at each stop and dictate a story. Two toots of the whistle, and they boarded again: we were off for the next stop. Sometimes there were sixteen stops in a day. Their tennis shoes (I had warned them to wear tennis shoes for the cinder-covered tracks) were being mutilated. But their stories were making page one, and the messages from the editors ("More on Lady Bird train") were a tonic to them—and to me!

One of the growing problems of traveling with that many bodies and no bathtubs for four days was sanitation. The one overnight stop—in Tallahassee, as I recall—looked like the best prospect for improving the atmosphere. The advance man must have been a little startled by the message I wired ahead: PRESS STINKS. PLEASE RESERVE THREE ROOMS AND 150 TOWELS FOR BATHING PERIOD AT NEARBY HOTEL. But he produced, and the gratitude of the train's grimy passengers was touching.

I was part of a third whistle-stop train, in October 1972, for the McGovern campaigners, but that trip we made, sadly, without Hale. Just as Lindy and I were making the arrangements, the awful word came that Hale's plane had been lost in a snowstorm in Alaska, where he had been campaigning for a congressional colleague. I sat with her in her Washington home throughout most of the night waiting for the call that never came. Among those who did call that night . . . that long, dreadful night . . . was a whole group of strangers, all seeking to help her find Hale through communication with a piece of his clothing. Send a tie, a comb, anything he had touched, and they would help her locate the body on some remote, snow-covered mountain. For Lindy, a deeply religious Catholic, these were well-meaning requests, if offbeat. However unorthodox, she quickly complied, but Alaska was too vast, the snow too deep. So the long search ended at last with a memorial at the great cathedral on Jackson Square, where presidents and leaders of Congress said good-bye.

Little surprise that the admirers of the Boggses encouraged Lindy to run for the empty seat. She knew politics and issues. She had handled Hale's campaign and worked in a dozen others. She knew the nuances of the Longs—Earl, Russell, and Huey—and how to contact their constituencies. She was old New Orleans and a political realist by association. She was widow, mother, saint. No wonder she won overwhelmingly.

"I suppose the hardest thing," she has since told me, "has been recognizing that I am the officeholder." For so long, she had been the caretaker, homemaker, and strength giver. Then a tragic moment taught her, as Browning wrote: "Love, we are in God's hands."

New Orleans is a city for all the senses: sound, smell, sight, taste. Eating is an orgy there, and on that final trip home, Betty and I dined in a way that would have shamed even the heroes of Frances Parkinson Keyes's books on New Orleans dining and her voluminous descriptions of gastronomic orgies—we had everything from crab gumbo through lobster thermidor to coffee diablo!

NEXT DAY, BETTY TALMADGE headed back to Georgia with her ham order book filled, and I continued the drive home, my niece Karen and my brother George at the wheel to keep me company for the last lap of the journey. I was entering a new phase.

Somewhat apprehensive of the slower pace, the new life that lay ahead of me, I was going back home—far-ranging daughter, back to my source—crossing the Mississippi and the Sabine, which my Robertson and Sutherland ancestors had crossed on horseback, by wagon train, and on riverboat 150 years before. It took them months to make the journey, years to settle into peace of mind. Ten hours by automobile took me from New Orleans to my destination in Austin. I wanted to renew my acquaintance with that large extended family to which I belong—I'd guess about 1,200 people in all, scattered over Texas—who still get together in groups and for big family reunions once a year. I wanted to listen more carefully to the stories of early times, dangers, panthers, Indians, Yankees. I had my own dangers now—isolation and discontent—but maybe peace would come to me. Being near kinsmen and exploring the making of my own person would be a comforting diversion from my enemy: self-pity.

As we drove, my brother and I talked of the stories we had heard in childhood. My niece listened, wide-eyed at times that a frontier past was so close in our family ties. George, who knows the stories well, was trying to make me feel lucky that I was traveling in the upholstered comfort of an automobile instead of at the back end of a wagon.

He remembered the frequently told story of the first Sutherland passage across the Mississippi and the Sabine. Three boats were lashed together at New Orleans and not long out, my ancestors spied their first steamboat. The passengers on the steamboat decided to have some fun: they put on such steam and pulled up so close it created big waves, tossing our relatives about. Our great-great-grandmother went down on her knees and began praying to the Lord to save them from a watery grave. Finally one of the men confessed to the ladies it wasn't the Lord making the waves, but the steamer. She rose from her knees and said, "Damn the steamer!"

WHEN WE FINALLY arrived in Austin we drove to Grass Roots (my house) and met the moving van and Ruth Baker, my housekeeper of seventeen years, who had flown down to stay for six months and help me get settled. She is a marvelous human being, a mixture of Indian and black, smiling, strong in body, and stronger in spirit. She knew how to make me feel right about this new lap of my life.

"Three weeks ago we were packing up thirty-four years of living, and here we are unpacking it," she said, shaking her head as boxes and pictures and furniture were being uncrated. "But it all seems to fit just fine."

I needed Ruth's enthusiasm and optimism. I felt scared and empty. Had I made a mistake in thinking I could divorce myself from that old life on the Potomac—from living in the center of things I considered important? I tormented myself about the decision that had so recently elated me. A driving November rain that persisted as a parade of my cherished belongings were marched through it only deepened my depression. Now, I grieved for Washington, too. I wanted to erase this Texas business and have my life just as it had been before.

I'll always be grateful for Ruth's support and "everything's right" attitude; and I'll never forget the moving van driver, a young man who loaded up in Washington, drove to Austin, then stayed two days with us, lifting and moving things into place— into my new home. It became a silent partnership: Ruth optimistic; the young man strong and helpful; and me, going through the motions.

Shortly before I had left Washington, I had a young Dallas artist, Lu Ann Bower, sketch my garden and an old friend, Lily Spandorf, sketch the house. I hung the pictures in my new Texas home to remind me of that other life—a little boy's swing, a little girl grown up to marry there in the garden. It tugs at my heartstrings still. But it is an empty house now for me, alive only in memory. In a few days, I felt that I couldn't bear to see those paintings each day; the wound was still open. So I moved them to the guest house out back and struggled to turn my thoughts to my new place and life.

Fixing up my new house to suit me became sheer happiness. I had some money to spend from the sale of the house in Washington, and I spent it, indulged myself in ways that I felt were important, since this would be my last house. I used white and yellow, soft pink and green, happy colors that I liked, tried to throw open the windows and let the sunshine in. You can mix outdoors and indoors in Texas, so I chose colors that brought the gray-greens of the live oaks into the house. I found myself eager to share my new world, so I opened the double glass doors etched with the grasses of Texas to a world of relatives, friends, writers, "characters," and all kinds of new people. I was eager to get on with life, and the house and people helped me do it.

One small consolation of widowhood is that you can see people that you like without clearing it with anyone else. Generally, couples entertain friends they agree upon, and this inevitably cuts out some of the interesting people one or the other would like to include. What a pity that we don't indulge ourselves more fully as people and individuals when we are a twosome. But I did now, and I didn't wait to be invited. I took the initiative!

"You sure meet some strange mixes in your house," one of my guests said to me, eyeing John Henry Faulk, well known as a foe of McCarthyism, in the same room with Ed Clark, ambassador to Australia: one a rootin'-tootin' liberal, the other the epitome of an east Texas conservative. But they didn't get in a fistfight, and the room sparkled with variety instead of succumbing to sameness.

In the process of opening my home to old and new friends, I learned to find a new life and new open spaces for myself. I rose early—so as not to lie in bed and worry and grieve—threw open the curtains and watched the theater of the early sunrise. In that first year I was hungry for news from Washington, devouring every early morning television show, watching the presidential press conference hungrily to find old friends, or calling long distance to ask, "What's happening?" Texas still seemed like an outpost, remote from *The Washington Post* and *The New York Times*, a thousand miles away from where "life" was happening, where politics was going on without me.

I couldn't cram my new life with enough people, enough action, to justify all I had left behind. Had I made a mistake by thinking I could just turn on happiness like a spigot? No gradual transitions for me—I wanted it all to happen immediately. I confessed this to my doctor, John Tyler, confessed it with tears that I couldn't stop.

"Stop racing and look around. Let your environment enrich your life," he said. "You have a place you love, so stay put long enough to love it."

One morning as I sipped a cup of coffee while I was on the phone talking with an editor in New York, I looked out the picture window and saw a baby deer walk gingerly by, sniffing at the pink geraniums. It paused, framed against the pink granite dome of the capitol of Texas in the distance. Here it was. God's world and my new world laid out before my eyes.

"I'll have to call you back," I hastily told the editor. "I've got to take this in."

And I sat there for a full five minutes gazing at the wonder of it all, reflecting that I had just learned how to move from loneliness to solitude. There is a vast difference.

That's what I had prayed for. That's what I had made the move for, and I had found it at last. God had really given me a chance at a second life, and gradually, in a different way, it became as full as the old life, the Washington life.

Eventually, however, I had a chance to return to Washington.

President Carter had recently appointed Federal District Judge Shirley Hufstedler of California to be the first secretary in the new Department of Education. I had met Shirley Hufstedler at the Aspen Institute several years before and liked her, admired her.

So . . . just when I had settled in to enjoy the blue skies of Texas, the deer feeding on my geraniums; just when my Jacuzzi had reached sensual perfection—the new secretary of the new Department of Education phoned. With a persuasiveness I had not encountered since Lyndon Johnson, she insisted, "Liz, I need you; the country needs you." I was about to tell her I wasn't all that valuable when I said to myself, who am I to contradict a cabinet officer? I was in Washington before the Jacuzzi got cold!

I went and I worked. My belief that in a time when so few things worked right, education above all things should work made me want to do it . . . and besides, I had grandchildren. "Education is a loan to be repaid with the gift of self." That is a line Lady Bird Johnson once used in a speech at Radcliffe, and it, like she, marked my life.

I was thrilled to be back in Washington and living that year in the home of the southern writers and my longtime allies, Doug and Libby Cater. All my senses were fine-tuned to the excitement of the city. It was wonderful seeing old friends so dear to me and visiting familiar places filled with memories of significant events.

But I soon found out that the bureaucracy was not the White House, where a single phone call could set people and things in motion. The bureaucracy does not work that way.

I became more aware of the city's noises. Had there always been that many ambulance sirens screaming through the night? Surely not.

It surprised me to find myself yearning for the quiet beauty of my hill in Austin. I will always be grateful for that year in which to test my decision to return to Texas. And after it was over, I never doubted where home was!

JUST THE OTHER DAY, I came upon a poem by Veronica A. Shoffstall that seems to describe what happens in the painful transition to living alone. Appropriately, she calls it "Come the Dawn."

> After a while you learn the subtle difference
> Between holding a hand and chaining a soul,
> And you learn that love doesn't mean security,
> And you begin to learn that kisses aren't contracts
> And you begin to accept your defeats
> With your head up and your eyes wide open,
> With the grace of a woman, not the grief of a child,
> And you learn to build all your roads
> On today because tomorrow's ground
> Is too uncertain. And futures have
> A way of falling down in midflight,
> And after a while you learn that even sunshine burns if
>   you get too much.
> So you plant your own garden and decorate your own
>   soul instead of waiting
> For someone to bring you flowers.
> And you learn that you really can endure . . .
> That you really are strong,
> And you really do have worth
> And you learn and learn
> With every goodbye you learn.

ROOTS

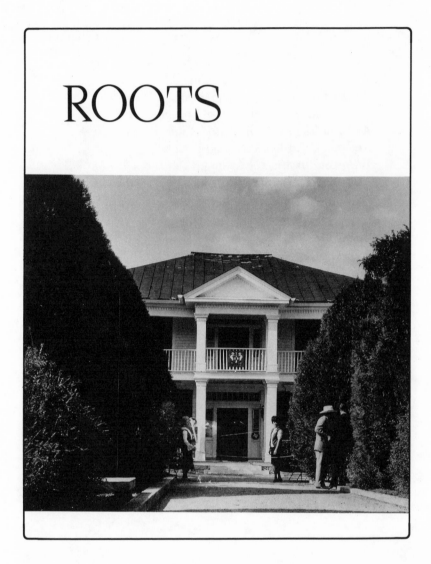

BACK IN TEXAS, surrounded by relatives and in reach of the land-marks of my childhood, old memories rushed through the corridors of the years.

"Remember who you are." The words so often spoken by my mother echoed down to me from the house where I was born in Salado. Just a dot on the map, if it's there at all, but important in early Texas history, and in my own.

There, beside clear springs, limestone streams, amid pecan trees and sheltering oaks, I was born in the big white plantation house of my great-grandparents—the Robertson homeplace— built in 1854 of cypress timbers hauled across Texas from the coast by ox cart.

All my life I have drawn strength from that place—Salado, a small village of 1,500 sitting alongside the spring-fed creek that flows along the Robertson place and continues through the center of town under a low bridge. From the bridge, looking upstream, you see the swimming holes under the shady pecan trees of the Stagecoach Inn. Downward, the stream branches out to the shallows rushing along the limestone shoals, curling among patches of watercress, and spilling out over pebbles and honeycomb rock.

In the 1920s, when I was growing up there, most people wanted to get out. Cotton was a nickel a pound, and cattle you could give away. Only a child could love it, and I did. On summer evenings my cousins and I would sit on the cool limestone front steps and watch the fireflies, listen to the crickets, and smell Aunt Gladys's fudge cooling in the kitchen or Aunt Birdie's divinity bubbling slowly on the wood stove. We would wait for hours, it seemed, before she beat it in the big porcelain platter from New Orleans, where all fine things came from.

Today, after a lifetime of seeing the world, of living intensely with the daily news, those who write it and those who make it, of walking hand in hand, as Justice Holmes described it, "with the actions and passions of the times," I love to go back there—for I need what it has always given me: serenity, a sense of what life is about, and an assurance of continuity.

A few miles out I see the highway sign and smile at the local wisecrack, "Where is Salado?" "Oh, about a quarter of a mile from Resume Speed."

Then there are the familiar landmarks. First comes the rounded grove of oaks at the brow of the hill, beckoning me on, and then, slowly, the top of the windmill emerges, along with the dark red tin roof of the house. And there it is, always the same, fixed in my life, indelible in my memory. Its porches reach out to me. On that upstairs verandah, my mother and her sisters used to brush their long hair one hundred strokes each night.

When I arrive, the ritual is always the same. I walk down the green corridor of arborvitae trees, their branches reaching out to touch me. As I count all twelve—six on each side, representing the twelve Apostles—I notice that Matthew needs water. John is taller; he gets more sun. Such an avenue of trees was a southern habit in those early days of church on Sunday and, afterward, dinner on the grounds. My aunt is there, Aunt Lucile, keeper of the welcoming doors.

This year, when Texas celebrated its sesquicentennial, I was invited to be "Salado's Favorite Daughter" and ride in a stage-coach in the parade with "Sam Houston." Sam Houston once made a speech against secession from the upstairs porch of the Stagecoach Inn. At the sesquicentennial celebration, his stand-in did just as Sam had done it then, and I stood there as my great-grandmother might have, wearing a long pink-and-white calico dress and wide-brimmed hat and carrying a pink parasol.

Earlier that morning, I had strolled to the bridge and, look-ing down, thought of the poet's words: "No one bathes in the same stream twice, for yesterday's waters have gone on to the seas." But I do bathe in the serenity of Salado. I find a peace I know in no other place, a reverence before this altar of ancestors. Like Brigadoon, the enchanted moments of my first home and my childhood reappear.

Coming to visit Salado is like breathing in the fragrance of rose petals in some old satin-glass jar, every corner a memory, every sound a familiar ghost. There, in the dignified old parlor and library, are the portraits of my family's heroes, the Confeder-ate generals: Robert E. Lee, the peerless knight; stoic Stonewall Jackson; Albert Sidney Johnston, who led the Texas troops. There are military commissions signed by Sam Houston, the hero of the Texas Revolution. Houston, that resolute Texan the critics could never change. He led a bedraggled army to win independence from Mexico at the Battle of San Jacinto in 1836, and twenty-five years later he stumped the state trying to keep Texas in the Union during the Civil War. Houston stood alone for manifest destiny and against secession. He was our Benjamin Franklin and Andy Jackson doing a multitude of public jobs, an Averell Harriman in buckskin: congressman and governor of Tennessee, then general of the Texas armies, president of our Republic—and, after we joined the Union in 1845, United States senator and governor of Texas, deposed when he refused to declare allegiance to the Confederacy.

As a child, I was taken down to Austin in an open-air Ford to visit the state capitol. Someone lifted me up and showed me the original Texas Declaration of Independence, written by my kinsman, George Childress. The knob was turned so I could see the names of two other signers who belonged to our family: Sterling C. Robertson and William Menefee.

I was shown the giant oil painting of the Battle of San Jacinto in the capitol's entrance hall. "That white-haired man by the tree is your great-great-grandfather, standing behind the wounded Houston," I was told. We then drove on to San Antonio and the Alamo. A hand guided my small fingers across the granite pillar where the names of the heroes of the Alamo were carved. "Here is your kin, William Sutherland. He was just seventeen."

"REMEMBER WHO YOU ARE. . . ." When I stand in the dignified, cool, and musty parlor of that old house where I was born, I know who I am, the descendant of two early pioneer families who arrived in Texas by horseback and riverboat before any of the fighting started—the Sutherlands and Robertsons, united in the marriage of my mother and father, Mary Elizabeth Robertson and Thomas Shelton Sutherland III. They were married in that gracious old parlor where nineteen women in my family have also stood to take their wedding vows.

This year, I have taken time to try to follow my mother's advice. Even though I've never had an identity problem, I have asked myself, "Who am I?" Some of the answers lie in family roots and records.

In them, I find the reasons I love Methodist hymn singing, why I feel intensely loyal (sometimes beyond reason) to friend and kinsman, why I love poetry, why I have a restless spirit that keeps drawing me to new adventures, why I like to lead rather than follow, why I am hardheaded and impulsive, why I am passionate about human rights, why I believe civilization moves forward with daring, and why I love my country. All my life I have been sentimental about the past, but I have also been a reformer, as they were, wanting to make the future better. I have never believed America was made stronger by standing still, by maintaining the status quo, by fearing new trails. All this is in my genes.

My Texas roots stem from two plantation houses on the frontier. One is Salado, the Robertson home. The other, no longer standing is Spring Hill, the Sutherland home, once the political and social center of the cluster migration of two hundred Sutherlands who settled in Jackson County. In Salado, they raised cotton and bred horses; in Spring Hill, sugar cane. There the house and sugar mill were long ago burned, rebuilt, and now have fallen into decay. Both houses shaped those they touched. I know them personally and through hand-me-down stories, letters, and journals which speak of hardships as well as happiness, struggle, purpose, humankind, and God.

The Robertsons came overland from Tennessee by horseback and wagon and riverboat to colonize Texas, bringing with them six hundred families. The group was led by my great-great-grandfather, Sterling C. Robertson, who did the colonists' business at the capitol in Monclova, Mexico, a month's journey by horseback. He was responsible for the six hundred families he had brought to the Robertson colony, and part of that responsibility included keeping peace with the Indians, who far outnumbered the settlers.

My Sutherland forebears arrived on the coast of Texas by homemade boats that weathered the storms of the Mississippi. They were known as the Alabama Settlement, a group of thirty families, mostly kinfolk, led by Major George Sutherland.

Once in Texas, the group established a thriving business at the fork of two rivers, the Mustang and the Navidad, in Jackson County. The core of this cluster of almost two hundred people became Spring Hill, a large, prosperous sugar plantation and home of Major Sutherland and his wife, until the Texas Revolution eroded the supplies, property, and family life of this new land.

The house is now in splinters. I saw its ruins quite by accident when I was campaigning in 1980 for Jimmy Carter and our bus of guitar-playing campaigners drew up in front of the courthouse in the provincial town of Edna, Texas. I got an idea of the attitude around there when I noticed the two mail sacks at the post office had crayoned signs that read "Edna" on one and "Rest of the World" on the other. After our group had set up the microphones and swept the courthouse for an audience, I spotted a familiar face in the small crowd. The man who belonged to the face was wearing a Reagan button and grinning at me. When I finished my spiel, he came over and said, "Liz, I'm your cousin Frank. I hope you don't believe all that hogwash you're saying." It was a typical Sutherland greeting, where kinship is stronger than politics.

"Y'all aren't going to get any votes down here, so if you have half an hour, let me show you the house of your great-great-grandfather."

So we made an unlikely motorcade, with Frank at the head, leading our big, cumbersome bus (which declared "Texans for Carter for President") over raw countryside, dry creek beds, and past falling-down cemeteries to the remains of Spring Hill.

After the 1836 Battle of San Jacinto, those who returned to Spring Hill found the house like this—in ruins, burned, cattle gone, fields barren.

RECENTLY, on Texas's 150th birthday, I traveled to the San Jacinto battlefield near Houston to participate in a celebration commemorating the date (April 21, 1836) and place in which Texas won its war for independence from Mexico; there, I tried to recapture the spirit of early times and kinfolks. Two great-great-grandfathers who, coincidentally, had fought with Andrew Jackson at the Battle of New Orleans in the War of 1812—Sterling Clack Robertson and George Sutherland—had stood with Houston that day in a battle that lasted only eighteen minutes and killed 630 of Santa Anna's Mexican army—fully half the expedition, which had been marched double time to wipe out the Texans.

Family legend has it that George Sutherland, grieving for his son killed at the Alamo, and with fear in his heart for his family, who were hidden in the forest, faced the retreating Sam Houston at San Jacinto and demanded that plans to retreat farther to the Sabine River be abandoned. The battle was fought that day where they stood. The victory was won and a vast empire gained.

Six weeks before, these Texans had signed a Declaration of Independence, written by my great-great-uncle, George Childress. I identify with Childress, for he, too, had been a writer-editor. He worked for a Nashville paper and had come to Texas to report on the migration of so many Tennesseans led by Sterling Robertson. It turned out to be a bigger story than anticipated—a war with Mexico, the need to declare grievances in a document ... Childress was the wordsmith present. I smile thinking how many times newswriters are suddenly called upon to put an issue into words and spread its message to the world.

Childress wrote the declaration himself, setting forth the reasons for the break with the central government of Mexico, which had revoked the guaranteed rights under which the settlers had migrated to the new land. These were not bloodthirsty men, but pioneers of civilization, men of education, substance, and leadership, who had come to this frontier that was part of Mexico, made contracts with Mexico, obtained land grants to bring families and settle here. Little wonder they felt betrayed by the

"Napoleon of the West," General Santa Anna, president of Mexico, who, by a coup, had established an authoritarian centralist government. He wanted to keep Texas and personally led the slaughter at the Alamo. Santa Anna's army put every man to the sword, including a seventeen-year-old boy, William Dupriest Sutherland. He was returning from Saltillo, where he had been sent to study Spanish, and was riding through with his uncle, John Sutherland, who had escaped the massacre because he had a broken leg and had been sent to find help in Gonzales. Help came—the immortal thirty-two—but to no avail. Santa Anna's troops attacked, and on March 6 the Alamo fell.

The invading force under Santa Anna had surrounded the Alamo, beginning "thirteen days of glory" that ended with the death of every defender. This history comes to life for me through the letters of ancestors.

Uncle George, writing to a friend back in Tennessee:

March 15, 1836

Dear Sir:

The unpleasant intelligence has just reached this place that renewed attack was made on Sunday the 6th, led by Gen. Santa Anna in person, that previous to the attack the Mexican calvary formed a circle around the city to prevent the escape of any person, that the infantry made an attack simultaneously on the four sides of the Alamo, which was carried by assault at sunrise—that the resistance of the garrison was desperate and the loss very great on the part of the Mexican infantry.

Every man died fighting except seven, who, when the place was carried, laid down their arms and cried out for "quarter and Santa Anna," but were immediately put to death by his orders. Col. Travis, the commandant, committed suicide as soon as he lost all hope . . . a price had been set on his head and he was determined not to be taken alive. Col. Bowie, who was very ill in bed, also put an end to his own existence. The bodies of the Americans were burnt as rebels, says the dispatch, and the blood-red banner of extermination now waves in undisputed possession of San Antonio. Alas, poor Crockett! He was among them!

You cannot conceive the state of feeling existing here—

it is electric—volcanic . . . you may depend there is now to be war in earnest. Santa Anna comes himself and will make it a serious business. . . . I have not time to add more,

Yours, Geo. C. Childress

Like a prairie fire, news of the Alamo spread across Texas, routing the terrified settlements into retreating before the on-coming army of Santa Anna.

Texans rallied behind Houston, whole families moving with his army in his now famous "Runaway Scrape." One witness de-scribed the mood of those traveling with Houston's army: "Tight-lipped women, prayerful mothers, squalling children, frightened slaves, the aged and infirm all fleeing by ox cart, sled, two-wheeled jig." Every able-bodied man in Texas was trying to reach Houston's army.

They retreated until the historic moment at San Jacinto on April 21, when Houston attacked the unwary Mexican army as it was taking its customary siesta. The Yellow Rose of Texas, Emily Morgan, kept General Santa Anna preoccupied in bed until the battle began.

I stood that day of the anniversary in the place of victory, looking at the flags flying over the battlefield, listening to General Houston's descendant describe the battle, hearing the band play "Come Unto My Bower." That tune had been played by a Czech fifer as Houston's forces marched into battle that day, surprising Santa Anna's men with cries guaranteed to set a Texan's blood tingling: "Remember the Alamo! Remember Goliad!"

I recently found a dramatic letter written by Frances Mene-fee Sutherland to her sister back in Tennessee six weeks after that battle, when Texas, now free, was battered and beginning to form its own government. It is one of the few descriptions of the Run-away Scrape.

June 5, 1836

Dear Sally,

I will try to compose my mind while I give you a short history of a few months back. The American army was on our frontier. We thought it prudent to stay at home and did so until the General [Houston] thought it proper to retreat. We, being on the frontier, were compelled to go. We went to the Colorado River, but after some time, the General thought proper to retreat farther, and of course we had to go too. We proceeded to the Brazos River. There we stopped a few days, but dread and fear caused another start. . . . I wish you could know how the people did as they kept going about trying to get somewhere but no person knew where they were trying to get to. Several weeks passed on without any certain account from the army. All this time you could hardly guess my feeling. My poor William gone, yes, sister, gone from me. The sixth day of March, in the morning he was slain in the Alamo. Then his poor body committed to the flames. Oh, Sally, pray for me that I may have grace to help in this great time of trouble.

I will now say our relations are only in tolerable health, tho' none very sick. Poor mother went the rounds not very well all the time. I was afraid she would not hold out to get back again, but she is much better. She stopped at Brother William's. Sister Martha lives there. We are still trying to raise something to eat, but I fear we will miss it. Brother Thomas' house was burnt with stable and corn crib. Mr. Sutherland's warehouse was burnt, also, his houses on the Bay. But if we can have peace and can have preaching, I won't care for the loss of what property is gone.

Your sister, Fanny

A pioneer woman's prayer: "If we can have peace and can have preaching"! It seems so stoically matter-of-fact, but I have relearned by reading these journals that pioneer women suffered so many hardships they were braced for daily disaster.

We may not easily comprehend the minds and souls of our forebears. Beyond the realm of civilization, these people awoke to hunger where there were no stores or refrigerators. The reality of the rising sun was work in the field with frequent accidents that maimed or killed. The chills and fevers, the fall of a tree or a horse, were common, and at high noon armed enemies often appeared in person. They trusted in God, prayed when night fell, and by day tried to look on the best side of things. One letter, written by my great-great-grandfather, Samuel Rogers, brought that attitude home to me:

> We were coming home [after the battle of San Jacinto], almost naked for want of clothing. We came upon Old Black Head, one of our milk cows. Never will I forget the joy and gladness of my two children. Catherine clapped her little hands while tears of gladness rolled down her cheeks, and said, "Papa, now we will have milk."
>
> Well, I learned that however dark the clouds that overshadow our paths, there is a silver lining to it.

The Civil War and the Reconstruction period ushered troubles into Spring Hill as well as Salado. Two great-grandmothers, both named Mary Elizabeth, had to cope with its increasing agonies as well as large families and husbands absent in the fighting.

In Spring Hill, Mary Elizabeth Sutherland wrote to her daughter:

> Trouble of so many kinds has so destroyed my mind, I expect I will forget part of what I wanted to say. I am sending some goblets which I want you children to divide. The reason I send them now is because I think it very possible the Yankees will get our things, and maybe by sending them, you can save them. We hear the Yankees will parole the prisoners at Vicksburg, and we have a great deal of bad news from the other side of the River [Mississippi]. I fear the enemy will be encouraged to overrun Texas. These are things I expected you to have at my death. I send my goblets one apiece for George Ann, Talitha, Frank, Ginny, Ellie, Barty, one left for my pore [sic] boy. Should he never come home, it is yours. I have not heard from him.
>
> My prayer to God is our safety, but if he has decreed our destruction, maybe he will give us grace to bear it with Christian fortitude. I have been asked to pray for the Army and even our great General asked me to pray for him, and of course I do. But O, the wickedness of our people! Will the Lord save such a nation as this until they repent.

As the war worsened for the southerners, a cousin, G. S. Gayle, wrote to his mother:

Just a few days ago I left Louisiana and went to Vermillion-
ville where the Yankees were camped. I saw several large
sugar cane patches without a rail of fence around them, cotton patches with no negroes [sic] to pick it, and no fence to-
keep the stock out. There was a very rich man lived there. He
had fifteen or twenty negro houses, very large, cane and corn
fields. The Yankees took every negro he had, burnt every rail,
and left the cane and corn standing after they took as much
as they wanted. Ma, you do not know what it is to have the
enemy in your country.

I grew up surrounded by Civil War history in Salado. I
played in the old slave quarters and, in the big house each evening, heard the stories of the original family of twelve: six daughters and six sons, raised by my great-grandmother Mary Elizabeth
and her husband, E. Sterling C. Robertson, whose spirits were
ever present.

Tucked away in a drawer of an old walnut table, I found a
faded piece of yellowing paper written by my great-grandmother,
a document freeing the slaves. Forty-five people had been enfran-
chised on that day in September 1865, freed to leave "due to the
failure of the Confederate cause and the operation of Mr. Lincoln's proclamation." It had not been necessary to write such a
note. Why had she done it? To formalize what was reality, stating
it for her servants and the oncoming Union patrols in acceptance
of a new order.

I wonder if Great-grandmother Robertson felt a sense of relief herself in being freed from the responsibility of running a
plantation, actually a small community of sixty adults, children,
and servants, black and white. The account books in the pantry
show endless responsibility for the flour, sugar, bacon slabs, and
coffee measured out for slave households as well as her own.
There was real managerial skill in women of the South, and I see
their legacy in the contemporary southern woman on the national
scene: Lindy Boggs of New Orleans, Betty Talmadge of Georgia,
Lady Bird Johnson of Texas.

Many slaves didn't leave. Slaves! The word was never used
in that house. Letters refer to them by name or as the servants.

Strong genes run in my family. My great grandfather, E. Sterling C. Robertson helped draft the state's constitution. Mary Elizabeth Robertson started the first literary society in Texas, in the old Robertson parlor. My mother (another Mary Elizabeth) and my father, Thomas Shelton Sutherland IV. A group of aunts and uncles during their courting days at a picnic on Salado Creek, my mother and father in the center.

When word spread in the wake of Vicksburg, the Union patrols, still called Yankees, were feared in Texas. And the plantation owners did what their parents had done in the Texas Revolution—buried the silver, putting it in fruit jars. One small black boy witnessed his father helping the women in my family dig the earth and place the silver in a gully east of the house. He told us about it as an old man.

The Yankee patrols did come all summer. A first episode was the sudden arrival of a southern general, Henry McCullough, on an exhausted white horse. Colonel Robertson gave him quick refuge, hid the white horse in the stable, and offered him a fresh black horse to ride. When the Union troops rode up, they asked, "Have you seen a man on a white horse pass by?"

"No," replied my great-grandfather, and they turned back.

The story was told and retold, and someone always pointed out that Great-grandfather had told the truth because the white horse was out back. It hadn't passed by.

On another occasion, a Union patrol camped overnight around the house at Salado. It was searching for a former Confederate soldier named Swan Bigham, who had shot a Yankee soldier in the Belton courthouse when he returned from the war and discovered that the Yankee had confiscated his land while he was away. Bigham rode quickly to Salado to the Robertson house, where he had friends.

My three great-uncles hid Swan out in a cave up in the back pasture. They set up a signal to alert him if the Yankee troops were nearby. The signal: one of the boys would call the cattle and salt them. This signaled Swan to go back to the cave. When the patrol arrived, the Yankees felt certain they were near their prey and were angry that they had missed Swan, their breakfast, and their lunch. So they set up camp near the house and started tearing pickets off the white homestead fence to make a fire.

My great-great-grandmother, Sophie Lynch, put her pistol under her apron, went out, and said to the sergeant in charge, "Captain, your men have just torn down some pickets from the fence when there is brush over there in the creek bottom they can use for making a fire. We are just a group of women here, and we can't rebuild a fence. Can't you please stop them?" He did, perhaps flattered that she had upgraded him from sergeant to captain.

I have thought a lot about those two women, Sophie Lynch and her daughter, Mary Elizabeth. I look at the pictures of Mary Elizabeth in a dark taffeta dress with her long curls, a coquettish, winsome expression, and holding a beautiful fan. She had grown up in Austin, met the young E. Sterling C. Robertson, who had already made a name as the Spanish translator in the new land office. Three members of my family have held that office, including my brother Tommy and my cousin Malcolm McLean, now head of the Robertson Archives at the University of Texas in Arlington.

Mary Elizabeth Robertson had beautiful eyes—the same eyes I saw in my mother, another Mary Elizabeth, and now see in my daughter—brown eyes, clear and unafraid. She saw things as they were. Her life revolved around twelve children, six daughters and six sons. Her home was the center of life in the area, and from it came the gift of one hundred acres of land for the First Methodist Church and another hundred for Salado College. All ideas were encouraged there. One caller, Mrs. Kate Orgain, later wrote about approaching Mrs. Robertson and her mother about forming a women's literary society.

"They sprang for the proposition, gave their hearty approval, and extended a cordial invitation to all interested to meet at their home. Married ladies as well as girls were asked. So an enthusiastic crowd gathered in the double parlors and began the literary society." The name was Ama Savourien Reading Society, meaning "I love to know."

The library of the homeplace itself has the leathery smell of well-read books: Sir Walter Scott's Waverley novels, Thackeray's novels, Robert Burns's poetry, Dickens, John Henry Brown's *History of Texas*, and once popular stories like "The Little Colonel."

Indeed, my mother had read all of the Waverley novels by the time she was eight years old.

RETURNING TO SALADO revives so many childhood memories. My cousins and I played under the trees and made houses between the graves in the family cemetery. At Christmas we would all go to the back pasture to find the perfect cedar tree. In the spring we fed the baby lambs with a bottle, and in the summer we cleaned out the springs. I would ride the tame mare to Norwood's grocery store for the mail and a few penny candies. All these memories rush over me as I stand on the porch of that old house.

On still, hot summer afternoons, my mother would find the coolest spot in the downstairs hall, and we children would sit on the floor while she read to us. I would crawl up next to her. It was a heavenly feeling being close to her softness and her lavender fragrance. The whole house smelled of lavender. Even now, we still cut a few sprigs to use in family funeral sprays. No matter how far away I am, I have never been able to pass a lavender tree without taking a leaf and rubbing it between my fingers to drink in, once more, that scent of home and family.

I grew up in a family of words, most of them saying something. We were a talkative, quoting family, one that liked literature. I once asked Harper Lee, author of *To Kill a Mockingbird*, how to be a good writer. "Read your head off," she replied. And that is what my family has always done, partly because they lived in the country towns of Bell County, where reading was entertainment and books were handy and visible. We valued them. No one would leave a book facedown to crack its spine without a sharp reprimand: "That is no way to treat a book!"

Poetry, because it is lyrical and easily remembered, was a natural part of growing up: Byron, Shelley, and Keats; Kipling, Wordsworth, Tennyson, and Browning. My mother was the biggest quoter because she read more than anyone else in the family. Like so many other women in that age of living in lonely ranch houses miles and miles from neighbors, she escaped the hum-

drum of household chores by quoting poetry over the dishpan as
the children dried the dishes. Loneliness was a common condition in rural Texas.

I WAS SEVEN when we moved to Austin so we could get a better
education in the public schools of a larger town and, later, at the
University of Texas. Like other Texas families, my mother packed
and moved us from Bell County when my oldest brother,
Tommy, was ready for "the University." My father helped move
us down, and then, because times were tough, he went to west
Texas to work as a small highway contractor. He came home once
a month, always bringing something special, a bushel of canta-
loupes or peaches or lots of big steaks. Daddy was a sometime figure in our lives, proud of us, strong, welcome, bursting with
presents, but the permanent presence was our mother.

Our house was on West Avenue, and we always called it by
the number: "1611." It was a yellow stucco house with a wrap-
around porch that stretched to accommodate everyone. It was
launching pad and thoroughfare for those who came to study at
the University of Texas, our "Athens on the hill." There were
three floors and a giant attic room that harbored cousins and
boarders with their books and crane-neck lamps, trunks, and
records pealing out, "Sooomewheeere over the rainbow. . . ."
Mine was the octagonal room in front, upstairs, where I could see
out in two directions for the slightest hint of a Model T Ford or,
better still, a convertible. They came in droves, filled with friends
honking, laughing, shouting. . . .

At least a dozen of us lived there, family, cousins, a para-
lyzed grandmother, a practical nurse, and an occasional maid. My
philosophical mother, amused, unperturbed, reigned over this
noisy house of banging doors, laughter, shouting occupants of all
ages, relishing the life around her.

Dinnertime was talk time. I wish I could relive those days of
endless debate and laughter. How little material things mattered.
The Depression was a fact of life, and you didn't let it get you

down. You simply got by on very little and were glad to share what you had.

The fare around the table was meat loaf, pork and beans, rice, hot biscuits, and molasses, but the conversation was ambrosia. No one talked trivia; we had no time for petty gossip. Local and national events offered plenty of exciting topics: the battle between the Board of Regents at the university on one side and the students, faculty, and President Homer P. Rainey, a mild and scholarly man, aligned on the side of free speech. We talked about Franklin D. Roosevelt and thanked God someone was trying to create jobs for the steady stream of hoboes who came knocking at the back door. My mother never turned one away— she always had a meal for them. She would hand over our stubby broom, and they would sweep the terrace of chinaberries from the umbrella tree overhead. We had no money to give them, just a plate of whatever was cooking. But I remember them as men with manners, middle-aged faces, and gratitude. It never occurred to us to be scared of them. They were victims of the times, men who were "just up against it," as Mamma would say. The Depression left its mark on all of us in politics; it made liberals out of a lot of us. It touched us in other ways, too. My mother and grandmother, who had learned to "make do," could never throw away ribbons or gift paper from a package. They would carefully unwrap their birthday or Christmas packages, smoothing out the paper to be used again, sometimes even pressing the ribbon. We kids collected unused milk bottles and later turned them in for five cents each, which meant admission to a picture show.

Austin had brought us a lot in new conversation, but we brought something from Salado, too: common sense—horse sense, my uncles called it—and a sense of roots and of the fitness of things. We also brought our code of honor and a devout belief in the magic of education as the entrance to the world, to places with bright lights like New York City and Paris, to places we had seen in picture books and on postcards. Austin was the pot of gold at the end of the rainbow from Salado. A new world began to take shape. We read the newspapers, listened to the radio, and heard talk about something besides the price of sheep, goats, and cattle.

I WAS ONE of ten thousand students enrolled at the University of Texas in 1938, and it was the most broadening experience I had encountered. Leslie Carpenter and I, both freshmen, headed for the journalism school as fast as we could and worked on the campus paper, *The Daily Texan*.

Our group of college journalists all fancied ourselves as characters in the movie *Front Page*, which was the rage then and influenced my era and profession as much as *All the President's Men* made Woodwards and Bernsteins out of reporters today. Starring Pat O'Brien, *Front Page* added to the glamour, typecasting, and romance of reporting. I can see it still: the sob sister with the big heart and cigarette dangling from her mouth as she perched on the desk of the city editor; newsman Pat O'Brien, hat on head and press card in the hat's wide band, writing frantically with the "hunt and peck" system of typing while someone "held the presses" on the story. Soon there would be extras on the streets.

Radio finally killed off the extra editions carried by small newsboys up and down the streets with the flashy headlines on disasters: "*Extrraaaa*, read all about it! Hauptmann guilty in Lindbergh trial!" "*Extrraaaa, Hindenburg* explodes over New Jersey!" "*Extrraaaa*, Hitler marches into Poland!"

It was a far simpler world than now: black or white, good or bad. It was a prepill world. "Nice girls" didn't "go all the way" with boys. We would lose their respect, and ultimately, they wouldn't marry anyone but a virgin. We danced, held hands, and kissed our dates good night, but heavy petting was out, especially for those from the Bible Belt. The innocence of my college days seems unreal now.

Throughout my school years I was drawn to people who were doing things, the girls active in campus activities, the boys and girls at work in campus politics, the students writing skits or campus plays. Les and I took a typewriter to the campus hangout to write a competition play for "Time Staggers On," the annual student spoof on itself. He was becoming a fixture in my life.

Dreaming aloud was as much a part of life as being a reporter-in-the-making. We avidly read Richard Halliburton's *Royal Road to Romance* and *Seven League Boots*, and they sparked our imaginations. We, too, wanted to swim the Nile by moonlight, see the Taj Mahal under the stars, and wind through the Casbahs of Morocco. Our classes in play-writing made us sure that one day we would produce a Broadway show together, and as we sipped Coca-Cola in the Texas Union, we dreamed of our names in lights. College was a place for dreaming. The day of counselors, aptitude tests, resumes, and college interviews had not yet dawned. We had every confidence we could make it to the top.

Campus politics at UT was, in those times, political campaigning with all the high jinks. I was the first girl to run for vice-president of the student body and get elected. My two male opponents were millionaires, both delightful and imaginative, and it took ingenuity to keep up with them. One, Jimmy Craig, owned his own small airplane and a convertible. His campaign slogan was "Free Airplane Rides with High-Flying Jimmy Craig."

In answer, I brought in an attention getter to spice up my campaign, a mother duck and her babies, and I put them on the main mall along with the slogan: "Keep Your Feet on the Ground with Liz." I also had a set of sorority sisters in Alpha Phi who went serenading the dormitories each evening after dinner. Their spokesman was Joe Kilgore, then a law student and later a congressman, a marvelous speaker who would, after a song or two, step forward and say, "Ladies of Scottish Rite dormitory, I come here to boost the candidacy of Liz Sutherland for vice-president of the student body." The dormitory windows would fill up with eager coeds cheering our performance.

I was blessed with energy and curiosity, and I am grateful that I've never lost either. I was in love with the freedom of thought a state university offered, and although it was a time of great problems worldwide, we were reaching for answers. We believed in government because we saw it working to lift people into opportunity. Roosevelt and the New Deal had put a leash on the Wall Street robbers. Hope abounded, and so did freedom.

Many future Texas politicians cut their political teeth—or fangs—at the University of Texas. We turned out governors, congressmen, senators, and judges for Texas. People often ask why I never ran for public office. Public office was not something many women sought then, but more important, I was swept up by newspapering. I took a side job on *The Austin American*, and it was there that I found politics.

I got my first political assignment by chance. No one else was in the city room of *The Austin American* when the AP and UP tickers rang, signaling "Flash! Big news!" Not just any news—Senator Alben Barkley was breaking with Franklin Roosevelt over the War Revenue Bill. It was noon, and everyone was gone except for the city editor, Weldon Hart, and me. He looked around for someone to send out to round up reaction. Our Democratic National Committeewoman, Clara Driscoll, was over at the Driskill Hotel, and someone had to interview her about whether she would side with FDR or Barkley. I was there, so I was dispatched to the hotel.

I had never been in a hotel in my life or even walked through the lobby without my father. You didn't want to be seen there in those days: hotels had a negative connotation. But I bravely walked down to the Driskill, went up to the suite, and knocked timidly. As I stood waiting nervously, "Miss Clara" opened the door, and she was . . . *smoking a cigarette!* I had never seen a woman smoking a cigarette before except in the movies. She was quite an imposing lady who carried a cane with a diamond in it. There was also a man there, Mr. Frank Scofield, the IRS collector and a political figure in Texas. And the two of them were . . . *drinking*—Manhattans, or something with a cherry in it. I had never been around people who drank, not even eggnog at Christmas. I was too nervous to sit, so I just asked my questions—Miss Clara sided with Barkley—and then I said good-bye and went back to the office. I had seen my first smoke-filled room

The second house to shape my life was a big rambling house in Austin — a launching pad for me as I went through the public schools and then the University of Texas. That was a house of growth and learning and dozens of cousins. There were no locked doors or minds. I graduated from the University of Texas with my journalism degree in hand and my virtue intact on a June day in 1942 and set forth to the world of Washington and politics. My beau and fellow journalist was Leslie Carpenter. We laughed and wrote our way through high school and college. I knew even then that if I did not marry him I would always feel I had missed the boat.

and felt the intrigue. I couldn't put that scene out of my mind. They were in the know, they had power, they got interviewed by reporters. I've been in a thousand smoke-filled rooms since and have learned something in all of them.

Years later, after the landmark Woodward and Bernstein Watergate investigation, I look back and laugh. I guess if I had been an investigative reporter, I would have asked, "What is the Democratic National Committeewoman doing having a drink with the IRS collector? Is it sex? Is it a payoff?" But I didn't ask, and I suspect that it was just as it appeared to be, two old political friends enjoying each other's company and talking politics. Maybe I missed a Pulitzer. I doubt it, but if I did, I don't regret it.

By 1941, I was a senior in college. I remember a Sunday— December 7, 1941, to be exact. On that early afternoon, I was having a hamburger and Coke with Les at our favorite campus meeting place, "Triple X." A student wandered in with news heard on his car radio: "The Japs have bombed Pearl Harbor!" How young we were! We knew it was important, but little did we know how it would shape our world. We even had to ask where Pearl Harbor was. No one was quite sure.

In the next two months, most of the boys on campus enrolled in ROTC units. Les joined the naval ROTC. Washington became the news capital of the world. My oldest brother, Tommy, moved his young family there and began working for the Board of Economic Warfare. War clouds began to hang over our lives. Ration books were issued for everything from butter to safety pins. Tin cans disappeared for the war effort. We saved the tinfoil from Hershey's bars and cigarettes, rolled it into tight balls of silver, and turned it in to a central collection station. Graduation ceremonies went on as usual. Our speaker was Lord Halifax, the British ambassador to the United States, who came down from Washington to make a plea for freedom, for a united front against the enemies, Germany and Japan. The United States was now in the fight.

It is strange how many details one remembers, the high

points or the first impression of an event or place. In assembling all my albums, clippings, and scrapbooks for this accounting of my life, I have come upon a line here, a memento there, that takes me back in time. My memory is often at odds with what actually occurred. One marvelous "find" is a suitcase of letters and cards which I wrote in the full flush of my girlish enthusiasm and romanticism. I am shocked at my bravado in a letter to my mother on Mother's Day, May 1942, written as I was about to graduate.

> I went to rehearsal for graduation today. It is hard to realize that only four years ago I stood gazing at the University tower in awe. I look around also at those seniors I started out with four years ago. For instance, Nancy, who has made Phi Beta Kappa, and achieved recognition in bacteriology, but who will probably marry this summer to be with that lazy poet. And there are scads more, some who've probably given and gotten far more from the University than I have. Nevertheless, I feel so much luckier. I don't know of anyone I'd trade shoes with. I ordered twenty invitations to graduation today, and I hope you'll give me a list of who to send them to.
>
> My plans for the summer I shall now state. I hope to heaven I can carry them out. After all, I deserve to get to do one thing I want after going through four years of hard labor. Jean, Elizabeth and I want to purchase a used car and travel all over Texas writing features. Dr. Reddick thinks we could make expenses. The experience and fun would be worth a million, and I know if we don't do it now, we never will. I don't see any difficulty in selling stories. The time is ripe and I certainly want to get in and do something I am inspired to do. It's a shot in the dark, but it may be a chance to become famous. . . . So I don't give a hang about coming to the capital where the rate is twelve women to every male and everyone is grabbing for a hunk of glory out of the national garbage can. Give me the wide open spaces, a Model T, and a typewriter, and I'll see you in the hall of fame.

I can't believe I ever called my Washington, which I love and whose every heartbeat I follow avidly, a "national garbage can." But there it is in my own handwriting. As it turned out, by mid-June I had my typewriter and was headed to Washington.

Four years of college were behind me. It never occurred to me that my learning was just starting, that it is what you learn after you think you know it all that counts.

Through the years I have heard hundreds of speeches about education, collected dozens of definitions. A favorite, from one of Lyndon Johnson's speeches: "Education is a companion which no misfortune can depress, no crime destroy, no enemy alienate, no despotism enslave. At home, a friend; abroad, an introduction. In solitude, a solace, and in society, an ornament. Without it, what is man? A splendid slave, a reasoning savage."

Lyndon Johnson, who was indeed the education president, said, "Education is the only valid passport out of poverty." He knew—as a young man, he had taught school in poverty-stricken Cotulla, Texas. One of his students there was a poor boy named Juan Gonzalez; eventually, LBJ took him back to Johnson City, where he and Mrs. Johnson gave the boy a home. Juan grew up to be a successful businessman in south Texas, offering the president firsthand evidence that a little faith and investment can transform the lives of the poor.

I'll never forget the day the first lady and I, along with Secretary of Health, Education and Welfare John Gardner, visited Canada Township, North Carolina, to see how the president's Head Start and Teachers Corps programs were working in Appalachia.

We stopped in to see Mr. and Mrs. Mathis and their seven children. Mr. Mathis, standing in front of the family's two-room shack clad in his best overalls, told us the four men teachers supplied by the Teachers Corps had helped a lot. The children's hair was cut now. They had new equipment at the school, and he and his "mizziz" went there in the evening for programs. Maybe his older ones would not quit school at the third grade, as he had. They might go down the mountain to the high school thirty miles away. He'd see.

Mrs. Johnson knew how to talk to Mr. Mathis about his garden and his crops, and before we left she put a jar of peach preserves from the LBJ ranch into Mrs. Mathis's hands. "Nothing tastes as good as when it comes from your own garden," she said. "We asked the home demonstration woman to come to the ranch and show us how to preserve this." The lesson was implied.

Before we left, someone asked Mr. Mathis what programs the family watched on television. "*Lassie*," he said, and listed a few more. Then, as an afterthought, he added, rather pleased with himself, "And we saw the president the other night. When he comes on, we don't turn him off. We leave him on jes' like it was any other program."

THESE DAYS there is an awful lot of penny-pinching going on in educational programs. We punish our public schools, we punish our public libraries, and yet their proud products are all around us. James Michener and Margaret Mead were the first two youngsters to apply for library cards at the Doylestown Library in Pennsylvania. What would most of us be doing had we lived in this country without the benefits of public libraries and public schools?

We are learning at last that education is for life, not just to obtain a skill or a job. I like the definition of education that Dr. Ernest Boyer of the Carnegie Foundation gave when he called for the educated heart as well as the educated mind. The educated heart embodies a reverence for natural and human life, a respect for excellence, an appreciation of beauty, a tolerance of and concern for others, a willingness to reexamine old assumptions that were drilled into so many of us during our formative years: mastery without arrogance, openness to change, attentiveness not only to what is spoken, but to what is omitted, and finding romance and excitement in the endless quest for learning.

Harry Emerson Fosdick, clergyman, author, and professor of practical theology, said he wanted to spend the last of his life living by a great university. I do that. There it stands framed by my window, across the city . . . sturdy, discernible. In some way, as a citizen and loyal ex-student, I want, I must, make my own input out of what I have learned. I must have enough nerve, of which I have never been short, to be a voice for a writers' center.

Sometimes education is the topic of conversation around my table as we look out at the university tower. We talk about it. What is an educated person? "What it is to me," Lady Bird Johnson once said in a way I shall not forget, "is knowing and caring about what is around me. That tree is a Spanish oak, aflame in fall. That bird is the red-tailed hawk, rare in these parts. There is a mesquite, newly discovered as valuable for hardwood floors. There are, if you look hard enough, the first tender green leaves of the bluebonnets poking up out of the ground. I would be a sloth not to know the things around me. Knowing them enriches my life."

Thinking things, doing things, experiencing sensations, responding to stimuli in ways that are not otherwise possible—this is education, and I hope I've acquired at least a bit of it in sixty-five years of living.

My lasting lessons in poetry and love of words came from my mother, forever urging us to have vision and acquire an education. She had opened doors from the secure limitations of small-town Salado. We made good grades because we became avid listeners, not because we were being pressured. The "mid-watches of the night," to borrow Thomas Wolfe's phrase, were where students explored into the wee hours all kinds of wild, Rabelaisian thoughts, stretching our young minds as never before. We argued and laughed and created crazy, wonderful ideas, short stories, fantasies. That freedom is something so joyous, you want to hold it forever.

LOVE

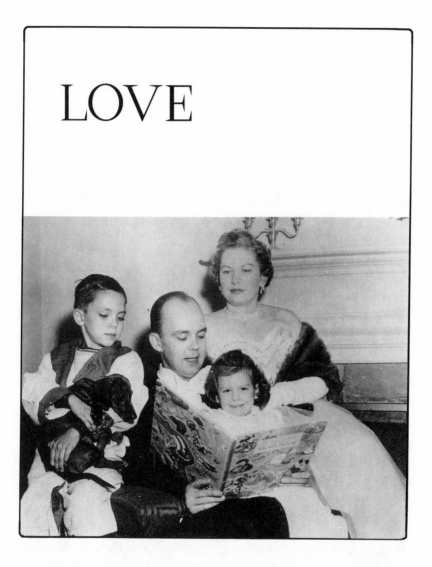

IT IS SIX A.M., and the deer aren't here. The corn has been waiting for thirty minutes. They are probably up on the top of the hill at Henrietta Jacobsen's rocky ledge. Yesterday when I told her that I lured fourteen deer for my birthday, I could see her gleam of envy. Generally four or five at a time is maximum. Later, I watched from my window as her car sped down the road. I knew she was bound for Buck Moore's feed store to get some sorghum pellets. Deer go wild for sorghum pellets.

Henrietta is my smart friend, once the mayor here in our West Lake Hills area. If she ran again, she could win in a walk. She still keeps tab on the environmental laws and zoning "regs" and rallies us to West Lake City Hall to protest a billboard or a power line now and then. She and I have a special friendship. We share the knowledge of "inside widowhood" as only those who have experienced it can. And we are friendly competitors for the deer who live on this hill, as well as the few male escorts available for women over sixty. Both are endangered species.

This hillside is unbelievably competitive for the wildlife. You may not see your neighbors for weeks at a time, tucked away as they are in their rustic settings. But if a painted bunting appears at anyone's bird feeder, phones start ringing all over the hill to pass the word. Imagine! You can gather a crowd with a bird. In my lifetime, I've networked on a lot of things: jobs for women, a place in politics, better salaries, and presidential appointments, but not until I moved back to Austin to live among the live oaks and the west hills have I networked on wildlife. A raccoon in someone's attic occupies us so thoroughly, it sets us back a week in work. We don't kill them. You'd probably be sent to the penitentiary for that. We call the wildlife woman with the Havahart traps, and she comes to lure them out of the attic or the walls when the babies are big enough to leave the nest. Sometimes it takes more than a week. Sometimes it takes as much as $50.

Most of my life has not been spent in such endeavors. When I first came home to Texas I thought it was crazy, and I wondered if I had settled in a nutty neighborhood of nature cultists. But they have won me over. Feeding the game does have its charms. I put as much enthusiasm into luring birds and deer as I used to invest in the great national issues of the day.

I wonder if Henrietta's new beau likes deer. Probably. After I finish this chapter today, maybe I'll have time to drive the ten miles to Buck Moore's and buy their new apple-flavored deer feed. That should win back my deer.

My friendship with Henrietta has a special dimension because we both know the insecurity that comes to those who have
loved and . . . well, *lost* husbands of many years and now live
alone. We keep each other's phone numbers handy in case of
emergencies like getting dizzy on a ladder, or breaking bones, or
strange noises in the night. It's like the buddy system at camp,
checking on one another. The other morning I saw an unidenti-
fied snake, and I called her. She was down here in a minute with
her hoe and had already summoned the West Lake police, who
arrived about the same time with a squad car and an officer who
had his gun pulled. All this excitement got my nephew over here
with his camera and some new neighbors who wanted to see what
was going on. Our little snake-killing party (we do kill poisonous
snakes) didn't amount to much because the snake didn't show up
again, having disappeared back into his hole. The gasoline and
mothballs I poured in failed to bring him up. All was not lost,
however. We served coffee to the new neighbors, and later,
Henrietta brought me a hoe of my own for my birthday.

We also share laughter, gossip, and a pipeline about available men. Alas, it is not a long list. It's not that we are interested
in getting married again. Let well enough alone! As for me, after
ten years I've finally straightened out my bookkeeping. I am now
categorized with the IRS and Seidman & Seidman as a single,
self-employed wage earner. I don't want to mess that up.

Henrietta, who has played tennis all her life, has just now
sorted out all her tennis partners and reserved courts for Mon-
days, Tuesdays, and Thursdays at the Lost Creek Country Club.
When she considers remarriage, she thinks about the perils of
trying to share in someone else's family love and obligations.
"Frankly, I wonder if I have what it takes at this stage of my life
to enter into a new husband's family togetherness," she explained
to me as we talked over our current file of gentlemen callers.

Of course, you hear a lot of horror stories about senior newlyweds with newly joined families. I have a friend who walked out
on the flimsy excuse that, at sixty-five, "I get nauseated singing
'Happy Birthday' to a bunch of children and grandchildren who

aren't mine." But you can balance the horror stories with successful marriages like that of Dick and Betty Hughes. They married long before he was governor of New Jersey. He had six children, she had six, I think it was, and, as Betty told me later, "Christmas was a carnival because no one got mad at each other, and even our old in-laws show up for family celebrations."

Those are the examples we relish. But we make the most of our "happy hour" time and take whatever adventures we can provoke out of life. We live in an idyllic spot for that. Except for the size of our stag line, it is sheer heaven up here.

The available men here (and, I suspect, the world over) divide into two groups. Group I are gentle, polite, esoteric, lifetime bachelors—sensitive, often witty, sometimes good singers, and always ready to cook up a culinary feast or take a weekend trip. But they are not all-purpose escorts. Alas! Group II are recently divorced or widowed men fresh from either the courthouse or the graveyard, bitter or bereaved. But if you give them time (not too much, for they tend to remarry at a faster rate than women because of the law of supply and demand), you may find a rare mate or escort. Never mind the jealous friends who say, "My kingdom, Edith's only been dead two months!" Most of my friends will still keep an eye on the obit pages.

Men aren't essential to later life. It's just that an all-widows world can get dull. It lightens things up to be looking forward to some male companionship at the end of the day. But finding them is tough. I took a head count of the ten men I know best who are nearby, and the result is depressing: two are close kin; three are widowers who will hang around and accept my hospitality and sympathy but will disappear when the bitterness or bereavement end and marry someone shapely and under forty; five are friends forever but will never marry.

I GO TO NEW YORK frequently to keep up with old friends; one day when I was lunching at Le Cirque with four of them, all worldly, successful women, we took up the subject of love and romance. Le Cirque is a fancy restaurant where you see and are seen. It is not the kind of place where you would normally talk about love. More likely topics would be money, fashions, face-lifts, or the Von Bülow trial. We got into love because we are all middle-aged romantics, and we had already finished pointing out everyone who was there—Bill Blass, at his regular table, and Gloria Vanderbilt, who is always seated in a conspicuous spot. Glancing around the room, we saw a lot of lady do-gooders, like the effervescent, ever-young Brooke Astor and that philanthro-pist-for-all-seasons, Mary Lasker. Both dispense money for good causes like the pope dispenses holy water. They make use of their widowhood and money to do public service and, with the effort, have found a good life. They also have a sense of humor.

I remember the day Brooke breezed in late for a committee meeting of wildflower enthusiasts. "I feel lousy!" she said breath-lessly.

"Well," I replied, "you look like a million."

She stopped, straightened up, and said with a giggle, "Well, I should!"

I like nifty women like that who don't just redo their own apartments or houses, but transform whole neighborhoods or schoolyards.

So that day at Le Cirque, love was our subject, and our loose-jointed conversation revolved around how to get it, how to keep it, when to shuck it, and, hardest of all, how to recognize the real thing and cherish and nurture it. I can't even remember who opened the conversation, but someone put forth the question: How many people do you know who can sustain a good marriage for fifty years?

"Or even an open-ended personal relationship?" Sherry in-terjected. "Yet we need to be loved more desperately than ever because it's a colder world out there, more anonymous, more dis-tant from friends and neighbors.

"The more successful a woman becomes," she continued, "the fewer chances she has. Where do you meet men—successful men—anymore?"

I repeated what Fleur Cowles had once told me: "Always fly

first class to find a first-class man." Or hit the health clubs. I know people who even jog for love. At least you get to see what you are getting.

"Not many of us are as successful as Margaret Mead," someone ventured. "After her last marriage, she said, 'I've been married three times and divorced three times. I gained something from each marriage. I'm glad I married them all, and I'm glad I divorced them all.' "

"It's absolutely true that some of the best marriages are second marriages," said Sherry. "You've learned from the first experience. You loosen up with the second."

"The hunger for love never ceases," Betsy said. "Mollie Parnis says that the first year she was a widow, she would have married practically anybody. But now she won't marry anyone and give up her independence and personal comfort."

Luvie took a deep drag on her cigarette. "Men have to marry," she observed. "They have been taken care of, and the older they get the more they need to marry. Everyone is very keen on Malcolm Forbes right now, but there aren't all that many Malcolm Forbeses with homes and yachts and wit and a circle of bright people. It's pretty bleak out there. Helen Gurley Brown says there are seven million extra women across the country, and they can't wait for Prince Charming anymore. They have to lower their sights."

"But how does my bright, thirty-five-year-old divorced daughter, who is smart, pretty, and well up the corporate ladder, meet someone who is smart, handsome, and as alive as she is?" I asked.

"You travel a lot and do interesting things," advised Eleanor, a wise and experienced woman.

I took from my purse an apropos letter I had just received from Fleur Cowles. Fleur is always polling her friends for her books about flowers. What kind of flower would you like to be? What is your favorite arrangement? I had polled her about love, and she'd scribbled off her own scenario on a yellow pad describing how she met her husband, Tom Meyer. I read it aloud.

Liz, dear,

I was in Iran visiting the Shah; Tom was prospecting the forests for him in relation to their 5-year plan. We were joined on the plane going westward—I to London before New York to break the long journey, he to go home to London, where he was born and bred.

He was very gallant on the plane—voluntarily clearing away the mess left in the pocket of the seat before me. We finally talked to each other and two things drew us into heated and happy talk.

1. I, discussing the progressive policies of Walter Reuther (whom I'd met and he so admired);

2. He, describing his life as a racing driver (something I'd have liked to do!) and we had a wonderful time passing the time as if it didn't exist. He was already "Mr. Timber" but raced in all the big timers.

Would he like a lift into London? Claridges was sending a car for me . . . I asked.

No—I'm being met myself. . . . But will you have a drink with me?

No, I'm sorry.

Okay, I'll pick you up at 7.

That's how it began, Liz, and oh, what a happy (30 years so far) ending.

Love, Fleur

I folded up her letter. The waiter brought another round of martinis, and Luvie began a poignant love story:

"You remember Paul Douglas, the senator from Illinois, and Emily, his wife, who was for a while a congresswoman from Illinois. . . . It happened after Paul, that tall, strong marine, was stricken with paralysis. He retired from the U.S. Senate and was confined to a wheelchair in Washington. Fortunately, he had Emily at his side. Theirs was a late and happy political and intellectual marriage. If you recall, Emily had been an actress before she was a congresswoman.

"After Paul's stroke, Emily became his constant nurse and companion. Twice each day, morning and afternoon, a neighbor helped her move the senator from his wheelchair to his bed. One day he reached out for something and toppled forward out of the chair. Emily ran next door for the neighbor, to find that he had left for work and wouldn't be returning for three hours.

" 'I knew Paul would be mortified,' she told me later in recounting that day. Mustering all the acting talent she had, Emily walked back into their house and announced cheerily, 'Paul, it's been years since we've been on a picnic. We're going to have one this afternoon.'

"She tucked a sofa pillow under his head, arranged him as comfortably as possible on the floor, then was off to the kitchen to pack a basket of sandwiches, a bottle of wine, two glasses, a blanket, and a book. For three hours, they lay on the floor, ate and toasted each other. She read aloud as though they were sitting beside a lovely lake. They were young again.

" 'It was one of the nicest afternoons we've had,' she told me, 'and when I heard the car on the gravel next door and my neighbor appeared, I hated to see it end. I think we both did.' "

We all were choked up, and then someone remembered a line from Tennyson's "Fatima," which seemed to say it all for the Douglases:

> O Love, O fire! once he drew
> With one long kiss my whole soul thro'
> My lips, as sunlight drinketh dew.

Oh, how the infirmities of old age overtake us! It takes imagination, humor, ingenuity, and some acting to cope.

Helen Hayes once told me about a Christmas when her husband, Charles MacArthur, gave her twelve pairs of eyeglasses and distributed them upstairs and downstairs and in the car so she would always be able to find them. "In about a month, I had managed to lose all but one pair," she said with a laugh

I remembered another couple who improved their faltering marriage when the husband, Burt, decided to "find things for Mildred." The Whiteakers are old newspaper friends of mine. Mildred has been women's editor of *The San Antonio Express* for thirty years despite a long bout with cancer.

When I asked them for the key to their happy marriage,

Burt offered an answer. "We've had rough times, really near miss times. Mildred was always losing things, and it used to infuriate me. Finally I decided I would just make up my mind to find things for Mildred. Now I make a game of it. I don't get angry when she loses her keys, glasses, notebook, sometimes even the car in the parking lot. I just stop and find them. We really get along very well now. I solved the problem by becoming Sherlock Holmes."

Having had my own around-the-clock marriage, a working partnership when Les and I were both engaged in newspapering, I think a lot can be said for that kind of marriage. You understand the demand, the hours, and share the same conversation and intrigue. It is part of both of you and part of the romance of living. In the newspaper world you see many intermarriages.

As the waiter brought our salads, Betsy took over the conversation. "If it is around-the-clock marriages you want," she said, "I give you the Lunts or George Burns and Gracie Allen. My kingdom, on his ninetieth birthday, after Gracie has been dead twenty-five years and George is still a big success, she is the one he still talks about and credits for his career. Despite all his braggadocio about girls, it is Gracie he still loves. George's longtime friend Carol Channing told me he got so lonely after Gracie's death that he went out and bought an electric blanket. At night, he snuggled under its warmth and pretended he was lying in Gracie's arms."

"Stage husbands are the unsung heroes of so many good marriages," Eleanor said. "For instance, Carol Channing and Charles Lowe, Dick Halliday and Mary Martin. Their roles are cut out for them, and they are not threatened by playing personal manager for the performer. Both Charles and Dick made it possible for Carol and Mary to keep center stage. They handled their bookings, their accounts, their appointments, interviews, their life. It worked out better to have all these details handled by a spouse, someone who was around all the time, rather than a stranger."

"Politics also makes good bedfellows," I interjected, bringing up a subject I know well. I have known many political marriages, many presidential marriages. The White House offers a high common purpose, as well as the solution to tedious household problems like enough space, household employees, and a schedule already planned by the American people. How to spend your time is no domestic issue. I've known and watched presidential couples since Franklin and Eleanor. Generally, the president and first lady arrive there knowing each other very well, having run the political gauntlet together. Suddenly they are on the national stage. The whole world is watching, and their bond is strengthened by their success and the nation's need for them. They feel their duty to country and to each other.

"Being in the White House is a unifying force if your marriage has any vitality in the first place," I said.

The couple and marriage I knew best, of course, were Lady Bird and Lyndon Johnson. They dared love each other as few men and women do, through all the years of campaigns, courthouse squares, barbecues, and election nights. As a reporter, I watched them operate from their days in Congress beginning in 1937 to Johnson's death in 1973. I saw them helping each other grow. Photographs of them invariably reflect his respect for her and her devotion to him.

Lady Bird saw her mission in life as "helping him," and she would have done that whether he stayed a schoolteacher, a rancher or became president. A shy woman, she took speech lessons to help him campaign; she was his constant morale booster, and he became heavily dependent on her judgment. He wore his love for her on his sleeve, and often, when he entered a room, he would kiss her impulsively in front of everyone.

They learned to crowd out people from their thoughts and be alone together. Once, riding in the backseat of the Lincoln Continental as LBJ drove her from the ranch into Austin to a birthday party, I felt they forgot I was there. She became a girl again, looking up at him, laughing, flirting, and he was kidding her, leaning over to kiss her. I didn't dare breathe or cough as I dug deeper into the upholstery.

Together they faced the heartaches of Viet Nam, enjoyed the heady moments of the civil rights bill signings in the East Room, the long laundry list of education and environment bills, and the battlefronts of the war they most wanted to fight, the War on Poverty.

A severe heart attack in 1955 nearly cost Johnson his life. I saw him alone once, soon after he came out of the hospital, grateful to be alive. He said, "Nearly everyone has disappointed me at some time, except Lady Bird. Do you know that while I was in the hospital, all six weeks, she slept in a bed near me. I never turned over in the night that I didn't hear her feet on the floor, coming to see how I was."

Years later, when the opportunity came, he wanted her to have her Highway Beautification Act passed—so he lifted Congress up by the ears and got it for her. He told me, "Probably when many things we did for the Great Society are forgotten, the environmental program will be remembered."

After leaving the White House, Johnson began to feel his health eroding and sensed that his time was short. He encouraged Lady Bird to accept every honor and board she was offered. He helped her prepare for widowhood, persuaded her to accept an appointment on the Board of Regents at the University of Texas, and fortified her with good friends and advisers before he died. It has always amazed me that even though this gentle woman was married to a man of so much strength and life that he overpowered everyone in his presence, she kept her identity, her commitments, her own priorities, and ultimately her individuality.

She is the first lady's first lady, the one appreciated for mastering the art of politics. Jackie Kennedy once said, in comparing her own difficulties as a political wife, "Lady Bird would crawl on ground glass down Pennsylvania Avenue for Lyndon." And I guess she would have. But she also would have emerged upright and unscathed.

I was wound up now, and although Le Cirque was almost empty, my listeners at the table were urging me on.

"The Fords' marriage grew while they were in the White

House, and Betty Ford emerged as a strong voice for the Equal Rights Amendment. She was the ultimate contemporary woman. She took her problems and walked them on stage with dignity and candor in a way that helped all other women facing the problems of a mastectomy, alcoholism, or even a decision about whether to have a facelift. She didn't try to hide her health, her weaknesses, or her vanity. America respected her and loved her for it. So did Jerry. She became an individual, loved by working women . . . well, any modern woman, because she carried their banner high.

"Then came the Carters. Both Rosalynn and Jimmy seemed like a couple of innocent kids from Plains who wanted desperately to practice their Christian brotherhood on the world stage. Unfortunately, the mad, mad world required more guile than they brought with them. They left Washington more cynical than when they came, but they were sustained by an unshakable faith and sympathy for one another. That also is love."

By now the love stories had drained us. Sherry gave the conversation a different twist.

"We might as well face it, all love isn't straight love. God knows in today's world, gay love abounds—the affectionate relationship of two people, two men, two women, for each other is part of the permanent scene. I always thought it was wretchedly unfair that Gertrude Stein's obituary didn't even mention Alice B. Toklas, who had for thirty years made possible her success, lived with her, loved her.

"I can think of a dozen gay couples in fashion, in literature, who have expanded each other's lives by loving, and giving. There's a line in Tom Robbins's *Still Life with Woodpecker*—it's not men who limit women, not straights who limit gays, not whites who limit blacks: what limits people is lack of guts; they don't have the nerve to star in their own movies."

"Obviously, gay love is part of the human condition," Betsy said decisively, "and should be accepted as such in a just and democratic society. And the fact that it is more accepted today may erase a lot of problems that existed before. It certainly must make life easier for those who are gay."

Our foursome at Le Cirque relished the subject of love in all its infinite variety. We were ready for another story. Eleanor recalled the moment that love left "the happiest couple I have ever known," a couple who had been married thirty-five years, John and Ruth, who adored one another and were always the "golden couple" mentioned when someone was asked to name a happy couple.

"Well, imagine my surprise the other day," she continued, "when John called me and said, 'You are the oldest friend we have, and I want you to know before you hear it from anyone else that I am moving in with a nineteen-year-old girl I met on a recent trip to South America. Don't tell me you are shocked. So am I. Yes, I love Ruth very much. She is a wonderful, wonderful woman, but I have analyzed it, thought about it, and when you get right down to the reason, I have a confession to make. I don't like aging flesh. I know it sounds awful, but I just don't like old flesh.' "

"What about your old flesh?" Eleanor said she asked him bluntly. "After all, John, you are older than Ruth. You are fifty-eight. How egocentric can you get? I just can't believe what you're telling me!"

"So what happened?" we demanded.

"That was six years ago. He has two houses in South America, and he divides his time between his wife and mistress. I saw him about a month ago, and he said, 'I know I am a shit, but I am a happy shit.'

"I also saw Ruth, who, incidentally, is the one with the money and is supporting this little escapade. It is no surprise that she feels demeaned, but so far she is not upsetting anything. She cares for their children and their grandchildren, and the dear fool cares for John. Meanwhile, his mistress has borne him a son. I asked Ruth if she is hanging on hoping he will come to his senses.

" 'I don't know,' she replied. 'I just take it day by day. I

don't want to give him up. I really don't know what he would do
if I did. He doesn't have any money, and I still love him.' "

We all felt indignant. Most modern women wouldn't put up
with that. Is love worth a damn after such a blatant betrayal and
all the hurt that accompanies it? Is respect, self-respect, a necessary ingredient to real love? Clare Luce once told an audience,
"Love, real love, the love that unites the mind as well as the heart
and body, can only occur between equals. When someone starts
treating you as his inferior, you can be sure he no longer loves
you, if indeed he ever did."

Cars arrived outside Le Cirque. I signed the check since I
was certainly going to put this information to use, and we said
hasty good-byes.

I have thought about that day around the table a lot, the
stories shared and the mixed emotions that love embodies. Love
stories keep crowding in on me. Old love can be good love. A favorite romantic figure in my newspaper days illustrates the point:
Ralph McGill, editor of *The Atlanta Constitution*, remarried
after he had been widowed in midlife. His story demonstrates
that mature love is based on more than lust. Although McGill
wrote thousands of words in his lifetime, leading the South,
shoving it out of its bigotry into brotherly love, he had never
written a love letter until late in life. He finally did because it was
an "assignment" from his wife-to-be, Dr. Mary Lynn Morgan.

McGill had to go on a mission to Africa and therefore had
to postpone their wedding. He asked Mary Lynn, "What can I
bring you?"

She replied without hesitation, "I'd like a love letter."

Surprised, he said, "That's a literary form I've never mastered." But on the flight, he mastered it.

True to a newspaper editor's style, the letter starts with a
quote. It is from a 1954 speech at Princeton given by Adlai Ste-
venson, a man McGill had always admired.

"What a man knows at fifty that he did not know at twenty
is for the most part incommunicable. . . . The knowledge he has

acquired with age is not the knowledge of formulas, or forms of words, but of people, places, actions—a knowledge not gained by words but by touch, sight, sound, victories, failures, sleeplessness, devotion, love—the human experiences of this earth, and of oneself and other men."

McGill elaborates on these thoughts in expressing his love to Mary Lynn: "This I think is applicable in some undetermined measure to you and me—the love I have for you is for the most part incommunicable in words—it is not the knowledge of why, or how, but a knowledge gained by touch, sight, sound, devotion, love—human experiences. I think the first knowledge, or coming, of being drawn to you, was one of sight—of liking the way you looked, standing, walking, of a certain style in your movements that appealed to me and made images in my mind. Other experiences, small and large, have been added until there now exists a composite of love and affection. Neither you nor I structured it consciously. It came out of human experiences and out of oneself—ourselves, separately and together. So I do not know in all its details why or how I love you, but I do. This surely is an odd love letter if we take the common pattern of them."

My grandson doesn't think about love at six years of age, but I want to tell him to marry a girl with spunk, intelligence, and spirit who will fascinate him and not let him become a boor, a male chauvinist, all macho. He shouldn't, as some do, be flattered into marriage by a doormat. As someone once said, "Doormats are for walking on."

So, Les, don't be a doormat, and don't marry one. In this increasingly complex and stressful world, with all its surprises and juggling of job and home, you want someone who can stand on her own two feet, not yours.

I often urge my granddaughter, Bonnie, and my young women friends to beware of men who are leery of formidable women. I may give the impression of being formidable, but I'll be damned if I want to go back to a magnolia mentality in the year 1986, when life is full and rich and is so much fun if you can be yourself. I can't play games anymore . . . I never was good at them.

It's possible the women's movement has prompted divorces in unhappy marriages that would otherwise have just drifted along. But it can be the salvation of others.

"As I start a whole new chapter in my life," a young woman friend wrote me recently, "I feel blessed to be starting anew. It is hard for a proud woman like myself to admit to a failed marriage when we knew how many people thought of us having the perfect marriage. You hate to disappoint others. I've had people come up to me, when they heard I was getting ready to leave Walter, and say, 'If you couldn't make it work, I've lost faith that anyone can.' You think I didn't feel a burden? Thank God the first half of my life is behind me. I feel I've jumped off a springboard and am in midair with my arms spread apart ready to grab hold of the wonderful things that are bursting out of me. I am no longer suppressed."

Her letter made me realize how awful it must be to live in a marriage where suppression is the norm. I have been blessed beyond belief, and at a time when feeling liberated wasn't a daily occurrence. All my life, all my married life, I felt cherished. I still believe in love despite all the hurt that goes with it. Thirty years of feeling cherished is a marvelous lot of life and love. Love makes it possible to do almost anything, like being smarter than you really are, because someone believes in you and encourages you.

I am so lucky I fell in love with someone who encouraged me to use all the talents I had, to be gutsy and part of the whole of life, including the rising tide of angry women. This was what was happening in the sixties and seventies. My husband knew, and I knew, that I didn't belong on the sidelines.

I never doubted for a minute that he loved me more than anyone else in the world. There was the time I made a speech at a big formal dinner for the United Press editors and barely got through it in time to go to the hospital emergency room. I ended up having an appendectomy in the middle of the night. Next morning when I woke up, there was my husband asleep on the floor in his tuxedo. The nurse couldn't believe it. "That's love," she said.

YESTERDAY, I finally summoned the courage to take down a big box of mementos from our thirty-year marriage: letters, cards, pictures of our life together. I haven't opened that box since I packed it up in Washington and moved it to Texas with me two years after my husband died. That was 1976. When I pulled down that box off the high shelf, I read its contents again with a new feeling of being loved but without the old ache. I was able to do what I had been longing to do, to look back in candlelight. Time had made the difference and, of course, being busy and wanting at last to tell about myself and my love. There were tears all right. Yesterday I shed buckets of them, but they were a joyous kind of ablution, a catharsis, washing away the cobwebs of pain. I found peace in that box of treasures. I realized that what Lady Bird wrote to me at the time of Les's death is so true: "Love never ceases to be."

She knew. Her love for LBJ never ceased. After his death she kept his clothes hanging in the closet, where they still hang. And for years his big brown terry cloth robe was behind the bathroom door. Once I saw her gently stroking it.

On one occasion she told me: "When I went back to work in my office at the LBJ Library, I didn't think I could bear to hear Lyndon's voice coming out over the speaker system describing his work. But I find it vaguely comforting. For, you see, I can never think of Lyndon at rest, but at work."

For ten years I had pulled the shade down on that box of mementos. It hurt too much to read them, but now it doesn't. Why? A willingness to stop racing and start sitting still long enough to really think about where I am emotionally is one reason. Writing, too, helps; writing for our grandson is a way of re-capturing what I once had.

There, on stationery from *The Daily Texan* office where Les and I worked together on the campus newspaper, was Les's first letter, the first one suggesting a future together.

It was 1942, and I was a brand-new newspaperwoman, working in Washington. I had graduated in June, and he was in the navy ROTC, soon to graduate and go to naval officers school. His letter came with six silver teaspoons in a silver pattern he knew I liked, King Richard. It arrived for my twenty-second birthday with a wonderful paragraph that I read and reread a thousand times.

> Dear Liz
> I started to have a "C" engraved on them but I decided against it for two most important reasons. One is that I didn't know whether you would like it—and probably you wouldn't. The other is the war—something that may sound trite, but it is true that I might not come back just like I go—or I might not come back at all. Dastardly thought!

Well, that was almost a proposal. Certainly I knew he loved me and I loved him that September 1, 1942.

By the time he was an ensign and stationed in Key West, Les was talking marriage. His letters, which once began with "Dear Mary Elizabeth" or "Liz," now opened with "My darling" and "One I love." I flew to Miami, where Les gave me an engagement ring. He then wrote a letter to my mother formally asking for my hand.

> Sept. 20, 1943
> Dear Mrs. Sutherland:
> For months now I've been wanting to write you this letter. For weeks now I've been writing you letters and, then, tearing them up. You see, Mrs. Sutherland, I consider this the most important letter I have ever written—that's why I've had such a time with it and why I want it to be so much more artistic than I'm afraid it is.
> When I met Mary Elizabeth in Miami I had a ring for her—now that she has accepted it and we are so gloriously happy, I am writing you because you must be happy too, to

make complete such an exciting and always-dreamed-about moment in life.

So trite and so ancient is the expression "made for each other," but I feel that it has a lot of meaning to it when there is someone who is so much of what you have always wanted that you can't endure the loneliness of being away from her, that you think of every little daily occurrence in terms of her, that all of your time is spent dreaming of a future which has a scope of enchantment that gives you such a desire to live.

Mary Elizabeth and I are so much more than two young sweethearts. We're companions, good friends—our love is one that developed from two people who like the same things, the same people, have the same ambitions, the same philosophy for living. We have a complete understanding of one another. We have shared so much in the past; we know one another so well. To me there could be no better combination—to me there is no better definition of what love is, what two people planning marriage should be.

This letter I have always been planning to write to both you and Mr. S., but since he is not well, I am writing only to you.

I anxiously await your answer. Deepest personal regards,

Leslie

I phoned my mother and told her that the letter was coming, and I instructed her to answer it right away. Instead, she wrote me explaining why she was not going to answer Leslie's letter for a while.

September 23, 1943
Dearest:

Leslie's letter arrived this morning, and I planned to answer today as you requested, but I don't feel settled enough in my mind to do justice to it today. You can tell Leslie he will hear from me in due time— He says he has been months writing this, so maybe he won't mind waiting a few more to get an answer. In the meantime both of you can spend the time figuring how you will fill what you imagine will be a void in your lives should I turn thumbs down on the proposition.

She included happenings at home and then tried to end her letter on a reassuring note.

> Don't think, though, darling, that I haven't thought of you every minute since our conversation. Much love, Mama

Les "anxiously awaited" her reply for what seemed an agonizing length of time, while she kept her silence. After three weeks, she finally wrote a very cautious approval, which sounded like, "I'll try to look on the bright side of it." I suspect she would have reacted the same way to anyone I had chosen to marry. But she didn't stand in the way. After spending three pages on an apology for not answering for so long, and then more beating around the bush, she finally got to the point.

> I appreciate very much your writing me. Some modern youths think that is a custom of the past ages, but I have always felt that it is only the respect and consideration due a girl's parents—I agree with you that it would have been easier to discuss it verbally than on paper, for this type of letter is as new an experience to me as you. There is one thing I am very glad of. It will not be a case of a stranger coming into the family. I think there is much more chance of a happy marriage that is founded on a long acquaintanceship and friendship than on a sudden attraction. There have been a number of weddings here of Austin girls and soldiers from the northern states, and I can't help but feel that there is a decided risk involved. When Mary Elizabeth phoned she talked to Mr. Sutherland as well as me, and his comment was, "Well, at least he's not a damned Yankee," so you may feel that he has given his approval also.
>
> When a girl marries her parents like to feel that when she goes from the shelter of her own home into a new one she will always be cared for and protected, when she no longer has her parents with her. I feel sure that her happiness will always be of first importance with you, as it has been with me.
>
> I hope that when you are married it can be here, and that it will not be for long that the condition of our country requires you to be located so far away. I want you to feel free to write me or consult me on any subject at any time for when anyone comes into any family they risk having advice

and counsel thrust upon them at all times. And I'll try to always have peanut butter in the refrigerator when you come.

With most heartfelt wishes for the lasting happiness of you both. I am,

Affectionately,
Mary E. R. Sutherland

Looking back, I know she feared my getting married would end my newly begun journalism career, which it didn't. Her own view of how marriage could diminish my potential is expressed in a letter that seems out of character for her.

There is propaganda when people talk about the "good old days." All the rest a woman had was to turn from Cooking the meals, Caring for the children, and Cleaning house (home was the original CCC Camp then) to the delightful diversions of working the garden and milking the cows. Didn't they really have a rollicking time? And the only new faces they ever saw was a small one every twelve to eighteen months.

We were married June 17, 1944, in the Washington Cathedral. I wonder what life would have been like if Les and I had not married. I can't really imagine it. Washington was ours together, where we did everything as a team, from working to raising a family. We were Liz and Les, part of the national media and the Washington merry-go-round, and life was good.

Among all the notes and cards in the box, I found the most heart-wrenching one, the last letter he wrote me just a month before he died of a heart attack at age fifty-two. The occasion was our thirtieth wedding anniversary, the date June 17, 1974.

My dearest Liz,
The last thirty years would have been unbearable without you. When I think of the many, many experiences we have had—including, most important, having our Scott and Christy, I feel sorry for everybody else. I love you very much, very much, and I am so proud of your many achievements. I've reached the point where I don't mind being called Mr. Liz Carpenter any more.

I thank God for you every night,
Les.

I liked being Mrs. Les Carpenter, and I hope he knew that. He made me the top of the coin. He was always there bragging about me, supporting my hopes and dreams. Why couldn't we both be at the top of the coin in the eyes of everyone? "Liz and Les" or "Les and Liz."

Most people thought of us that way. An old friend told me the other day, "You didn't think of one without the other. Like Amos and Andy." We were Liz and Les in each other's eyes, although there were awkward times when I was getting the lion's share of attention in the newspapers. He didn't mind too much.

Marriages, twosomes, allow for two people to be themselves more now. I think when the women's movement was new, the insecure man was scared to death. My husband wasn't. He urged me on, he liked the women who came to our house for meetings. He knew, as well as I did, I would be a voice, a leader, in the movement, because that is the way I am. When he died, there was a "Men for Women" campaign button pinned on a suit in his closet. So I knew he wouldn't have wanted me to be any different. I probably couldn't have been different.

Oh, there were explosive moments. Sometimes there were volcanoes of fury! But I'm convinced that letting off the steam is the best way. Chemistry sees you through a lot of that. Humor, too!

In that box I found so many different letterheads that came with the notes of sympathy when Les died. Dear God, I hope he knows how many people loved him and wrote these marvelous letters about him. He would be amused that so many of the letters came from my "women's lib" friends: Abortion Rights Committee, North Carolinians for ERA, and Women in Sisterhood.

One of the most sensitive letters was from Gloria Steinem: "The closest person to me to die was my father, and the only way I could handle it was just to realize that time was what there is, and I should make the most of the time before me. That I could do in memory of him."

One particular paragraph from Lady Bird's letter was great comfort: "Liz, the question that keeps coming on, I know, is

'Why now?'—and there is no answer anybody can give you—but I do know love is good while you had it. Remember, you made him happy, and proud, and made your life together fun."

As I find love still alive in the words and memories of those years together, I try to think how to explain exactly what it was with us and perhaps for all who love.

To me love is a moment and a lifetime. It is looking at him across a room and feeling that if I don't spend the rest of my life with him, I'll have missed the boat. Love is working together, laughing together, growing together. It is respect for each other and the people each cares about, however difficult it is sometimes to like his kinfolks or his friends. Love is wanting to shout from the rooftops the successes, little and big, of one another. Love is wanting to wipe away the tears when failure comes. Love is liking the feel of each other. It is wanting to have children together because they are the exclamation point of love. Love is laughter, especially in the middle of a quarrel.

Love is lots of "nots." It is not having to have the same friends. It is letting go for an evening as well as holding on. It is not having to measure the equality because that becomes too mechanical and wipes away trust and common sense. Love is not always equal because life and talents are not that even. Some people need more loving, more touching, and knowing that they are important. Love is knowing our own shortcomings and hoping they'll be forgiven. Love reaches out, grasps your hand, pats you tenderly, and envelops you so completely that, in its ultimate moments, nothing else is there.

WOMEN:
Then and Now

AS A CHILD my ears always perked up when anyone started talking about the women in the family. There were a lot of indignities done to women, even on their pedestal. My blood boils when I remember the story of my Robertson grandmother, in labor with her seventh child, politely asking my grandfather to please hurry up and saddle the horse and ride to town for the doctor. He, just as politely, continued to shave because he wouldn't leave home unless he was completely barbered. This was the same grandfather who, when he married my grandmother, wrote a friend that he was filled with joy "because I have the quickest gun, the fastest mare, and the prettiest girl in the county."

Poor Grandmama Robertson! I remember her standing in the doorway to welcome cousins, uncles, and aunts to homecomings—delicate, serene, smiling, dignified. At Christmas, her gift-wrapped packages were always the prettiest and smelled the sweetest. She outlived her husband, thank God, though there were few satisfactions in her later years; most consisted of visiting her children and grandchildren. As a little girl, I handed her tiny hairpins to her as she dressed her long hair, and I admired the beautiful amethyst brooch she wore that signified her February birthday.

My mother, the oldest of seven, treated her with such devotion and respect that all the rest of us knew she was a special person. After suffering a stroke, she lived the last two years of her life in our house. No one would have thought of having her anywhere but home with us.

All of the women in my family, whether delicate like Grandmama Robertson or strong-willed like my great-aunts, who were leaders in the suffrage movement, favored women getting the vote. Many baked pies or cakes and served them near the polls to influence the male voters in the customary way—through their stomachs.

As I grew older, I became fascinated with the portraits of the women in my family. What a parade of strong women march across my counterpane. My mother, a strong force in all her gentleness, immersed me in her love of history, poetry, and seeing the "entirety of life," as a cousin once described her outlook. Mama used to talk about the great-aunts, particularly Birdie and Luella, daughters of Mary Elizabeth Robertson who were born and grew up in that dear house at Salado. So last night, I took the photostats of their letters, written one hundred years ago, to bed with me and read the delicate handwritings with all their curlicues until my eyes would hold no more. Long-dead, these aunts speak to me like old friends, and I yearn to know them better.

The two older daughters who grew up in Salado, Luella and Birdie, both beautiful, graceful, and intelligent, married the smartest men in Texas. My eye falls on the wedding announcement of the marriage of Luella on April 4, 1877, and the sheaf of letters she wrote home to her mother from Austin. She was full of excitement about her husband, Zachary Taylor Fulmore, promising young lawyer and affectionate bridegroom, eager to show her the city and introduce her to his friends.

He had found his soul mate in the brilliant young woman who had stood on Salado College Hill two years earlier and delivered a two-hour essay to the first reunion of Salado College. She was the leading graduate and chose her subject: "The Mental Capabilities of Woman and a Plea for Her Higher Education." He must have been impressed with her research, as I am, as she made her passionate plea in behalf of the equal education of women.

The status of women in education in the United States was not acceptable, she said, because the school and college courses prepared for them were shorter and inferior to those of men:

> Young women are graduated at the early age of eighteen when the young gentlemen are just beginning to enter upon their education in earnest. Her early marriage and household duties prevent her from pursuing the treasured schoolbooks of girlhood, from diving deep into archeology, and by light of the mental vision, from adjusting the telescope to survey the wonderful dimensions of heaven's great arcane.
>
> A girl may warble Italian airs with the practiced skill of a Malibran, or play "like a professor," she may dance with all the lightness and grace of a Fanny Elssler, or rival the coloring of nature's pencil in her elaborate embroidery, and yet be miserably educated; indeed, her very perfection in these accomplishments is, perhaps, the strongest evidence that she is lacking in judicious mental training.

Luella listed her models, whom she called her "Temple of Fame," women who have exhibited determination, rare intellectual and conversational powers, and achieved high positions. Among them, Mary Somerville (the mathematician and astronomer), Madame de Staël, Hannah More, Elizabeth Barrett Browning, Mrs. Washington, Mrs. Polk, Mrs. Mary Curtis Lee, Hypatia (teacher of the Platonic School), and Lady Jane Gray. She added the queens: Semiramis of Babylon, Zenobia of Palmyra, Cleopatra, Isabella of Spain, Elizabeth and Victoria of England.

Rising to what must have been an eloquent moment, she pointed out:

> Woman, the mother of John, the forerunner of the light of the world; the mother of Jesus of Nazareth; the first at the foot of the cross, the last at the tomb of the Son of God . . . that she shall not be educated in common with man . . . is a disgrace to the age in which we live and falsifies the Declaration of American Independence, granting freedom of thought, speech and worth to all the institutions of this country.
>
> Fathers, if by one feeble word of mine, I could disperse the mist which hangs like an incubus around you, and cause you to view more plainly the necessity of education for your daughters as thoroughly as your sons, I would feel this essay had not been read in vain.

How, in this backwater town of Salado, did this young lady of twenty become so knowledgeable? Here in this quaint, lost village she rose like a phoenix from the ashes of the Civil War to speak for the human spirit, as have a galaxy of women writers across the old South: Carson McCullers, Eudora Welty, Katherine Anne Porter, Harper Lee, Flannery O'Connor.

She was blessed with a gentle, understanding father who encouraged her and a thirst for knowledge—which did not discourage a following of young men of the social centers in Austin and Galveston. The young lawyer Zachary Taylor Fulmore came courting all the way from Austin, sixty miles away. What a union it must have been—those two together, marrying in the old parlor, bidding her parents good-bye, then moving to the political capital. To her mother and father back in Salado she writes with breathless happiness of her new home, a "commodious" room in the famous boarding house of the day, and of every detail of her new life.

April 6, 1877

My dear Mama,

We had a delightful trip down, reaching Round Rock several hours before the stage. We drove around to Mrs. Millet's—our home—and oh, Mama, such a delightful room as we have, 'tis upstairs and we get a splendid breeze all the time from the south and east, and the little portico in front is so nice. The Capitol is just in front and I sit and watch Mr. Fulmore as he passes through its grounds until he is out of sight. He spent yesterday with me, and is spending this evening with me though he was at his office all morning. I am very, very happy, and I find he is quite a favorite here.

I must tell you about our bridal presents: Mr. A. P. Wooldridge and Lady sent us a beautiful silver teapot with a little lamp beneath it, a silver sugar bowl and cream pitcher. John Wooldridge sent us a beautiful bronzed bouquet holder . . . but above all, Mama, do I prize my dear husband's present—two large volumes, beautifully bound, "Picturesque America," edited by Bryant. I asked him their costs and he said fifty dollars. I appreciate them all very much, but the oddest thing was to see them addressed to Mrs. Fulmore.

Five days later, she writes glowingly of the honeymoon, even though she still calls him "Governor" or "Mr. Fulmore."

He went to his office Monday morning and goes every day now but not until he kissed me nearly to death, my lips are becoming habituated to it. Yesterday evening, he took me down to his office, we also went in the court room and then on top of the building from which we got a splendid view, but he is coming early this evening to take me down to the courthouse, from which we will get a view of the Capitol. I had to stop writing this letter on account of callers. Just think of it, Mama, sixty callers already among the ladies and half as many from the gentlemen.

What an intellectual life they had, writing home to Salado so frequently of their happiness, their newfound friends, the daily social life of their new home in the capital of Texas, where they were making a popular reputation and name for themselves!

The gifted genes were strong in the females of the family. Aunt Birdie, thirteen years younger than Luella, was making top honors at Wesleyan Female College in Macon, and she returned to Texas to marry Cone Johnson, the promising state senator from Tyler in 1888. Organizations for women were appearing, and Aunt Birdie led the way for the Quid Nunc Club, one of the first literary clubs in Texas. . . . In 1897, it became the Texas Federation of Women's Clubs and Aunt Birdie was elected president, a job that took her throughout Texas and other states meeting women leaders. Her masses of prematurely white hair and her elegance, according to the social writers of the day, were her trademark. But it was her perception of public issues that guided her leadership right into the fight for women's suffrage and into politics in Austin and Washington. In an article for the newly organized federation, she placed the greatest emphasis on education and praised Congress for passing several laws of interest to women concerning education, child welfare, and pure food evaluation. This before the turn of the century.

Politics was her mission and the Democratic party her home. Her husband became embroiled in a bitter fight for power with Joseph Weldon Bailey, the great orator of the state. In a struggle for delegate control, Birdie's outspoken support of her husband made her an overnight celebrity in Texas political circles and the newspapers. As his chief political adviser she warned Johnson that Bailey supporters were planning to charge him with sexual improprieties and excessive familiarity with black voters.

"They are only trying to make you angry," she hurriedly wrote him. "Now don't pay any attention to it and don't take your time too much while speaking to explain these things, for that is what they want. Tell the people the question is not what you have done but what Bailey has done. Do noble deeds! Talk noble things in the love and fear of God, and He will make his light to shine on you, and work confusion to those that assail you. I want you to be known in Texas and loved as the preacher statesman." So successful was her help that Birdie and Cone returned from his campaign for governor to find ten thousand people in their hometown of Tyler turned out to see their arrival. They circled the courthouse square twice, and Birdie, the local paper reported, "was radiant with pride and happiness, and she waved a flag in acknowledgement of the applause." They must have been deeply disappointed with his defeat later that night, but it was on to Washington and the Wilson administration: the suffrage battle for Birdie and a subcabinet position as solicitor general at the Department of State for her husband. Cone's position was quite possibly aided by Zachary Fulmore, attorney for Colonel House, adviser to Wilson, who named two other Texans to the Wilson cabinet.

I would have liked to experience the Wilson period, for it was filled with Texans, my aunts, the battle for suffrage, and the concept of the country as a world peacemaker under a brilliant, idealistic president. I wish I had been there with all of the newsmakers, wish I had known my politically minded aunts and talked with them. Maybe I was in some unseen way, for I have never wavered from the desire to be where the action is.

I have searched and found my catacombs, my lavender leaves and satin glass urns. In my ancestors, I keep finding me. I keep finding that their causes are my causes. Aunt Birdie was the first Democratic National Committeewoman from Texas, and I was one of several forty years later.

SOME OF THE BEST days of my life have been several of the wilder days of the women's movement. Trying to win equality in law and in practice and trying to get women elected and appointed to public office is the most exciting endeavor of our times. It is only natural that it would follow the labor movement, the civil rights movement, and the youth movement. Women have always participated in movements for equality and put themselves, in customary fashion, last in line for it.

My personal journey into the women's movement began fifteen years ago on a July weekend in 1971 when the National
Women's Political Caucus was born in the Statler Hotel in
Washington, D.C. It was a day that changed my life. Life would
have been easier if I had not gotten so deeply involved, for I
poured fifteen years of energy into it, and I'm still at it. But I
would have missed out on so much, so many friendships with remarkable women of all income levels, so much learning as we
hammered at the doors of Congress and the legislatures, so much
understanding of my own country and how the other great movements for fairness and equality took place. How wrong it would
have been to have let it happen and not be part of it! Many gains
have been made. I still rub my eyes in wonder. Can it really be
... us ... doing all the things we are now doing? Still struggling,
yes; it's wretched how hard we've had to struggle.

It was the spring of 1971. I had been out on the road selling
my book, *Ruffles and Flourishes: The Warm and Tender Story of
a Simple Girl Who Found Adventure in the White House*. It had
sold amazingly well in view of the fact that my span of time in the
White House was with a president who had an unpopular war on
his hands and whose own popularity was low.

A phone call from the writer Shana Alexander, an old friend
from *Life* magazine, alerted me: "Betty Friedan thinks the feminist movement has gone as far as it can go until it gets some political clout behind it. You know more about politics than anyone I
know. Will you talk to her if she calls?"

"Sure, I'll talk to her, though I haven't even read her book,"
I replied. "Tell her to call."

She did, about ten minutes later, spouting forth in the rapid
staccato that is Betty's native tongue the need to elect more
women, the need to pass legislation that would help women
work, the desperate need to make Congress aware of all of the in-
equities the working woman faces. I was impressed with Betty's
sharp mind and intense focus on the problem. "There's going to
be a meeting next weekend with a core group on the Hill. All the
women's organizations will be represented there. Three congress-

I have never been a sideline sitter. I like the heat of battle, and I got it with the women's movement where I learned so much from (above) Alan Alda, Sey Chassler, editor of *Redbook*, and Judy Carter, the daughter-in-law of President Carter. Jenny Joseph, the English poet (left), taught me "to run my stick along the public railing." At the ERAmerica salute to First Ladies Rosalyn Carter, Betty Ford and Lady Bird Johnson (below), with cochairman Elly Peterson in the center; at left, Betty Friedan.

Marching in Florida—one more go for the ratification of the Equal Rights
Amendment.

women, Bella Abzug of New York, Shirley Chisholm of New York, and Patsy Mink of Hawaii, and, of course, Gloria Steinem. I hope you'll be there, too," she said.

"Can I bring my daughter, Christy, who is visiting from Brown University for the weekend?" I asked.

"Sure," she said.

I had plenty of other things to do, but I thought the experience might bring me closer to my daughter. I called her as soon as I hung up with Betty, and she said she'd like to go.

So, we went—Christy and I—and were met by Bella, who was the hostess, dispensing coffee and sweet rolls. My eyes scanned the room. It was full of women I had seen on Capitol Hill through the years—wonderful women, who walked the halls for all the women's organizations that worked for better legislation, a scattered contingent of women from the peace groups, young women with their backpacks, fresh from the marches against the Vietnam War, black women, Hispanic women, and representatives from the new women's groups—Women United, NOW, and so forth.

Bella opened the meeting by asking everyone to stand up and say why they were there. Of course, all eyes were on Gloria in blue aviator glasses and miniskirt, dramatic and cool with her soft voice and waist-long blond hair. These trademarks were already making news in *W* and other New York literary media. Betty Friedan, a very different type, sporting frowsy blouse, long skirt, and an "earth mother" look, was a best-selling author, full of a sense of purpose because of the heavy mail she was receiving from women, especially housewives who had read her book and felt they were meant for more than blowing noses and scrubbing baseboards. It is ironic that the first self-labeled "feminists" were college-educated suburbanites who read *The Feminine Mystique* and wanted more "fulfillment." That was the big word. They felt it was a message for them and the years they were "wasting" on nothing but carpools and the dreary sameness of household chores.

We were a mixed group, with our different backgrounds

sometimes putting us at cross purposes. The Business and Professional Women's Club wanted an Equal Rights Amendment out of Congress and ratified; Congress has been dragging its feet for forty-seven years. The peace-seekers, the Women's League for Peace and Freedom, wanted to be represented at the peace tables; there were lots of "Make Love Not War" buttons around. The NOW group was already pushing abortion, and the League of Women Voters and AAUW were more genteel in their approaches, but not moving fast enough.

It was an exciting kaleidoscope of the sounds and fury of women, and I didn't miss a word. When Gloria spoke everyone was quiet. "Looking around this room, I see there is at least one thing we all have in common—a vagina." I jumped about two feet. I had never heard that word except in my gynecologist's office. But I noticed my daughter didn't move a muscle. When it came my turn I introduced myself as having covered the Hill for sixteen years and worked in the White House for Lyndon and Lady Bird Johnson for the past five. I could feel—or was it my imagination?—a cold resentment when I talked about LBJ, and as time went on I felt it even more except from the black women, who let me know they were his friends. It was a lesson on how you inherit both friend and foe from close identification with others. I really didn't mind, though I resented their resentment and was determined to show them I wasn't going to be run out of any movement because of their disapproval of a man I admired.

LBJ had been good about pushing his cabinet to include women in government. On one memorable day—soon after he had decided that women were being discriminated against with respect to high-level government jobs—he called his cabinet together and told everyone: "I'm sure there are plenty of high-level positions available for qualified women in your departments. And I am sure there are many women already on your payrolls who have been waiting for promotions for a long time. So, go back to your departments and see what you can do. Then, report back to me next Friday how many you have placed."

Not waiting for the reports, the president began the talent search for women himself.

I was lying in bed on a Saturday evening enjoying Mrs. Johnson's favorite TV show, *Gunsmoke*. Just as Miss Kitty was about to step in and stop a gunfight in the Long Branch Saloon, the phone rang, and it was you-know-who.

"Liz, are you watching television?" he said.

"Yes, sir."

"There is a terrific woman on television," he continued.

"Not Miss Kitty!" I panicked, wondering privately how she would perform as U.S. treasurer, a post LBJ wanted to fill with a woman.

"This woman is on a panel show," he said, as I breathed a sigh of relief, "and she knows a lot about handling money. She has been supporting her children as a lady banker since her husband died. I haven't the remotest idea whether she's a Democrat or a Republican, and I don't care. But find out who she is and see if she will do."

I did find her, but as it turned out, the U.S. government couldn't afford her. Undaunted, the president continued his search and in typical style ended up naming fifty women in one day to top jobs to dramatize how he felt about them. For his sake, I felt it was important to represent the Johnson camp at this women's meeting.

At the end of the day another meeting was set to be held in early July—a big one, to form a National Women's Political Caucus. We dispersed, slightly suspicious of each other, hailing taxicabs on Pennsylvania Avenue.

"What did you think of it?" I asked Christy.

"It was interesting to me that the only congresswomen there were the three minorities: Bella, Shirley, and Patsy Mink."

"Why do you think that is so?" I asked, for it had not occurred to me.

"Because they're used to putting their names on the block," she said. "They've been through the civil rights movement."

Christy went back to college, and I was slightly disappointed that she seemed to take the meeting for granted. I couldn't think of anything else. And I wasn't permitted to, for Betty and Shana were on the phone over the next few weeks, and a small group of us kept meeting long hours in grimy offices that all seemed to have Spartan straight-backed chairs. We met wherever we could find space. There was a growing tension between Betty on one side, and Bella and Gloria on the other.

Although they have since mellowed and made peace, their strong and clashing personalities and enthusiasms burst out like gunfire in our long, tedious nightly meetings. Betty, having energized the women's movement with her book, was understandably possessive. Bella, whose clout as congresswoman from New York gave us all greater entrée and a podium, was unyielding in her own strong beliefs. Gloria, softer spoken and conscious of her large following among young women throughout the country (Gloria lookalikes were everywhere, wearing aviator glasses, long hair, ribbed turtlenecks), was equally unrelenting in her position that the women's movement had to embrace every female issue.

It was a period of all chiefs and no Indians . . . except, perhaps, for Shana, who needlepointed her way through the heated sessions like Madam LaFarge, and me, who knew that each woman there was needed for different constituencies and different public appeals. All of them brought something, but Betty felt that Bella and Gloria were "separatists" and "antimen," narrowing the movement with the radical chic clichés of the time. She saw the movement more as part of the general drive for equality and civil rights.

"They talk so . . . well, strong," I said once to Shana, dismayed at the shouting and dissension.

She calmly continued with her pillow cover and said quite matter-of-factly, "These are strong times."

The heavy combat bothered and yet fascinated me. I had never been around so many strong women shouting at each other, but I had never been around a revolution before. I felt a long way from Salado, Texas, but I also felt exhilarated by these bright, determined women. Experienced enough in politics and public images, I knew that we needed to stick together to show a united front, not discord which the press would label a "cat fight."

In a few weeks we did indeed gather together on a July weekend in the Statler-Hilton Hotel, two blocks from the White House, to form the National Women's Political Caucus, which shifted the fighting front of the women's movement to the political arena. It was reminiscent of what I've read about the meeting in Seneca Falls in 1848 when American women first declared themselves equal and began what historian and author Eleanor Flexner calls our "Century of Struggle."

That July weekend in 1971 we were born again, born this time shouting to be heard. The room was a strange teeming mixture of women: some identifiable leaders and some scrubby-looking stragglers out of other movements of the sixties. There were highly intelligent respectable women, newer, noisy, more irreverent representatives from the National Organization for Women, and half a dozen groups young and old from the peace and civil rights marches. In the crowded ballroom, in the corridors of the hotels, in the powder rooms, were women, women of all ages, personalities, and talents. The hum of voices filled the entire hotel mezzanine. Everyone was talking. Everyone was angry—not only about injustice, but newly aware that as women they had to fight for their own equality with their male colleagues in the common movements for civil rights and peace. This had come as a shock to the college girls, just as it had come as a shock to women one hundred years before in the battle for abolition of slavery and in the temperance movement. I see their faces still, the bright young women from Radcliffe or Berkeley, or the University of Wisconsin, or Smith, dismayed when, after marching together for peace, their young male friends had still sent them out for coffee while they, the *men*, plotted the strategy and made the decisions. "I realized then," one young woman told me angrily, "I had to fight for my own rights, too. That's why I'm here."

So there we were. It was an embattled weekend. I had been "drafted" by Shana and Betty to be the contact person with the press. I expected it to be explosive, maybe an embarrassing failure. My White House years had taught me the value of measuring an event in the eyes of the "average reader." I had asked my neighbor, Ruth Shook, to come with me and give me the level view. Ruth was the quintessential housewife and mother of three, the kind of good neighbor who could fix a hem or stir up a pitcher of lemonade in a jiffy. Her side porch was the gathering place for our neighborhood, women who wanted to talk or solve problems, children who found her company full of laughter and ease. We all loved her and sought her out when we had problems, and I had one. That morning at seven-thirty I backed out of the driveway and stopped in front of her house to pick her up and take her with me. She came out, predictably, in a neat navy-blue dress with a Peter Pan collar, her eyes twinkling as she got settled in the car.

"I'm excited about going," she said with a smile. "You know, I've never seen a lesbian before."

In our naive generation lesbians were remote from conversation and visibility. We expected them all to look mannish and be athletic.

As we walked in the door, I started counting the heads at the press table. Many were women, well-known reporters. I noted happily that the two wire services, AP and UPI, *The New York Times, The Washington Post, The Washington Star, Newsweek,* and *Time* were all there, and there were a few TV cameramen setting up. This in itself built tension, excitement, and, I knew from experience, troublemakers. But despite the misapprehensions of those of us from "The Establishment," we were full of anticipation and hoped desperately the inevitable dramatics would not get things off the track.

There was Bella, smiling; Gloria, moving into a corner conference with her confidantes. Betty Friedan was trying to get the meeting under way with the Republican leader we had picked as pro tem gaveler, Kay Clarenbach. There was Shana quietly needlepointing. There wasn't much trust in that room, and we found ourselves battling each other in every imaginable grouping: the youth caucus (those under thirty), the prime-time caucus (those thirty to forty), the black, Chicano, working women's caucuses.

We needed each other, but we had been left out of the action so long, we were suspicious. So we were shouting: about poor women and poor wages. About peace. About ERA.

At the press table, the reporters were up and down watching what was happening and, like me, rubbing their eyes in wonder, half-glad, still somewhat unsure of what was happening, where the story was going. Everyone had a different issue—peace, wages, civil rights. Everyone was angry at something. It was Gloria, Bella, Betty, and Shirley Chisholm who set the agenda: top priority was to run for office and win voices in Congress and in the state legislatures, to create a caucus in each state, to find women who would fight for women.

My role that day was a small one. I had been summoned to help advise on politics, and incidentally, would I handle the press? I sat there wide-eyed. It was the most interesting, the most thrilling meeting I had ever attended. I knew I was in it to stay. Reporters frantically tried to keep up with what was going on, and I tried frantically to give answers in the confusion of events.

It was late that night when I dropped Ruth off at her house. "Well, what did you think?" I asked.

"I thought it was fascinating," she said. "I couldn't keep my eyes off it. You know, Bella is really prettier than her pictures. She has a beautiful face. And I don't know if I saw a lesbian or not."

At midnight when I got home I knew the first person I would telephone would be my daughter, and I knew she would be glad and we would be closer. The morning papers bore proof that even if the words "sister" and "right on" did not come trippingly off my tongue, I was at least a successful press agent. We made history that day and the next one. We were in politics to stay.

News was slow that weekend following the July holiday; the president of the United States was in San Clemente, and we were a big national story. Monday morning, the story of our meeting and the five-column picture of the speakers ran on page one in the *Times,* the *Star,* and the *Post.*

What a picture! Betty Friedan, jubilant that the feminist

movement was going to get some political clout and attention. Bella Abzug in hat, looking determined and purposeful. Shirley Chisholm, mellow and wise. Gloria Steinem, looking younger and more serene than any of us.

There were the doubters among us, some not so sure we should "go public," but there was no holding back the able women writers like Eileen Shanahan of *The New York Times,* Isabelle Shelton of *The Washington Star,* and a somewhat startled young man *The Washington Post* had sent over. His mama had raised him right—he wrote a great story.

Meanwhile, in San Clemente President Nixon met with his cabinet and found that Secretary of State Bill Rogers had arrived that morning from Washington with the eastern newspapers. Rogers threw the papers on the table for all to see. "It looks like vaudeville," someone said. "Who is Gloria Steinem?" asked President Nixon. Secretary Rogers replied jovially, "Oh, she's one of Henry Kissinger's girlfriends."

Helen Thomas from UPI, who was within hearing distance, pounced on the words and the wire stories began. Next day came another news story from New York as Gloria firmly replied, "I am not now, nor have I ever been Henry Kissinger's girlfriend." It was a wonderful quote.

The press was not idle, and they kept the story of the noisy new women's political movement and its impact moving on the wires and throughout the country for weeks, quizzing political figures on what they thought of this new force in politics. Nor were the women idle. The state caucuses began springing up. The first formed in Florida, where I was asked to be keynoter because I was from the South. then came Texas, where the second Women's Political Caucus was founded. State Representative Frances "Sissy" Farenthold, who had created national attention attacking corruption in the Texas legislature, was my co-keynoter there.

It was then that I first met Sarah Weddington, the blue-jeaned Methodist preacher's daughter with beautiful red hair to her waist. At the time, she was a law student at the University of Texas. Her voice was calm, and she helped hold the meeting together. It was this same Sarah Weddington who at twenty-seven would argue the landmark abortion case of *Roe* v. *Wade* before the United States Supreme Court . . . argue it, win it, and later be punished for it when antiabortion groups tried to bar her appointment to public office. But she was never one to falter or give up.

Now, fifteen years later, I am still deeply involved in the women's movement, a graduate of the experience that comes with what seems like a million meetings and a million miles since that weekend when, to my mind, the contemporary women's movement was born.

I was ignited by the two hundred and seventy-one women who crowded into the ballroom of the Statler-Hilton on that weekend to form the National Women's Political Caucus and begin, in a serious and organized way, to fight for ERA and to urge women to run for office. It was a day to remember. Those of us who were there may forget our Social Security numbers, our ZIP codes, our area codes, our children's ages, and sometimes their names, but every detail of that day and the months and years that followed is forever part of our lives, our very souls.

What happened in the years of traveling the United States as we chalked up the victories and losses for ERA and shoved women into running for public office? A day spent in Sunflower County, Mississippi—campaigning for Fannie Lou Hamer in her bid for the state senate—came to epitomize the agony and ecstasy of my life as circuit-rider for the women's movement.

I had first met Fannie Lou Hamer at that July 1971 caucus. She stood five by five, a black earth mother in a cotton smock. And her voice—my God, what a voice! She could quote Scripture or burst into a hymn and sweep an audience into her spell.

The daughter of a black sharecropper family, Fannie Lou had managed to rally the black people of Sunflower County into organizing a freedom farm "so no one would go hungry."

"We feed everyone who comes by, black or white," she told me. Her presence on the national scene was an embarrassment to the Jim Eastlands of Mississippi and other white, male, status-quo southerners who have never put the Fannie Lou Hamers of the world on their agenda. I had particularly admired her gracious sense of fair play during a stormy caucus meeting when she demanded the noisy women stop their cacophony of boos and hisses and give Dr. Benjamin Spock a fair chance to talk. Even though many of these women had been his ready followers in peace marches, they saw him now as Dr. Spock the baby doctor, who wanted to keep mother home tending the baby, who wanted to preserve all the built-in put-downs that have shaped women and their daughters since the beginning of time. So they booed and hissed, and suddenly up stood the hefty black woman from Sunflower County, rising out of the crowd and defying the audience to turn and listen.

"I'm ashamed of you," she lectured her white sisters. "I know what it is to be harassed."

That was all she needed to say. In the course of the meeting, one of her cards, "Fannie Lou Hamer for State Senate" got pressed into my hand. I wrote her a note of admiration.

Five months later the telephone rang, and it was Fannie Lou asking me to come down and help her campaign for the state senate. She sounded desperate. There were only three more days before the election, and it looked like a futile gesture.

Fannie Lou Hamer had put her neck on the civil rights block early in the movement and gotten the Mississippi delegation seated as rightful delegates to the Democratic Convention of 1964. Fannie Lou had made a national name for herself at the convention, and as time passed and black men began running for office, she was a rallying point for them. Now she sent out the call for help and found them too busy. In desperation, she turned to her women friends in the caucus. The irony was, only the women answered this brave and remarkable woman's request for help— not the black men she'd helped elect. Many of them resented the fact that a woman was running. They had taken her seriously when she brought attention and power to them, but now, when she was using her know-how and strength to run for office herself, they were conspicuously absent.

I have always had misgivings about outsiders campaigning in the South, because I am southern and I know the old resentments against political "carpetbaggers."

So I asked her, "But will it help?"

"Honey, anything will help," she said simply, and that cinched it for me.

"I'll land in Memphis tomorrow night and spend the night with my brother Bill," I told her. "Tell me how to get there."

"Come straight down the Memphis highway until you hit Yazoo. Drive slow or you'll miss the whole town. Turn left at the light and you'll see a whole bunch of small frame houses. Just ask anybody and they'll tell you where I live."

When I told my husband I was going to Mississippi he said flatly, "They shoot people in Mississippi." Then he added, "Well, get Bill to go with you."

Fannie Lou was waiting in her neat frame house. The smell of frying chicken welcomed us. A dozen of her campaigners were seated all around waiting to board the Winnebago camper to start out the day's campaigning. On the walls were awards from universities and civil rights groups and pictures of her heroes: Bobby Kennedy, Martin Luther King, and Jesus Christ.

There was no shortage of campaign workers from the freedom farms, but I wondered how many of them had actually registered, how many would make the effort to get to the polls that day. If all the blacks were voting, Fannie Lou was a shoo-in. In the final campaign, I knew every hand and voice should be working at more than frying chicken, so I suggested they get on the telephone and start calling every name in the phone book, politely asking the voters to go to the polls for Mrs. Hamer.

They looked at me as though I were from another planet. "I think that might be resented," Mrs. Hamer said gently to me. Was it that in Mississippi black people still couldn't call white people on the phone and ask them to go to the polls?

So we did what we could. All of us piled into the Winnebago camper, my brother followed in his car, and we went barreling along for six hours through the cotton patches into half a dozen small towns around the sleepy courthouse squares with their stately old magnolia trees and the inevitable two or three old men whittling aimlessly. We stopped at the radio and TV buildings, always the newest, most prosperous-looking buildings in town, and tried to buy time. We were a strange-looking troop marching into these stations, one white woman and a handful of blacks, but I noticed that the receptionists at each building made an effort to look polite. They always knew Fannie Lou and always called her "Mrs. Hamer." As for getting on TV, it was hit or miss. But as an outsider I could make two contributions to the candidate that day. First I was an oddity, therefore a news story—a former White House aide in Mississippi, helping a black woman in her campaign. This sometimes brought us free air time. Second, I knew about equal time provisions in the Federal Communications Act and was a threat if the station refused to sell us time. More than once I found myself having to remind station managers of this law.

Fannie Lou had some money, about $2,000 wrapped up in an old handkerchief, to pay for air time. Having worked in well-organized campaigns, this, to me, was a sad, pitiful way to buy time on TV, but it was the way it went in Mississippi that year. This was one thing the caucus could do to help the Fannie Lou Hamers of the world, I thought. We should be in a district two months before an election with the know-how and experts who would buy the time for the last week, who would have placards printed and each election day assignment taught and rehearsed. There were plenty of available candidates around—they just needed someone to show them what to do.

One time, at a small TV station in the delta, an interviewer said to me rather curtly, "What are you doing in Mississippi, Mrs. Carpenter?" He really couldn't have cared less what I was doing in Mississippi; he was really asking, "What's an uppity white woman like you doing in Mississippi campaigning for an uppity black woman like Fannie Lou Hamer?"

Trying not to sound uppity, I answered him, "I am here because I am southern. Because I am white. Because I am a woman.

Because, hopefully, I am a thinking American, and because Fannie Lou Hamer, one of twenty children from a sharecropper family, knows more about the problems of Sunflower County than anyone else, and she'll do something about them. I am here because county lines don't count anymore, and Sunflower County can't be hidden behind some mystical curtain of yesterday's establishment and left to rot on the Mississippi River."

What I felt like saying was, "And because, you idiot, women are going to get uppitier and uppitier. And if we don't win this one, we'll be back!" But the idea of women working to get other women elected was still a phenomenon he couldn't understand.

I'll never forget that day in Mississippi or my new campaigning friends. Breezing along the road, that ribbon of cement that separates the cotton fields between the towns, we sang lots of the old, old hymns that inspire faith and hope and were so much a part of my own Methodist childhood in Salado. The Cokesbury hymnal is a bond between black and white in the South. "Amazing Grace, how sweet the sound!" Fannie Lou's voice was clear and magnificent above all the rest. She taught me that lovely hymn: "His eye is on the sparrow, God watches over me." I can hear it still, and I hum it quite often, but never does it have more meaning than when you sing it in a cotton patch campaign on the delta. Of course Fannie Lou lost the election, but we had only just begun. Today black candidates often win in Mississippi.

THE NEXT FEW years and months brought a whole new wave of women into the movement, and one of the most delightful and helpful was Erma Bombeck. She was loved by millions of readers for her humor column and books. She had drawing power, and she had guts. "I have respect for that woman out there that I'm writing for who is standing over the dishes and the stove," she told me. So she became part of the weekend forays we would take to the five or six unratified states where the change of a few votes would make a difference.

The Equal Rights Amendment had been hanging around

the corridors of Congress for forty-seven years with few champions. Labor was against it, and that certainly affected most of the Democratic senators and most especially Congressman Emmanuel Celler of New York, who had long been chairman of the House Judiciary Committee. He was an avowed enemy of ERA. Many women's groups of high standing had been against it, because they had fought to win special treatment for working women in regard to working hours and conditions. In writing labor reform laws decades earlier, the effort had been made to abolish child labor and grant special privileges to women. What women didn't realize at the time was that special privileges meant less pay and fewer hours in which to earn pay. For instance, an employer at a restaurant could gallantly send the waitress home before dark, just when the good tips started. And he wouldn't bat an eye when charwomen came in to clean the place up at two in the morning. Ironically, women didn't see that they were being taken. While we were being protected against heavy lifting jobs, we were daily lifting our one- and two-year-olds, who often topped the allowable weight for men.

I have often wondered how different things might have been if, in the formative days of our new country, John Adams had heeded Abigail's advice to "remember the ladies" instead of brushing it aside. Later, the all-white, all-male group in Philadelphia writing the Constitution for the fledgling country refused to receive any petitions concerning equality for sex, including one that merely asked for slave girls to be educated equally with slave boys.

"Equality of rights under the law shall not be denied or abridged on account of sex." Sixteen little words! And an allowance to give states two years to put it into action. But to get it out of the U.S. Senate would require, not a simple majority, but a two-thirds vote. Then it would have to be passed by the House and get past the powerbrokers in two-thirds of the states. The forefathers made it possible to amend the Constitution because they knew it was not perfect and in a growing, changing America could not remain the same. But they were too preoccupied with their own agenda to do what Abigail Adams, certainly one of the most brilliant of the colonists, had asked.

So here I was in Arkansas in April of 1978 riding through the fringe of a tornado in the company of Erma Bombeck and Judy Carter, daughter-in-law of the president. We had been all over Little Rock asking Arkansas to ratify the ERA. By eleven o'clock that night our work was over. We were bone tired and cold as we drove through sheets of blinding rain looking for a red mailbox, which marked the home of our long-awaited dinner.

Starvation had set in, and I stuck my head out of the window to try to chew the rain and get a better view of our landmark. "Watch those two-dollar permanents," warned Erma. "They frizz!"

Fortunately, the red mailbox loomed just ahead, and we took off our shoes and sloshed through the rain to the house, filled our plates at the buffet table, and plopped down in more comfortable surroundings to ponder the question I had put to them: "Why are we here?"

"Because," said Erma, "when my grandchildren ask, 'In the battle of the sexes, what did you do, Grandma?' I don't want to have to reply, 'I gave at the office.' " She continued, "I'm tired of all the stereotypes being applied to those who are for the Equal Rights Amendment. I don't want to be 'justa' anything . . . 'justa housewife' or 'justa writer.' "

What about Judy? It would be easy enough to assume she was there because the president had sent her. But that was underestimating Judy, who had enthusiastically logged hundreds of hours and thousands of miles on behalf of the movement.

"Women have reached the desperation level about ERA," Judy said. "We can't give up. Coming here, making appearances to rally women, is what I can do, and I'm going to continue doing it for my children and their children and myself."

And me? What was the number-one flying coward doing bouncing over the skies between the last fifteen unratified states? Not just that day, but ever since 1972, when the ERA passed through Congress. I was doing it because I couldn't *not* do it. We were so close to a victory after two hundred years, and it was countdown time on ERA. I was doing it because of indignation—that women were left out in the first place and have always fought other people's battles in lieu of their own. I was doing it because I figured life had been good to me and I was being given the chance to say thanks in this one area of human progress. The Lord wouldn't like me very well if I didn't. And I wouldn't have liked myself, either.

When you get right down to it, I think the answer for so many women in those turbulent years was the same: we believed that justice and equality belonged to all of us, that women should be able to go as far as our aspirations and abilities could take us, and we thought that our efforts could make a difference.

Well, ERA got beat back during the Reagan years as the right wing moved in. But one day it will pass.

Last Thanksgiving I spent some long days lying on a beach with two young women I have known a long time and love dearly. One, my daughter, now struggling up the corporate ladder in New York; the other, a good friend from ERA days and a thoughtful writer.

And in the dreamers' talk that comes on a beach on such a sun-filled day, we mused about whether we had been someone else in another life and what we might like to be in our next one. Kathleen Currie, my ERA co-worker, and I were quite sure we'd been there with Elizabeth Cady Stanton or Eleanor Roosevelt.

But when my daughter spoke I caught my breath to hear her say, "In the next life, I think I want to be a man. It just makes things so much easier—to be a man." My own daughter . . . the lawyer with the high grades and the fifty-thousand-dollar education!

I suspect there are many young women who would agree with her. What a wretched situation that this is so. How, in our democracy, can the freest nation in the world—in the twentieth century—still be making life so difficult for women that they would find it easier to be a man?

Does our long struggle add up to nothing? We simply can't let hollow and bigoted people make this so. I have spent too much of my life in politics—given too much of myself in the women's movement—to believe that. So what is the answer for young women today?

"Putting it all together into a satisfying life is the challenge. For those of us out in the work world, it's hard to balance your personal life and your profession, and maintain a well-rounded life," said Christy. "For so many years, men have been there, but they had this wife at home going to the grocery store, picking up the clothes from the cleaner, doing all the detailed errands. A person like me has it tough."

"Does that make you want to be a wife?" I asked.

"No! I just want a wife," she shouted, laughing. "And we are getting there. Computers will soon be offering services like ordering groceries."

Where are women now? I put the question to my daughter-in-law, who is staying home now to be with my grandson. She has held a high position in the workplace, and I asked her if she misses it.

"I miss the self-esteem. I miss getting paid for what I do, and I fight daily to feel like a person. On the other hand, I have chosen to be home. I'm not forced to be here. And I have the pleasure of really knowing Les and being here when he gets home from kindergarten eager to tell me about his day. He's fun to know. Each year makes it easier, and I am looking for a ten-to-two job, because I could handle that and still be with Les."

The answer is different for each person, but part-time work and good day-care centers would ease the strain.

Where are women today? I called up my ERA traveling friend Erma Bombeck to toss it around.

"I want to say women are in limbo, but it's not quite that. We've got a generation now who were born with semiequality. They don't know how it was before, so they think, This isn't too bad. We're working. We have our attache cases and our three-piece suits. I get very disgusted with the younger generation of women. We had a torch to pass, and they are just sitting there. They don't realize it can be taken away. Things are going to have to get worse before they join in fighting the battle."

"One more Donald Regan and his put-downs of women ought to do it," I interjected.

"Yes, and it will probably happen. However, I do see women our age who years ago were saying, 'I'm not a libber.' They are into the whole thing now, and I see young women quite often opting to stay home. What makes the difference is that staying home is their own choice now. It wasn't before. Women were put there and stuck there. And you can't be happy when you are just put someplace.

"What was it I did before I had this plateau of planes, and speeches, and writing columns and plays, and television?" Erma asked. "What was I doing that was worthwhile? And the sum total was saying to myself, Wouldn't it be amazing if I was doing the most important thing on earth: unleashing a whole human being into the world. Liz, I wrote a column about it, and you should read the mail that came in. The difference, simply, is that we helped give them that choice. I guess what I'm trying to say is that something good has come out of the women's movement, even though I wish this generation were fighting harder. Complete equality is going to take that."

We cannot lose our sense of rage, those of us who lived through the embattled years for ERA. Nor should we blame our own shortcomings for its failure to pass. We lost ERA because three state legislatures didn't move it. Not a governor, a lieutenant governor, or a speaker was able to rally enough votes to get it through. At the start, in 1972, when Congress passed the amendment, Hawaii stayed in session all night to be the first to ratify. Thirty-three states followed quickly, and then the stall of the last three set in. Too much time elapsed. The right wing rallied behind one woman who was able to cast fear in so many hearts about false ramifications. The ludicrous threat of homosexuals raising children in some sort of fantasy state was introduced. Oh, yes, introduced in state legislatures through a well-organized campaign of fundamentalists, Mormons, and pink-lady followers of Phyllis Schlafly, who was determined to kill the amendment. I faced one of her followers (I will call her Mrs. Tippy-toes) in a legislative hearing. She stood on her toes and, in a high, almost vaudevillian voice, whispered into the microphone: "I love my husband, I love our two children. If something happens to both of us, please don't leave our two children to be raised by a homosexual couple." Can you imagine anything more absurd being voiced in a state legislature?

The ladies in pink descended on legislatures, passing out cupcakes and literature, leaving an imprint. By the time our side had begun electing and rallying the women in these legislatures to power positions, the ballgame was ending. A few leading ERA supporters claim that if we hadn't had to stage marches with the always present lesbian contingent, it would have been easier. We looked a lot scrubbier than the pink ladies in their hats and gloves. These arguments were used back in the suffrage days when even white leaders like Carrie Chapman Catt thought it wiser if her black supporters avoided the public efforts. But how can you justify a battle for inclusion when you exclude some of your own? The ERA movement was not just for neat, tidy suburban Junior Leaguers. It was for all women, black, white, gay, rich, poor, young, and old. As a result, we came on strong—too strong for easily intimidated men.

The early suffragettes faced the same dilemma in their quest for equality. There was my great-aunt Birdie in Washington during the Woodrow Wilson administration. She was a favorite of the society writers, who praised her good looks, "which have the piquancy of a Watteau canvas with her sweet dimpling young face surmounted by amazing masses of snow white hair, always arranged with elaborate distinction." While the society writers never missed her parties to see notables like Mrs. William Jennings Bryan, what they missed was that Aunt Birdie, for all her Watteau piquancy, was busy lobbying for suffrage on Capitol Hill and, back home in Tyler, Texas, taking out prosuffrage ads in the town paper. In 1912, she began rallying women for Woodrow Wilson, who was just beginning to realize that they meant business about getting the vote. If they got it, he wanted it cast for him.

There was her sister, Great-aunt Kate, who as a girl growing up at Salado shocked the town by riding astride and annoyed her brothers by outriding them. A volatile and energetic woman, she spent some time in Washington marching for women's suffrage.

I heard my aunts and uncles arguing about Birdie and Kate and their aggressive suffragist activities in Washington. The two had not agreed on tactics. There were two camps of suffragists, the "Axe girls" which included Aunt Kate, and the "Wiles girls" which most certainly included Aunt Birdie, who had a husband and the power and contacts to confront her victims face to face. She would don a long white dress, pick up her matching white parasol, and step into her buggy to be driven to the national Capitol to sweet-talk senators into voting for suffrage for women. She was horrified that just as things looked like they were going well and the Wiles girls had been promised the necessary votes, the Axe girls, including Aunt Kate, would get disgusted with President Wilson's stalling and march on the White House to toss rotten eggs.

I have often wondered if, had I been there, I'd have ridden to the Capitol with Aunt Birdie or pelted eggs at the White House with Aunt Kate. I have a little of both in me, as do the women I came to know in the battle fifty years later for the Equal Rights Amendment. We had Axe girls and Wiles girls. It took both, and both were not quite enough.

Will ERA ever pass? It will come as soon as we make it come, and that will require continued election of pro-ERA supporters. No man or woman against equal rights for women belongs in a lawmaking body of the twentieth century. I suspect it will take several years for the weeding out to put an ERA landslide in motion. But it will come, and we will look back, as we have on the days when blacks sat at the back of the bus, and wonder why anyone was ever against giving women equal rights under the Constitution of the United States. This I feel in the marrow of my bones.

Meanwhile, I am grateful for the umbrella of ERA, which brought us all together and taught us to love, respect, and work with one another. Never have women learned so much, moved so fast, been so alive with their own vitality and worth. We have learned to laugh at pomposity and cry at injustice. Every mile we have walked, every microphone we have spoken through, every check we have written, every friend we have made—and there are thousands—all are building blocks and will count in the future. The issue still burns within us. The fight goes on, and I will go on with the fight.

FAMILY TALK

I LAUGHED AND RUSHED to the phone when I came across it in the old cardboard suitcase. "Tommy, you've got to come over now! I don't care if it *is* raining."

It was a cold November night, but the letter I had found— his letter written to me on my thirteenth birthday—was hardly an accurate forecast of my life to come, and I was eager to tease my brother about the advice he had given me so many years before. We already had a long postponed date to talk about men and women as they are today, to probe our own attitudes now that we are both past our salad days.

"You certainly can't make predictions," I teased him. "Listen to this!"

September 1, 1933

Dear Mary Elizabeth,

Congratulations on having gotten into your teens. It's about the swellest age to be in and has twice as much excitement as all the rest of your life put together. Of course, the rest of your life is put together anyway. I say put together because a girl doesn't have to do anything but entertain herself. A boy has to worry about what he's going to be—not that he'll ever be anything, but he has to decide and make up his mind and answer people's questions about it until he hardly has time to do anything exciting enough to get whipped for.

With girls it's different. They get away with anything; that's the nice part of being a girl. Girls don't have to worry about anything because they know that all they have to do is grow up and then some boy falls in love with them and marries them and makes them a living so that they never have to do anything, only have babies as fast as they can.

And girls while they are growing up have nothing at all to do or think about except have fun from morning to night. They don't have to be good, like boys, because people just take it for granted that they are good and never want any proof. When a girl wants something people won't give her, all she has to do is jump up and down and chew the bed clothes and cry and people just have to give her what she wants right away to stop her, because you can't hit her over the head like you can a boy. And besides, boys aren't smart enough to think of such a way of getting what they want. Girls are smart, and no matter what they do, even to using their big sister's smelly perfume, they can lie out of it just as easy as falling off a calf.

Happy Birthday! My love to all, and especially to mamma because she's the kind of mamma who sends me $10 instead of $5.

Tommy

"Did I say that?" he laughed. "Well, if you were thirteen, I was twenty-two, and in 1933 I was just about to take on the responsibilities of marriage and family at the height of the Depression, and I had not lost my innocence. I was making a bit of whimsical fun out of some envy on my part. I was being forced to get a job before I got married. All right, I'll come over. It's a good night for chili-making—a three-dog night."

A "three-dog" night is a phrase Tommy learned in Mexico that describes how cold the weather is. It refers to how many dogs you must sleep with to keep warm. Thus, a five-dog night is bitter cold, a three-dog night just plain cold.

I thought the letter was "hilariously chauvinistic." Chauvinism can be hilarious when it is so blatantly ridiculous. But maybe that is the way men saw their roles fifty years ago—as forced breadwinners.

However, life didn't work out that way for me. I have worked all my life, wanted to work all my life, needed to work all my life. And, unlike the letter predicted, I had seldom used tears to get what I wanted. It would be fun to analyze our viewpoints, I decided, and it was a perfect time for a good talk. A norther had blown in.

I PUT A LOG on the fire, a really good dried-oak log that Lady Bird had sent from the LBJ ranch with a pile of mesquite. "Liz, I can't believe all you want for your birthday is firewood," she had said last September. Texans are finicky about their firewood. Mesquite is the hottest-burning wood; oak embers are the best. A combination is perfect for a good fire.

Tommy is a marvelous talker, loves family history, likes to have it read to him, which is necessary now that at seventy-five his eyes are gone for reading.

We are both single. I am widowed. He is twice divorced and father of two sets of children: seven daughters by his first wife and two more girls by his second. Thomas Shelton Sutherland V, his long desired son, was born after Tommy was sixty-six. His first batch of daughters are all grown and working, and most are married. College graduates, they have become editors, anthropologists, real estate agents, and social workers, and all are philosophers of a sort. Two more nieces by my younger brother, George, round out my circle of "little women" who fascinate me as a living laboratory of contemporary women.

Tommy arrives by taxicab and mixes two margaritas—mine without salt. I find the right pot for his chili and turn the kitchen over to him while he does what he loves to do: cook with an audience. Cooking is one of his pleasures now that his old passion, reading, is no longer possible.

While the chili sizzles slowly with the six cloves of garlic he considers essential to two pounds of beef, he pulls out his pocketknife. "You don't have a decent knife in the house," he says, peeling avocado for the guacamole salad. He drops in more garlic and mashes it into the mixture, then drops the avocado seed in, too.

"The seed prevents the avocado from turning dark. Something about the chemistry," he explains.

While he bends low over the frying pan to examine his culinary concoction, I settle down nearby with the letters, ready to talk family.

A recurrent pattern in American history, and in our family's history, has been the quest for a new Canaan. The pushes and pulls generating such quests have, for some families, led to, not only one, but a series of moves. America moves incessantly today for new job opportunities. A hundred years ago the Sutherland family from Jackson County was pulled by the availability of cheaper land and pushed by the "fevers," as they called malaria.

We had heard our father describe it: "We boys grew up swimming in the Navidad and the Mustang, where there were still alligators . . . where the mosquitoes said, 'Q-u-i-n-i-n-e,' and the bullfrogs answered, 'Double dose, double dose.' " Daddy would tell this story in a low-pitched voice, imitating the mosquitoes and bullfrogs, which always set the relatives laughing. Grandparents and uncles and aunts moved out to the remote Nueces Canyon in southwest Texas to raise children, goats, and sheep and to find better health. They took their savings, bought ranches of five thousand acres for $15 an acre, and moved into the ranch wilderness with their families, some including ten or fifteen children. The new Canaan was not easily discovered.

Even now it is hard to keep all the families straight. But in my mind's eye I can still see an old quilt pattern—the Wedding Ring—with three rings symbolizing the three families: Laura Lizzie and Tom, Minnie and Bob Lee, and Willie and Emma, all Rogers and Sutherlands. Three Sutherland brothers married three Rogers sisters, uniting in marriage and purpose the children of the original Alabama settlement of their grandfather, Major George Sutherland, and their father, Samuel Rogers, both of whom lived through the Battle of San Jacinto. My father was the oldest of all the thirty-two double-first cousins.

"Tommy," I say, "you realize how young this country is when you learn that your father knew his grandpa Rogers, who had witnessed and described the scene of the 1836 Battle of San Jacinto. Daddy was five when Sam Rogers died," I point out. "It is strange to think that our own father knew someone who had been alive in 1836; strange to think that I knew a great-aunt who was born in 1849." Tommy knows I am referring to Aunt Talitha, who was (appropriately) called "Aunt Lifey": she lived until 1934. "I don't know whether these facts point up how young our country is or how old I am."

"It was country that was hard on men, women, and animals," Tommy says matter-of-factly, looking up from the stove. "The life expectancy was about forty-eight years. Yet this hardy group, despite multiple childbirths and godawful hardships, survived, many of them living on past eighty, some past ninety."

Hard on animals is right. One of these letters tells about a storm—a real gully washer—where the rain gauge registered 21.45 inches in twenty-four hours. One horse swam four miles downstream before emerging. A cow came out forty-two miles below, I don't know whether it was dead or alive. And eight hundred goats were drowned. Weather shapes people more than we realize.

Life after sixty holds so much. Times to be with my
Seattle family—Bonnie, Jean, Scott and little Les; my
oldest brother, Tom; and my other two brothers, Bill and
George Sutherland, at a family reunion. There is also
time to entertain, with (right, above) Jerry Earle at the
piano and hymn singers Barbara Jordan, Don Rives and
Bill Moyers; and (center) former White House aides who
gather in my hot tub: Leonore Haag and her husband,
Budd, my neighbor Henrietta, and Simone Poulain. Relaxing in a favorite caftan and on a favorite couch in
front of my favorite view.

The Nueces Canyon is a land of extremes: too little rain or too much. Streams are either full of catfish or they are dry creek beds. Roads are narrow and muddy through winter and parched ruts in summer. But there is a beauty to it all, too—sycamore trees along the river beds, some maples and cottonwoods, and wildflowers when the rains come. Houses are still few and far between, even now, and there are no great expanses of pasture for grazing. The livestock has to eke out its food, the same as the people.

What was life like for people out there? The letters my grandmother Laura Lizzie and her sisters wrote home to their sister-in-law Bell, who had remained in Jackson County, describe the love and loneliness and hardship.

"These letters begin in 1895, Tommy," I say, "the October when Grandmama and Grandpapa Sutherland moved out to the canyon. But what is confusing in reading is that everyone is named Tom."

"That's the 'in' name in our family," Tommy says, laughing.

Grandmama called Grandpapa "Tommie" and she called my father "Tom"; he was eight years old when she wrote the letters, one of four children, and seven more were to come during the fifteen years they lived out there. Grandmama was only twenty-six when they moved, still a young woman self-conscious enough to have a cousin come over to curl her hair before she took the train west for their new adventure. They all—the three Rogers sisters who married three Sutherland brothers and moved to the canyon—wrote back home to Aunt Bell in Jackson County.

The letters reveal a far different life than I had envisioned for the period. There is surprising tenderness on the part of many men in my family, moving love letters, more feeling than I would have guessed.

What surprises me most in reading these accounts is how much interchange of responsibilities and chores occurred in order to survive wilderness hardships. The men weren't John Wayne or

Tom Mix all the time, and the women were more than Betty Crocker and Whistler's mother. They talk of men washing the heavy sheets and nightgowns while the women did the rinsing. I learned that in letters from Lizzie Laura written in 1895, which relate a saga of hard life in a hostile land.

> Dear Bell,
>
> We arrived here yesterday morning and all have very bad colds. I don't think I would have been able to get to the train at all if a lady hadn't offered to carry Mary for me. George went along crying to go to sleep and I carried John. We all have very bad colds. Little Tom was a help. Tommie very near sick. I believe he had a pretty bad case of Catarrh. I have nettle rash all over me. . . .

Three weeks later she wrote:

> Tommie saw the man that once owned the ranch where we will be living. He told Tommie that he was sorry he had brought horses, that it is too rough for horses, but it is a splendid hog ranch. They made good crops every year. They never failed, but it is very rough, and I am afraid we have no road to Utopia.

Tommy interrupts, "Do you have any onions?" I shove them toward him.

"Utopia, Tommy! Don't you think that's prophetic, how they thought that Utopia was ahead?" I tell him, irritated because he is missing the point.

"Utopia is a town about thirty miles down the road in another canyon," Tommy says in disgust. "But it's ironic that they were searching for it, geographically as well as symbolically, since the place they settled was a stretch of the Nueces River that cuts through boulders and rugged, rocky country. But land was cheap."

Aside from no heat and lousy water, there were panthers around. Grandmama wrote about those, too.

> Tommie went hunting with Mr. Box and killed a young panther. Mr. Box has killed four panthers and three catamounts (or leopard cats I should have said) since we came here.

Tommie says the house at Mr. Box's is really not fit to live in, but we will have to put up with it until we build our own. Young Tom has been crying to go back home and George is very anxious for us to find our house. I am afraid he will be disappointed. But I am very anxious to get moved. "Be it ever so humble there is no place like home," even if it has to be a rented one. Some of our furniture has been setting outdoors since we first came. We have had it covered with an old tent cloth which protected it some. . . . Santa Claus is last thing at night with the children and first in the morning. Poor children. They will be very much disappointed, I think. I tell Tommie that Santa Claus bothers the children's minds as much as he wearies himself about making a living.

"I don't know whether it's the onion or the letters, but something's making my eyes water," Tommy confesses. "Can you put some more ice in my glass?"

"Aunt Bell apparently sent a Christmas box, thank God," I say, filling up his glass and glancing at the chili.

By now the meat is gray, not brown, just the way he likes it. He adds water, tomatoes, and spices.

I continue. "In January 1896, Grandmama writes:

Dear Bell,
    I must at least write and thank you for the books you sent the children. Little Mary almost knows her book by heart. The children are a good deal of help to me. They clean up the dishes real nice. I am trying to get me a Mexican girl or boy. I will need one very badly after a little. [She is expecting her fifth child.] Please send the draft of your house. . . . I am satisfied Tommie will want to build a place of his own by fall. There is a very cheap place fifty miles from here that would be much better for his stock and more healthy but we hate to go. It is a long ways from there to any place except two or three near neighbors.

"When she says 'draft for a house,' that was the term for floor plan," Tommy offers. "You can see that already she is yearning for a home of her own and getting homesick away from her people."

In February, she writes:

> Tommie is very busy with his goats, kidding. Has only fifteen
> but more will be coming on. . . . I am expecting Mamma on
> the 20th. Tommie will go down to Uvalde [a two-day trip by
> wagon]. . . . The day after she gets here Emma's and Rosey's
> families will come to see mamma and we will have a gobbler
> for dinner as Rosey sent me one up this evening. Little Tom
> will have his hands full attending to the kids [young goats]
> while his Papa is gone.

After reading these letters I can better understand my father,
the get-up-and-go man. At the age of eight, he was tending to a
whole ranch and a family of brothers and sisters while his father
was away and his mother expecting another baby soon. He never
talked of this as hardship but in later years would recall stories of
life in the canyon with humor. Everyone laughed over hardships
to avoid sinking into depression.

In March 1896, Grandmama writes Aunt Bell about the
new baby.

> Our little girl arrived. I guess I am doing as well as possible.
> The children are delighted. . . . We still cling to family
> names. . . . We will call the baby for you and Minnie . . . the
> full name, Minnie Bell. Enclosed you will find a lock of your
> namesake's hair.
>
> She is a perfect little beauty to me. I think she is very
> much like her papa and you. Especially when she is
> asleep. . . . Today is wash day. Tommie does the rubbing of
> the sheets and nightgowns while I rinse.

I recall a similar scene in my own family during the Depression of the 1930s when my little brother Bill was born. It was
Washington's Birthday and Daddy was home between jobs. He
washed the clothes in the bathtub. He was cheerful about it, too.
"Washing on George Washington's Birthday!" And then repeating it: "Washing on George Birthington's washday!"

"The unwritten law, you see, of all these people was to pitch
in and get the job done," Tommy points out.

"That was before job descriptions," I reply, and remembering some of the accusations made by antifeminists, I add sarcastically, "No one thought you lost your femininity by carrying a rifle or plowing a field."

What I hadn't realized was just how much couples counted on children to help. In December 1896, my grandmother writes:

> We have been so busy since moving, but I am always busy and never get through with all my work. Besides I have been sick since we came here and my physician tells me I can never get well and drink the well water in this ground cistern. I am taking medicine, drinking boiled water. . . . Minnie Bell is teething. . . . I am trying to teach the children a little, which takes most of my time in the evening. Mary has learned her large letters and is now learning the small ones. George knows a good many and has a splendid memory but does not apply himself as well. I find it harder to teach Tom because he does so many jobs such as watering horses, going to the goat camp, bringing in wood, washing dishes and various other things too numerous to mention. Mary cleans the lamps. George minds the baby while I am in the kitchen and washes potatoes and puts them in the stove. John brings in wood and Minnie Bell . . . well, she makes us attend to her. They help a great deal for little children. . . . I would get along well if it were not for the washing and sewing, but those two things I am not physically built to stand. . . . You can't conceive how rough it is and open. We are anxious to improve it some, but like all people without money, we have to wait.

"What a contrast to the children today, who stay glued to TV and ask to have their food brought to them," Tommy says, laughing.

"Not to mention the old folks," I offer, knowing that Tommy can't sleep through a night and keeps the TV going more than his children do.

"I know. I know, but it is entertaining and I can turn on to the whole world from my pillow. I have never liked to sleep in a great big room. I've been so used to big family noises that silence bothers me."

I turn back to the letters. By February 1897, life had become even more difficult:

> We went to Willie's for Christmas. . . . Only three times have I been off the place since we came here. The roads are so rough. I dislike to see people live to themselves but there is little time to spare for visiting. . . . We are all homesick. I want to see you all very bad, but I think sometimes that I don't want to go back until I can stay. Of course, this country is good for the goats and hogs.

That's the way my father talked about it years later . . . good for goats, but not for people. And lonely, lonely, lonely, even with the big families.

> Tommie is just as homesick as can be. I know he tries to keep it from me just like I do from him, but he knows it too well. He tells me I think more of it than I acknowledge, which I guess I do, for it does no good to let him know it. Just makes him feel bad because we could not go. As long as no one has the "blues," so to speak, but myself, I can stand it, but I can't bear to see him get low-spirited. I always think whenever he seems the least that way that I will try to be cheerful no matter what the circumstances are because I think Tommie hates very bad having his family out here where we have so little association. It is not so much homesickness as it is tired of the sameness of things. But don't take this for a "blue" letter for I am not feeling that way at all, but I do think more here about it because I see so few people and Tommie is seldom here at the house, only at meals.

What would she call a blue letter? I remember her and my grandfather years later at a family gathering. He was speaking of how much he liked the canyon country when our grandmother suddenly blurted out, "Oh, you didn't like it. I remember you cried like a baby when someone played 'Home Sweet Home' on the piano."

Tommy laughs. "Loneliness and the sameness of things was a common problem. Right now I'm ready to go to the well for a horn."

"You mean you're lonely for another margarita. If you put the chili on the table, I'll mix more."

While I mix the tequila, triple sec, and lime juice and set the table, I tell him a story about Lucy Goodnight, alone for weeks at a time on the famous J. A. Ranch in the Palo Duro Canyon back in the 1870s. She looked forward to having cowboys stop by, and when they did, she cooked dinner for them. One brought her several live chickens as a gift, to use as she needed them.

She kept them for pets and wrote her sister, "You have no idea how much company a chicken can be."

Tommy nods his head. "I have heard of another ranch woman whose child died and, to keep from going crazy, for she had no one to talk to, she made a 'crazy jug,' pasting pictures of children's toys from magazines on an old bottle she found. I once saw that bottle in a west Texas museum. It was a sort of awful memento to the stark desperation of that country."

Sam Rayburn understood loneliness and used to talk about it often. In a speech he made in Congress promoting the rural electrification program, I was struck by the moving way he described life in the country when he was a boy.

"Many a Sunday I sat on the front porch just waiting for someone to come along. God help the lonely," he told the Congress.

"Are you lonely, Liz?" Tommy asks directly.

"Lots of times, aren't you?" I answer.

"Not when I'm making damned good chili," he replies. "But yes, of course, in the way you can be lonely when life lacks something. And what life lacks for us is a lover. The highest form of companionship is someone who loves you physically as well as spiritually and in harmonious thought."

"Well, I'm fresh out, and so are you," I say with a laugh. "I do not find men who interest me readily available. The interesting ones are married and they die before their wives. Now, you, Tommy, have less of a problem at seventy-five than I do at sixty-five. You are not considered shelved. You are a man."

Tommy brings up another reason we don't have anyone. "We are picky. You especially. You've learned how to protect what is yours. You are protecting yourself from a bad relationship that might rob you of the independent life you have mastered, even though it means being lonely."

Some families have trouble communicating. Not mine. We are candid and outspoken, particularly with kinfolk. It sometimes has its advantages. Tommy is probably right that increased judgment and financial independence prevent a woman from accepting anyone who doesn't meet her qualifications. I hang on to what I have and am afraid to risk my property or emotions. I don't want either to be damaged.

"I think what we yearn for is an alter ego, someone to share our thoughts and our bed. It is very hard to find that person after you're past the point of lyric love," Tommy says.

"Lyric love" . . . that's why I love talking to Tommy. He can still come up with those phrases even at his age.

"Maybe what we need is more cluster migration—families together and providing the companionship that substitutes for lyric love," he adds.

It seems strange that we live in the same town with a family of more than fifteen relatives who are close kin, yet we have as hard a time seeing them as our grandparents did out in the Nueces Canyon.

"I think the era of the self-sufficient person began to diminish when the automobile came, when land wore out, when America moved to town and the frontier was gone," Tommy philosophizes. "Our grandparents may have lived in one or two homes. I've lived in fifty. The civilization of the automobile uprooted us of home and of affections. Men moved reluctantly to town, began to build roads and sell gasoline. The women got teacher's certificates and business school diplomas and headed to the cities, where the eight-to-five jobs were. Women were happier because they had more opportunities; the men were miserable because they had lost their individual importance—their kingdom: land, horses, independence. They had lost the kind of woman who relished being called Mrs. Tom, or Mrs. Willie or Mrs. Bob.

"I suspect those women missed it, too," he continues, "but they all wanted something better for their daughters and their sons. Less drudgery. Less sameness. They fought for more education, associations, and social graces."

Ever the teacher, Tommy sends me to the bookshelves to get Walter Prescott Webb's *The Great Frontier*.

"Liz, find the part where he asks, 'After the land, what?' "

I turn to the section he means and read: "As society thickens and becomes more closely integrated, its members more interdependent, governments become stronger, using more compulsions. There will be a tendency toward socialization, as in the United States and Britain, or toward absolutism as exhibited by the fascist states and by Russia. The loose democracy belonged to a frontier stage of society. The individual will become less important and tend to lose his identity in growing corporate life."

"It's hard to beat that for a prediction," Tommy exclaims. "And I heard him say it once. That's what happened to men. They have been swallowed up in corporate life. The frontier of today is a frontier of the mind. The new corporate world, predicted by Walter Webb, is still cursed by loneliness and sameness. Webb could look clear-eyed into the future, but he looked, literally, with tears in his eyes when he spoke of the loss of freedom and individual greatness that would come with the end of the physical frontier."

"Well, Tommy, we saw that in our own father. I have a poem you sent me that you wrote about Daddy when he was old and helpless. Like lots of your poetry, you may not remember it, but it is great—one of your best. I can't read it without weeping."

> *This old man . . . bedridden now,*
> *broken in body by time,*
> *by all the ravages of living,*
> *was once a rider . . .*

He knew,
he seemed by knowing to possess
the streams and waterholes and rolling country,
the river, roads and ranges,
from short grass to the coast,
and from tall timber to the thickets.

He was a good hand
at working cattle . . .
and once in Belton on July the fourth
he roped and tied a calf
and won the money.

. . . Your daddy's fast,
a man told me.
But I said
It was the best bay horse in Texas
that put him there.
(that's what I'd heard him say)

Now while his frame's all bones,
his hand unsteady,
I watch and see the look
the old look
I knew when he was undefeated. . . .

Seeing his eyes alone,
I think he may be going out the house
in hat and spurs
to ride off on Old Fiddler
down a trail
that only they remember.

We both wiped tears from our eyes after I'd finished reading the poem, and then Tommy asks me, "What is your first memory of Daddy?"

"It was when I was about three. I was lifted up by Daddy and placed behind my grandfather Sutherland on his horse. I wrapped my little arms halfway around his sturdy waist and rode as he walked the horse slowly around."

"That was Betty," Tommy says, "a marvelous mare. Betty could almost hold a fox trot at ten miles an hour all the way from Salado to Belton, a distance of ten miles. She could reach Belton without tiring the rider in an hour and a half."

"What did you sense or feel about these first men in your life, Daddy and Granddaddy? Can you remember?" asks my older brother.

The memories are there, but they are nebulous; I try and sketch them for Tommy. "Size, strength, voices that were so deep and stern in contrast to the softness of my mother's and grandmother's that they put a child on edge. I saw their tender side on rare occasions. It was there, but I think life had taught them a reluctance to express it."

"Those men lived by a code of unwritten law, a code that came all the way down from Moses through European history to the American frontier," Tommy says. "That code, for them, was that they gave justice as they understood it, and expected justice; that they were forever loyal to their own people; and that they never flinched from the pain of life."

Tommy wants to go back to what the swallowing up by the city does to men and women. "The history of America has been thrilling but anti-intellectual. The theme is not thinking. We are doers, not thinkers. Now we are confronted with thinking—for women are now free and eager to think, and men are now required to confront it and adapt to it."

"I don't think the jury is in yet," I say. "But I do firmly believe women are better off. Adapting has always been easier for women because we do it daily as mothers. At last, women, hungry for intelligent conversation with men as well as women, have a group of choices before them which were missing before."

"What is missing for all of us now," Tommy says, "is the solidarity of the human race that was found in ranch country families and their churches."

Over dessert, which is mango ice cream, we return to philosophizing about our own predicament, the lack of a companion-lover.

Tommy lays it on the line. "At seventy-five years of age, I'm still looking for a woman who is in love with me because of me, not because she's liberated or has lost her fear of flying."

I quickly point out what I think is true: the women he is looking for, that every man of every age looks for, are twenty- and twenty-five-year-olds who have firm bodies, who are still willing to play flirtatious games, and who don't have any of the experiences that he has had. Historically, they can't even remember Bobby Kennedy.

Sex is more than sex, I tell him, and older women like myself have physical as well as companionable love to offer. We were there when you were—in the Depression, in the high and low moments of this country. Doesn't that count for something in the bedroom?

Tommy nods. "True, other than a stolen kiss or very brief moment of sex, there is little interesting in a woman under thirty, although women get smart very fast."

I interrupt. "I got phone calls from my kids the night they saw a TV documentary about the Alger Hiss investigation back in the fifties. They spotted their father and me at the press table covering it. Both were amazed. 'We didn't know you were there.' "

Tommy laughs. "It doesn't help either when the girl you are waltzing calls you 'sir.' Or the boys at the bar call you 'dad.' "

"But that is bound to change some with better health and longer lives," I reply optimistically. "We are adults for sixty years, and life can be rich for a long period of time, so how do we get rid of the old emphasis on youth and make men appreciate the appeal of women over fifty?"

Tommy quips half-seriously, "There ought to be a law that after fifty, men and women meet only in total darkness like the fish in Mammoth Cave."

"But that's insulting," I retort.

"No, what I'm talking about is the intellectual achievement of putting physical emphasis out of the mind," replies Tommy. "Just imagine removing the Dallas Cowboys and their pep squad from the TV screen, and think of an after-dinner colloquium where there is a feast of wit and flow of soul, where there is a discussion of Emily Dickinson or Robert Burns. The younger athletes would lose yardage to any average citizen over fifty. Yet we are too proud and too proper to run an ad saying something like 'Available, one sixty-five-year-old loving woman who wants good talk, good food, understanding, and warm bedtime love.' Why don't you put an ad in *The Wall Street Journal*, Liz?"

"Why *The Wall Street Journal*? Are you thinking money or security?" I reply indignantly. "Do you know that money is last on the list of requirements for a mate for women of my age, perhaps any age? We don't depend on men for security anymore; we do depend on them to support other needs, and we seek the security of their love. I trust they depend on us."

It's late and Tommy has called a cab, but I push him for more conclusions:

"Before your taxi comes, do you have any thoughts on how we can use a new frontier of thinking, of getting men and women to love each other in a more sensible and intellectual way?"

"Well I will now try to think of how men and women can stand each other after fifty," Tommy replies sarcastically, for he says my pontifical questions always come just as he is ready to leave. "They have to psych up to it like a football team before the big game. They have to think of themselves as winners the way they did when they were young. And they have to ask. You know what the country boy said about his approach to girls: 'I ask all of them. I get slapped a lot, but I get a lot of loving, too!' "

PONDERING THE CONVERSATION of "the three-dog night," as it is now known in family talk when we repeat it and, in Sutherland style, argue it back and forth among nieces and nephews who come around to do just that, I know that the world of our grandchildren will be far different. They don't have as many physical hardships, they don't have to fight as hard for education, for company. How can they make their relationships, so necessary to human happiness, work over sixty years of adulthood?

Comedian-pianist Victor Borge once said, "The closest distance between two people is a laugh." So maybe we should look at our situation today and laugh more about it, laugh our way through the sour and suspicious moments. It will take more than that. Respecting each person's right to individuality is another must.

The men I have known best respected women. My father never made his daughters feel less than their brothers. Yet I think he would have choked if he'd had to say "Ms.," and he quite honestly believed that there are some things women shouldn't do, like fix a flat or drive alone at night, and that there are certain places women shouldn't go. But he gave me my drive, my get up and go, and my impulsiveness, and I am ever grateful to him for it.

My husband was "sensitive" long before that was a catchword for nonmacho men. We were working partners and equals in our news bureau. His attitude toward women was as influential as mine in shaping my son's. Jean, my daughter-in-law, says she married Scott "because he is the only man I met who respected women, and I give you credit for that, Liz."

Scott credits his father. "Daddy's respect for you and your abilities had more to do with my attitude than any particular thing you said or did. I grew up in a home that assumed women were equals, and it never occurred to me to discriminate. Our house was full of your working newswomen friends, professional women. Today, I don't think women have to stay home, and I don't think they have to go out. It's like a skirt length. You can choose any way you want to go."

I know my children were raised in a special environment that would not have been there if I had not been working and involved in my work.

Scott fished with Sam Rayburn and, on one occasion, caught far more with his hook and worm than Mr. Speaker did with his fancy tackle and flies. Whenever I ran into the speaker after that, he would ask, "How is that fisherman?" He didn't relish the experience as much as Scott, however, who, at age ten, had outfished the master. To our public horror and secret amusement, Scott shouted from one side of the lake to the other, "I got another! I've got more now than he has!" He carried the long string of fish home and wanted to hang them on his bedroom wall.

Then there was the evening when Congressman Wilbur Mills, chairman of the powerful Ways and Means Committee, came for a backyard picnic supper. Christy was heavily into Tinker Bell and Peter Pan, and she enlisted this man, who fortunately has raised two little girls himself, into the role of Peter flying behind her across the lawn and shouting, "We can fly! We can fly!" Mills played Peter Pan with humor, a sheepish smile, and perhaps the realization that Tinker Bell was the daughter of the correspondents for *The Arkansas Gazette*, the political bible of Mills's home state. Another sacrifice for politics!

But was I enough of a mother? I am still haunted by a nagging sense of guilt.

Recently, I called Ruth Baker, my friend and helper from those days, now working in a Washington bank.

"Don't you feel any remorse," Ruth said when I surprised her with my question. We talked an hour about our days in Washington when my children were growing up. "You did enough, more than many mothers who don't work outside the home. You were always a phone call away. If a child called you, you dropped what you were doing and talked, when a lot of mothers might have said they were too busy to talk. Scott and Christy grew up knowing a lot of people. Had you stayed home, they wouldn't have been so knowledgeable. During dinner I'd listen, and it wasn't you and Mr. Carpenter talking over their heads. It was a four-way conversation.

"You and Mr. Carpenter built your vacations around what they wanted to do. Remember the time Christy and Scott wanted to go to Mexico and you all had planned something else? You canceled your plans and went to Mexico.

"Now let me ask you a question. Why now? Why are you questioning your life now?"

I stumbled around for an answer and finally told her that I

suppose I was feeling guilty and was looking for assurance that I'd not done the wrong thing by working so much while the children were growing up.

"And I just guess I've always wondered if I should have stayed home. I had a marvelous life. I really had it all. I just wonder if it cost anyone else too much."

There was a certain fire in her voice now. "Don't even stop to do that. It was a home of love. You were a loving and devoted wife. The years I was with you and Mr. Carpenter were great years. Just stay prayerful. You know that poem, 'Lord help me not to worry about the things I can't change?' Well, put it on your stove or refrigerator. I have it and I see it every day and it helps me. But no remorse."

I put down the phone, which seemed much lighter now. Maybe I was the victim—children all raised and I'm still worrying if I did right by them, feeling good because I had such a great time, but also feeling I may have missed some moments of being home with them, of seeing them grow each day, moments that are now gone. I believe I would have been too much in the way sticking around the house, feeling frustrated and shelved, trying to pick up my writing and work after letting it and me drift into total motherhood. And yet I'm so grateful my daughter-in-law, Jean, has opted to be home while my grandson is little. I guess I'll never know for sure, just keep worrying. But I do think I'll stay prayerful, as Ruth suggested, and find Reinhold Niebuhr's "Serenity Prayer" to put on my refrigerator.

I once got up enough nerve to call and ask Scott if he thought the fact that I worked affected him in a negative way. Did he feel neglected?

"Not at the time," he told me frankly. "My life was my life. My home was where I was. But looking back, I feel some lack of nurturing. After all, you and Daddy were covering the White House, and I was vying for attention with the world. Don't let that put a guilt trip on you, Mom," he said with a laugh. "But I think it's the reason I need such constant affection now."

We all need the reassurance of steadfast affection. It is needs like these that encompass and anger you as you lose men through death or divorce. You lose not only the man you built your world around, but the world he provided entrance to, through business associates or friends. So we ourselves have to seek the entrance that someone once provided for us. That is difficult.

For me, men seem to have disappeared. Not just because I have outlived many of my male peers. Not just because I am strong and outspoken—"formidable," some say, though I don't feel formidable at all. I think of myself as a warm, lovable, sexy woman. I can still work up a temper and my blood pressure over men and their retrogressions to chauvinism or over women who bow to it. But what I really want is for men and women to grow together and find the comfort of loving one another.

Margaret Mead once told a reporter, "Men have always been afraid women could get along without them." But I don't think we can and be happy, too. Gloria Steinem says, "Women have become the men we wanted to marry." My worry about men is not only quantity but quality, and what seems like a cowardly reluctance on their part to make a commitment with the many bright women who are out there now.

What's wrong with men? Or is it us? Did we run them off permanently in our obsession with finding ourselves and establishing our rights? Perhaps there was a period of time in the seventies when we women became so engulfed in our newness as people that we stopped being interested in anyone but our gender, our new growth, our new options and discoveries. We found each other's new worlds more interesting to talk about than the old conversation in the world of men, which had barely changed. But now that we have made the point, if we have, we want them back—improved. In the interim, groups of women gather together not just for lunch, but for an evening together. They do it because these evenings feed their souls and brains in a way their husbands do not. My niece Carol and some of her friends laughingly call their weekly gathering "the Board Meeting." Another group calls theirs "the Poker Club." They gather once a week and pretend to be playing poker since this is the male justification of a night out. But they don't play poker. They talk and talk, not of recipes and children, but of politics, business, investments, and, of course, personal problems. They bare hurts and scars as men never do. Why is it that women can do this and men seldom reach this point of intimacy? They can talk sports. They can talk business. They cannot talk soul. They are much more likely to open up, if they open up at all, with a woman than with a man.

Men have gone through a whole series of stages and adjustments since women became—what was it they called us?— "noisy, strident" feminists? What have their reactions been? For a while they sulked. At least the old macho types were sulking and ridiculing, but deep in their hearts they knew the game was over. They were frightened, too. Some men tried to be all we seemed to want them to be. "The feminization of men," it was called, but it couldn't last because it wasn't real.

We have redefined women . . . the new woman, the contemporary woman, but we have not found a definition of the new man.

Sitting in a think tank at the Aspen Institute for the Humanities, I heard James Brooks, the Hollywood writer and producer of *Rhoda* and later *Cagney & Lacey*, clarify the problem.

"We can define the new man. He isn't formed yet. Every morning in Hollywood ten or twelve writers sit around a table, trying to make the new man out of Rhoda's husband. He is sympathetic to women and their cause for equality, but the new man has got to be more than that. And he isn't. So we are going to have to write him out of the script. They've got to get a divorce."

Now, ten years later, we see *Cagney & Lacey*, and Lacey's husband, the sturdy, blue-collar, loving, and considerate husband of the woman cop, is convincing. Perhaps because it is apparent that they need two salaries and he knows it. He loves her for earning half of it and helps her make it, emotionally and physically.

This sets me thinking . . . Hollywood style: my father was John Wayne; I married Alan Alda; and I'm still looking for Lou Grant!

In the sixties, there was a lot of yelping about wives going to work, but I don't hear it anymore. In fact, some men have pitched in with the chores to make sure that their co-breadwinners don't give up. Two salaries are better than one. A more interesting wife is another result and worth the added tension.

"No decent man wants to turn the clock back," says my thirty-six-year-old friend, Howard Burris. "I don't think I could deal with coming home to a cupcake, waiting for me to make her life begin. I don't want to be anyone's steward, and that's what men have been."

The revolution has brought a relaxation of traditional sex roles, not only for the young, but even for liberated men and women over sixty who, because of death or divorce, are dating again. One of my women friends has no problem at all going off to play tennis while her beau cooks dinner. That would never have happened when they were in their twenties.

These past weeks, I asked several men I know and respect what impact the women's movement had on their lives. These were men of varying ages, old friends, new acquaintances.

Admiral Bobby Ray Inman, czar of the microcomputer companies here in Austin, is quick to applaud what happened in the women's revolution.

"What did the women's movement do to me? I've learned where the washing machine is. When Nancy went back to school and we altered the way we were doing things at home, our sons saw their mother as something more than a sock washer. We are a more balanced family now. It had a very positive effect."

I see the Inmans around town, and always there is a glow about this couple. They are active in the community, there is lots of laughter between them. They have found the secret of equality and a happy marriage that still eludes so many. There are still surprises: each Christmas he gives her a mystery trip. She knows it will be some sunny place, but never knows where until she finds the tickets and the hotel reservations in her Christmas stocking. At the end of the day, they are off for a new adventure.

Then there are the disappointed ones who yearn for this sort of transformation in their married lives. A longtime friend called up to invite me to her wedding anniversary party, and I put my question to her: "What impact has the women's movement made on the man in your life?"

"None!" she shouted in disgust over the phone. "You want to know what Jake gave his son for Christmas? A knife. You want to know what Jake's son gave Jake for Christmas? A gun. So what's new with men?"

I ran into the most outwardly macho man I know, H. C. Carter, at a Christmas party. H. C. looks like a drugstore dude except for his designer shirts and jeans, $600 Tony Lama boots, $150 Stetson, and his ever-present toothpick. At heart he is still the cowboy from Sonora, but he moved from the range to Austin and now is a rich developer. He does the developing for money. For love, he keeps a herd of longhorns on a working ranch he has—a spread thirty miles from Austin—and when the magazine writers come here to write about Texas, H. C. is their man. You can never catch him in a bad pose. He looks the part, more at home on the range than in his penthouse office. Every town needs an H. C., just for color if nothing else. So how has women's lib affected him?

"All my life I have tried to impress girls," he replied. "From the time I was six years old, riding a tricycle with no hands, I was trying to impress some girl. I've busted my butt riding broncos, trying to impress girls. Well, since they all went back to school, it takes a lot more to impress them now.

"Recently, I gave some free office space to a women's group, and the other day they asked me down to lunch to thank me. They were effusive. 'What in the world can we do to say "thank you," Mr. Carter?' they asked.

"Hell, I don't know why I said it . . . nothing else to say, I guess, but I told them, 'Well, I've got some buttons that need sewing on and some socks that need darning, and if you all could handle that, it would really say "thank you" to me,' " H. C. recounted.

"You can't imagine the silence that followed. The president of the group moaned. 'I can't believe you would do this to me.' I guess that wasn't what they had in mind."

H. C. will never win any Alan Alda awards, but at least he has a sense of humor about his passé attitude . . . and that, I suppose, is progress.

Sey Chassler, former editor-in-chief of *Redbook*, has done more thinking about liberated women than any man I know. He says the women's movement has raised the male consciousness in permanent, lasting ways. Sey was born a twin, his sister arriving seven minutes after he did.

"I always knew I was given preference for some reason, and that it wasn't right," he told me. "It was more apparent to me than most boys because I had a twin sister and I was very conscious of the differences in my behalf." The essential difference, he said, "is that men have the right of grants. Women do not. To be thought of as being as good as men are is what the whole discussion is about, and every man knows this, feels this, fears this."

Out of the last twenty years, in the anger and struggle of the women's movement, we are emerging from a period of bitterness to working things out. Things are still not perfect. There is still a distance, but the conversation is improving and the by-product of women trying to be thought of as individuals has paid off for men. We are beginning to see men as people, too—not just as providers and protectors, but as friends, in the same way we fought to be thought of as more than "justa" housewife, mother, sex object.

Our circle of male friends has widened, while our circle of marriageable males has narrowed. There are fewer "threatened women" who try to body-block your friendship with their husbands. I feel a real friendship with husbands of many women I don't like nearly as well as their mates. The husbands are interested in my world of political talk or literature, and I love to lunch with them. I feel no reluctance to call these men for lunch or for escort service when their wives are out of town.

I also find that I seek the companionship of many men who are single, gay or straight, because I do not like an all-woman's world. I feel no hesitation in having professional lunches with men, married or not, and the business of who pays the check is long past. Age gives me the freedom to invite men to share a vacation, to come for dinner.

So where are we women now? We are still on a new frontier, but life between us is looking up and relaxing. These last few years have not been easy, and we miss each other more than we admit.

We are burned out from the battle, but we don't want to surrender the gains or even consider a truce that will wipe out further gains. We aren't there yet. Too often, we are still having to reinvent the wheel on women's rights. But women know something is missing, as men know something is missing besides a balance of duties between us.

Men suspect they are not as important as they once were, so they can't feel as self-important. They have been up against the wall these last few years. Some retreat to celibacy, abandon women, or hide in the gentler gay movement. Some still sulk and think that Ronald Reagan or Donald Regan will make things all right again.

The predicament we're all in, men and women alike, is that we need each other, need love, both physical and mental, and we need it throughout our lives. We are in a world where love is in short supply, and life without love is desolate. So, how do we have both love and equality without men feeling threatened and women being suspicious?

The biggest myth is that women like sex less than men. Most women want more sex than they get. I'm not talking about "conquests," but romantic sex. "Man's love is of man's life a thing apart, 'Tis woman's whole existence." It's been true since Byron's day.

At my age the circle of men to marry is practically zero level, yet I am more interesting and have more time. "They're out there," said my friend Jean, who recently found one after four years of widowhood.

"But who wants to nurse an aging man?" I asked. "It's too late for marriage."

She reminded me that he might be nursing me in the years ahead rather than the other way around, and that would be a comfort. I doubt it. It sounds cruel, but most men at sixty-five seem older and less sexy.

She countered, "A statistic shows that when older men are widowed, they remarry younger women in record time—often within six months of their spouses' death—and sex surveys indicate they are virile."

My friend has recently married a great guy ten years her senior. At seventy-three, he is happy, healthy, and ready to travel anywhere except Libya. I would like to clone him.

She set me thinking. What do I like in a man today? Since a pencil was handy I made a list. It is not the list I would have made at thirteen or eighteen or even thirty. I wouldn't have had enough experience to know what really counts with me, but I know now:

• Intelligent and liberal, even if he's a Republican. He's got to be progressive. Don't offer me a Jerry Falwell–Jesse Helms type. If he's a Republican—and I can sense that I am weakening on this point—he's got to be at least a Rockefeller Republican.

• Good at cooking something so we can enjoy cooking together. Eating and creating good food is one of life's joys, and I'll be damned if I want a lot of calorie counters around me. I'll walk my two miles, I'll lay off the heavy sauces and butter, but I am not going to be weighing the food on scales . . . or me, either.

• See the funny side of things and bring laughter to my life. What is nicer than sharing a headline about some fool in the newspaper? What is better than telling anecdotes or reciting the day's events and seeing the humor in them? I am so hungry for that.

• Like the feel of me . . . be physically drawn to me. And I am hungry for that, too.

• Refrain from talking about his own health all the time. If there is anything that bores and ages one, it is hearing about someone else's ailments. It gets you to thinking about your own. I remember what my Sunday School teacher Lena Hickman told me at age ninety: "It's a good day when you wake up with nothing new hurting you." Men are worse about complaining over ill health than women are.

• Have enough money so I won't feel used. Some of the tightest men I know are bachelors. I don't want any more possessions. There's no more room for them. But a movie, a bottle of wine, a dinner out, are welcome escapes, and I don't want to worry about picking up the check, although I am glad to do my share.

• Like long weekends together. I enjoy someone with a sense of adventure, who would like to see the place where the eagles nest, or browse in Salado, or roam the river walk in San Antonio.

• However old, make me feel young; however young, make me feel younger. My darling old friend Ernie Cuneo is a marvel at inventing ways to do this. When I am in Washington, he calls me for lunch and is waiting with chilled champagne, has two or three wicked stories on hand to tell me, often about Madame Pompadour. In his mobile days, he would stroll with me hand in hand. "There is nothing nicer than having a companion to walk slowly with," he would say, pausing now and then so he could catch his breath and using the time to expound on Einstein, Freud, or his days as Walter Winchell's lawyer.

What do men want? I suspect their list might be like mine, maybe not quite as fanciful. I made the mistake of asking Tommy after my long dissertation, and he replied defiantly, "Blind devotion and loyalty."

I shot back, "That's why they end up with dogs instead of women!"

ENTERTAINING

IT HAS BEEN rainy and foggy now for a week, which goes with my gray mood. Wonderful things have been happening to me, and I should be happy, too, yet something is missing . . . Les . . . and the happier I should be, the lonelier I am.

The blue skies were last visible two weeks ago when we planted a mesquite tree in honor of the arrival of Bill Moyers, longtime friend, soul mate, and TV commentator. He had come to my home to film a CBS television interview about growing old—me, not him. While we were out admiring the tree, from somewhere in the distant sky came a faint honking sound. Sure enough, way up above was a majestic flock of wild geese flying in perfect V formation. I hadn't witnessed that since my childhood. Too high, alas, for the camera crew.

It was easier than any interview I have ever done. We chatted for an hour or so to provide enough material for a twelve-minute piece for Charles Kuralt's *Sunday Morning News.*

Bill and I are on the same wavelength; we had established that relationship when we both worked the same side of the fence in the White House. Bill was press secretary to the president, while I was press secretary to the first lady, and we shared the brunt of reporters' wrath when the news was not fit to print for one reason or another.

Once, when Douglas Kiker of NBC was doing his share of complaining and asked sarcastically, "Why are we getting so much news?" Bill replied, "I intend to confound you with the truth."

The repartee between Moyers and the reporters was something to listen to. He managed to cut most of these exchanges out of public transcript, and thus they were never read by the president, but a few choice copies survive.

REPORTER: Bill, can you tell us if the president prays?
MOYERS: He does.
REPORTER: When? Before meals?
MOYERS: That depends on what he's eating.

REPORTER: Bill, has General de Gaulle's message arrived here yet?
MOYERS: No.
REPORTER: Why do you suppose it's taking so long?
MOYERS: Maybe the general is chiseling it himself.

REPORTER: Bill, was the president on the lake yesterday?
MOYERS: Yes.

REPORTER: Boating?
MOYERS: He just went for a walk.

Bill had a great wit. When a memo went out in the White House urging us all to save anything that might be interesting for the LBJ Library, Bill picked up the chicken bones off LBJ's plate following a luncheon. He wrapped them carefully and labeled them, "From these bones, LBJ gained nourishment for the ship of state," and dispatched them to Dorothy Territo, Johnson's archivist and assistant at the White House.

I loved his sense of humor then, and with age it has improved.

The day after Bill left, the rains came, as if the geese had carried a silver curtain in their flight. (Maybe if I think of the fog as "silver" instead of "gray," it will lessen the gloom.)

This morning I can hear the raccoons rooting around in the big can outside where I keep the food for the deer. Let them root. It's better than hearing them in the attic, where they have been making a nest. They sounded like a couple of Japanese wrestlers the first time I heard them, and it almost scared me to death. But now, I am experienced in the ways of raccoons. I just buy mothballs and get a delivery man to steady the ladder while I climb up and pitch a few through the attic entrance in their direction. The mothball fumes make them scurry out. Delivery men who drive to this hill do so at their own risk. So many of us who live by ourselves up here must wait to get the climbing and heavy lifting jobs done when an unsuspecting delivery man shows up. They are nice about it, though, and we try to compensate at Christmas. In a way, this hill resembles a giant, green, landscaped condominium without a "super." My hidden neighbors and I live alone together up here on this wooded hill and have to depend on each other. Maybe that is what we must do everywhere . . . learn to live alone together. On this hill we compensate with friends, having them and being one, very much like living on a frontier. We are self-reliant, ingenious, yet dependent upon one another.

My raccoon discovery was an excuse to call Seattle and tell

my grandson all about it. He was full of advice. "That's not the way to get rid of them, Grandma Wiz," he said. "You take a piece of meat and tease them out, then toss the meat outside and slam the door very fast."

I asked him where in the world he had learned that method. He said he just thought it up.

I have been down all week and feeling guilty about it. Why am I blue when so many nice things are happening to me? I've been inducted into the Texas Women's Hall of Fame this week with all the frills that entails: parties, lunch at the governor's mansion, sitting on stage with eleven other women who are being honored, and hearing their stories as they receive their handsome crystal awards. That is always inspiring to me, listening to the stories of remarkable women. What a bounty of experience sat on that stage.

One of the honorees, Willie Lee Glass, a seventy-five-year-old black woman from Tyler, Texas, said her father had told her when she was a child, "Don't ever let anyone stop you from talking." And she didn't, even though we were limited to two minutes. But it was worth hearing every word she said. She introduced the doctor who had sewn her foot back on after it was cut off by a train when she was a child. "It is good as new," Willie Lee told us. "I've walked in every county in Texas, all 254 of them." That is a lifetime of walking. She had been the first consultant for the Texas State Teachers Association, and that led her to look in on how teachers all over the state, black and white, were doing. "I kept on walking and talking," she said. Everyone from her hometown had come to see her, and she proudly wore the orchids they sent.

Another award went to Edna Whyte, eighty-three years old, still a pilot and still running a flying school. She flew herself up for the ceremony. "When I grew up and found out I couldn't vote because I'm a woman," she said with a twinkle, "I decided I'd become a pilot." She has spent her life teaching her students how to compete in aerobatic competitions. She holds 127 trophies for doing loop-the-loops. I got airsick just hearing about it.

Dr. Benjy Brooks, who in 1958 became Texas' first woman pediatric surgeon, said she had learned early in life that "it is easier to ask for forgiveness than it is to ask for permission." There is wisdom in that admonition. You can waste a lot of time asking and waiting when you could be doing.

We were a real mix of the women of Texas. Ann Richards, our state treasurer who looks like a Junior Leaguer but thinks like a Roosevelt New Dealer, reminded us that women are like Ginger Rogers. "Remember, Ginger Rogers did everything that Fred Astaire did, but she had to do it backward in high heels."

When my turn came, I tried to talk eloquently about the field of communications. That is what I was honored for. I wanted to encourage young women to keep working for national ratification of the Equal Rights Amendment. As it is now, women are at the mercy of the whims of the Supreme Court. I don't want women to stop trying until we are in the Constitution. It is infuriating that after all the years and all the struggle, we are still left out. We came very close. Five votes in three states could have changed it. I am proud that Texas ratified ERA and reratified it when certain legislators tried to take it away. Most of the credit goes to the outspoken women of Texas and those men who were not threatened by openly supporting us. Oh, we have our "good old boys" network, too, but so far we've been able to overpower and outnumber them.

I came home with the beautiful crystal award with my name etched on it. But the emptiness of the house was overpowering. That is the way it has been each day, celebrating Texas Women's Week. As I zipped myself up in my new clothes, getting ready for each event, I asked myself, "Where is everybody?" I needed someone here. I should not have told the children it didn't matter, not to come, that they should save the money. Honors, applause, even a praiseworthy letter, need to be shared.

As these thoughts went through my head I felt something I hadn't felt in a long time: real depression about Les's death. I thought I had put it behind me, that I wouldn't feel that awful emptiness again, but there it was—casting a pall over my life. I kept thinking how much he would have enjoyed the whole week, kept me buoyed up, helped me write my words of acceptance, zipped up my dress, had me at all the events on time. I reminded myself that there are many people in the world who have nothing, who suffer great agonies—so dust yourself off, Liz, get on with life and quit feeling sorry for yourself. I caught myself humming the song, "What'll I do when you are far away and I am blue, what'll I do . . ." I couldn't stand it another minute, so I called Henrietta.

"I understand, Liz," she said quickly. "This month is hell on me, too, because it's when Jens died, so the whole month reminds me of how much I miss him. I was going to play tennis tonight, but something happened to my partners . . . all of them are sick or injured."

Thank goodness I called her. You never know when someone close by is suffering the same widow blues. We decided to get out of our houses, immersed in fog, and do something daring like go to Donn's Depot and listen to Loy Blanton play country music. Would you believe that despite the music, we sat there talking about women and our troubles? That's what women do a lot. Miss men and talk about women!

"The statistics are all against us," Henrietta said. "We live longer than men. Most women will spend more than a third of their lives alone, so we all have to learn how to prepare for it. Staying busy is half the battle."

Together we talked it out, and my mood brightened as I reasoned, "You and I are lucky, Henrietta. We both had good marriages. We are both independent thinkers. We know we can support ourselves. We can create our own busyness, but still, admit it, we feel robbed, robbed of something dear to us that we were counting on to make the last of life wonderful, when all the kids were grown, the deadlines finished, and we could just enjoy each other. There are thousands of women who don't have the resources even for what we are doing, having a glass of wine to drown our sorrows. I still wake in the night, lying there an hour or so wishing to God I could go back to sleep."

"It's the same for widows the world over," Henrietta said. "My solution is to turn the light on and read material about city planning which I keep by my bed. Sometimes I can turn off sadness by mentally trying to solve the septic tank problem for West Lake Hills."

"Septic tanks don't do it for me, Henrietta," I confessed with a laugh. I prefer handy bedside reading: a funny book by Erma Bombeck or Art Buchwald, two old friends whose printed words have seen me through many a sleepless night. Sometimes a pretty magazine does it, pictures of rooms and gardens that set me thinking of what I might do next time I make some money giving a speech and can afford to redo a room in my house. The main thing is not to just lie there depressed. It won't go away until you erase it from your mind, and that takes some action.

"Why don't we plan a singles party?" Henrietta suggested cheerily.

So, with a pen and a napkin, we started making the list, and the blues went away. For a while, anyway. Soul-searching a problem with sympathetic women friends is a marvelous help to women alone, young or old. Women have become friends. The women's movement did that.

I LOVE PARTIES, love to give them, love to go. Small things make a party go—a clever invitation that makes you want to come; sometimes a theme that is carried out in decorations and food; a special guest; and music, especially "arrival" music to set the mood from the start. I've used everything from my own congressman playing the harmonica, a lone accordion player, some out-of-work guitarist who needs a job, and my cassettes to a twelve-piece steel-drum band!

When I arrived back in Austin in 1976, I didn't wait to be entertained. People are likely to overlook singles, particularly female singles, particularly aging female singles. The Lord made too many of us. You could have the brain of Margaret Thatcher and the wit of Joan Rivers and still be forgotten by hostesses who think that parties, like Noah's Ark, are meant for pairs. So I do the entertaining. This keeps me popular and broke.

I started with the group I want to know best: writers. I created a series of small gatherings for writers, literary lovers, and listeners, including some I didn't know. It's surprising who will show up because they like the idea. James and Mari Michener, for instance, I nervously met the first time at my front door, books in hand, to join less notable writers who were reading poetry around my fireside. It's intimidating to read your own work to famous authors like Michener, but Texans overcome that quickly. It's a form of communication—words are—with people you don't know well. It surpasses the "what school did you go to?" conversation when you are trying to find common ground. It's a way of guiding us to a more literate world by bringing out the "closet" writers and poets. People seemed thrilled with the idea and started a round of parties in their homes, inviting friends to bring a poem or manuscript and share their thoughts. There is always a nugget of truth, a memorable line, and you find new dimensions in friends you thought you knew. A very slick public relations friend turned out to be a sentimental poet. Eventually, it helped bring about a much needed Writers' League in Austin.

Another kind of literary gathering I had was a storytelling party where each guest brought a "Tall Tale of Texas." We followed the frontier theme, using quilts for tablecloths, mason jars for wildflowers, and tin plates and cups that fit the simple Texas barbecue and beans menu. On the bar was a round of cheese, Andy Jackson style, with my brother's pocketknife collection luring guests to slice into the big wheel. A large jar of boiled eggs in beet juice, such as you would find in a country store or saloon, added to the atmosphere. Old-fashioned kerosene lanterns lined the edge of my rock terrace, transforming it into a stage for the evening. The storytellers—some of Texas's best liars—had to compete with the crickets and katydids. But it was sheer magic to hear about cattle drives, crazy people lost in the Texas big thicket, and ballads like "Little Joe the Wrangler" amid the fireflies and under the stars.

Meanwhile, in the past ten years I have met most of Austin and four surrounding counties. Now the parties seem to have grown from happenings to productions.

Once, after we had introduced charades and assigned two-person skits for the guests to perform, Harry Middleton, director of the LBJ Library, grumbled to Shirley James, my assistant, "Dammit, can't we ever come to Liz's and just eat and drink?"

No! Left to their own devices, guests tend to talk about their children and their ailments or, in this academic town, their tenure, none of which interests me at a party. So you do something to keep boring chitchat to a minimum. What gives parties a lift is a theme, a focus, and an interesting mix of guests. I can't bear parties that have the "company stamp" on them, whether it is all academe, all corporate, or all anything. Mixing guests from different professions and incomes gives everyone a chance to learn something they didn't know when they arrived. So I have flaming liberals and toss in an occasional wide-eyed conservative. They often eye each other suspiciously the first fifteen minutes, then decide I did it out of ignorance. It does give the guests something to talk about. One person even told me, "I see people at your party that I never see anywhere else." Great! It's high time they crawled out of their shell.

Nothing is more boring than sameness. I like the advice Alice Roosevelt Longworth once gave: "If you owe a bore a dinner, send it to him."

I can't do that entirely, so often I open topics to bring out a bore's best, even if I have to shock him into being charismatic. Some thought-provoking or just plain interesting questions can be written on the back of a place card, hidden in a fortune cookie, or simply assigned by a vocal hostess.

"What is the most remote place you've ever been?" Invariably, you learn about their experiences. "If you were in a hospital room, whom would you like to share it with for a week? For a month?" This produced a tie between Brigitte Bardot and Hubert Humphrey. "What is the most unusual place you've ever had sex?" (You do have to choose your crowd for this one.) The answers ranged from Union Station in Washington, D.C., to backseats in a parking lot, atop mountains, to the steps of the U.S. Capitol. But the prize went to the couple who claimed they set their private plane on autopilot and had at it at twenty thousand feet.

When you have mentally lively guests, sans bores, you can have the fun of a continuing story with everyone around a table contributing to it. This happened on an impromptu Sunday evening simply because it rained heavily and would otherwise have been dreary. I called up several friends, asking each to bring a covered dish, and ended up with a feast. My Polish friends brought Polish vodka, which improved the story fest. After dinner we began with, "It was a dark and stormy night when Alexander met Lady Sarah stealing her way through the streets as though she were trying to escape from someone or something. . . ." It fired the imagination, and thirty minutes later we had survived a murder, a marriage, and a volcanic eruption so the couple could live happily ever after.

One of the most unique parties I ever gave, which was fun in the planning and doing, was to introduce a new bride to the political life she was destined to live with her bridegroom, our former city councilman, Lowell Lebermann.

By party time, my house resembled a national political convention with red, white, and blue bunting draped across the entrance and over an alcove that was the stage for the "performance." Balloons, streamers, and straw hats were issued at the door along with red, white, and blue campaign-style buttons promoting the bride as the candidate—"Pat for President"—and appropriately naming the groom "Lowell for Treasurer." He's performed that service for most of the political candidates in this county for the last fifteen years.

The bride entered into the spirit of it all and displayed her own sense of humor (thank goodness) by showing up in a veil and carrying a bridal bouquet—the veil was a $3.98 lace doily hastily purchased at K Mart.

The invitation read:

> You're Invited To A Select Grass Roots Caucus
> To Introduce Pat To Lowell's Wonderful World
> Of Politics and Strange Bedfellows!
> Trickle Down Libations
> Pork Barrel Dinner
> Campaign Singing
> Stump Speaking

Food and drinks were given political names, which we listed on colorful "campaign" posters and hung on the walls. The house was packed with hand-clapping friends who could appreciate all the political innuendos, including the three candidates running for governor in the Texas Democratic primary! I had assigned certain acts before, and as I know a lot of "hams" and would-be "playwrights," they went at it with abandon! I had also lined up spirited singers along with a combo. We rehearsed the "show" for a week—and we were a hit.

A well-known local banker surprised everyone with a vaudeville hoofer's act, singing "Do a Little Sidestep" as advice on being a good political wife; and a lobbyist warned the happy couple about the "Little Tin Cup"—and so it went. Each had cleverly paraphrased the words of a song to fit the couple and the occasion.

When it was time for the toasts—a tradition at my parties and dinners because they give focus to the event—I delivered mine in the form of a nominating speech, extolling the virtues and attributes of the bride. Some of the candidate guests were just as happy she wasn't really running for office—she could have gotten anyone's vote that night!

I GOT MY INITIATION into spectacular entertainment in the big time. Evelyn Walsh McLean died shortly before I hit Washington, and I'll never forgive her for it. The town was still full of talk about her parties at Friendship, the name of her great house. In earlier, grander days, the lavish dinner and dancing ended with cigars and brandy, during which time her husband would pass the word by liveried butlers that upstairs there were several French "ladies of the evening." On those nights, guests left thinking of the house as Close Friendship.

In my time in Washington, the reigning hostesses were known as "the Big Four": Perle Mesta, the oil and steel heiress who inspired the musical *Call Me Madam*, was one. Her rival, Gwen Cafritz, focused her attention on Dali paintings and the opening of the Supreme Court from her modern Foxhall Road home. Polly Guggenheim (later Logan) could seat sixty at her dining room table for caviar, blinis, and Russian vodka—and this was only starters. She had one white-gloved footman for every two guests. The fourth and grandest was the elegant Marjorie Merriweather Post Close Hutton Davies May Post—she lost one husband to a maid, another to a valet. Her fortune, which began with Post Toasties and continued through all the General Foods products, allowed her to offer up, among other entertainments, an entire ballet company performing *Swan Lake*. Marjorie entertained from three homes and a yacht, *Sea Cloud*, with its 36,000 square feet of canvas. Her Washington homes were Tregaron and Hillwood, now the property of the Smithsonian Institution because of the treasures she brought back from Russia when husband number three was ambassador. Her Adirondacks home was called Camp Topridge; she stayed there during the summer, arriving after the "boys in green," her camp keepers, had trained the chipmunks to eat out of the guests' hands the peanuts that were placed handily about. Fall and early spring she spent in Palm Beach. The residence there was the creation of the husband she liked best, Edward F. Hutton, who made his money and hers in the old-fashioned Smith-Barney way—he earned it. Well, more or less. The house was called Mar-a-Lago (between sea and lake), and that it was. I was lucky enough to have spent time at all her homes, partially because Marjorie loved Texans. Her fa-

Watching the party Les staged on my
fortieth birthday are Perle Mesta of *Call
Me Madam* fame and Speaker Sam Rayburn. The Speaker, Les and me (left). A
moment of wisdom with Walter Cronkite (below) on the *S.S. Enterprise*, Governor Nelson Rockefeller and Happy. At
my farewell from Washington at Ford's
Theatre, Scooter Miller, Nancy Dick-
erson, Jack Valenti, Carol Channing and
Pearl Bailey. Below, fellow Texan Van
Cliburn, who once borrowed LBJ's white
tie and tails.

FRANK WOLFE

Like a charm bracelet, old friends encircle my life. At a Roaring Twenties Party at the LBJ Library, Scottie Fitzgerald Smith, Lady Bird, and I don our best flapper girl outfits. Then, James Michener, who took on Texas, Alaska and the Caribbean, gives me advice about literature. Mrs. Sadat had me over to her home once at the Med in Egypt.

I am blessed with a group of friends who are willing to turn "ham" for a cause. Syndicated columnist Liz Smith tunes up with the band and belts forth "How Little We Know." Erma Bombeck and Cactus Pryor softshoe a number at an evening for the Liz Carpenter Distinguished Lectureship, which brings important writers to the University of Texas. My children, along with Lady Bird and the Governor of Texas, Mark White, gave their time and cash to make it go.

TWO PHOTOS:
DALLAS TIMES HERALD:
ANDY HANSON

ther, C. W. Post, had discovered Postum in Post, Texas, and the profits formed the basis of his fortune.

Queen Maud of Norway once told Marjorie, "You live like a queen." And she did. At all of her homes, table settings were varied several times during the customary stay at her house parties. A plane—the *Merriweather*—was sent for guests. The plane always had fresh flowers and souvenir travel bags bearing its name. She gave a book-signing party for me at her Palm Beach home when *Ruffles and Flourishes* was published. Guests were invited to hear me review the book in her drawing room and, after champagne and caviar, stroll through the terrace. The sales were impressive following her marvelous introduction of me, which was like being introduced by Mayor Daley in Chicago. Incidentally, the terrace was embellished with polished black stones, thousands of them. She and Ed Hutton had picked them up on a Long Island beach and shipped them in train loads to Palm Beach. Regal to her fingertips, Marjorie could still come forth with a down-to-earth "golly" or "gee whiz," the slang words of her youth.

Once, when the *Sea Cloud* was harbored in Miami, she scooped up all her guests and took them down to see the yacht that had once been hers. She was an old lady at the time, but when she stepped aboard she became a girl again, the young, beautiful "Mrs. Hutton," who had planned and executed every magnificent detail of the yacht to perfection: brocaded bedrooms, marble fireplaces, tables and desks built from her design. At full sail, *Sea Cloud* sported twenty-nine sails and a crew of seventy-six; she looked like a cloud on the sea.

"Isn't she lovely? She was a dream, you know?" The dreamer showed us every inch, lovingly fondling the railing. She asked the captain "to bring down the lace" and told us about sailing the South Seas on it. We had arrived by a unique motorcade—two Cadillacs and one Rolls—stopping off for hamburgers at Howard Johnson's en route. That was a typical Marjorie touch. But before we left her dreamchild, she turned to the captain and in a moment I shall never forget said, "You have no idea what a rewarding day this has been for me. I am eighty-two now, and I won't be building another ship. If you would care to have the name *Sea Cloud* permanently, I will make the necessary arrangements."

In Washington, social events were for a purpose, to get people together, to raise funds, to salute a head of state, to laud a cause, a special day, or a special event. You would eat strawberries and clotted cream and toast the queen's birthday—she was not present, nor was it her birthday. But it was such a big bash that I once saw a woman dash into the shrubbery to heed nature's call while 1,500 guests failed to notice . . . the powder room was simply too far away.

Embassy parties were always especially exciting. My first encounter with this entertainment was in 1942 when a cousin took me along to the British embassy, that piece of the empire that sits majestically on Massachusetts Avenue, the British flag displayed and lions guarding the gates. I could hardly wait to write home about it.

> The party was very picturesque. There were two Scotch bag pipers who wore green plaid kilts, tams, etc. The place was filled with British soldiers, WAFS, and Canadians. Edward Arnold, the movie star, spoke and was very good. An opera was held on the steps of the Embassy.

Years, later, when I was seven months pregnant with Christy, I went to the Russian embassy for their October Revolution party. The party was in honor of Foreign Minister Andrei Vishinsky. Les and I wanted to go and write about it. He promised that if my labor pains started in the Russian embassy, he would drag me off Russian soil so I could bear a U.S. citizen. It was 1949 and elected officials were somewhat skittish about attending, but we did, and I wrote home about it.

> Going behind the Iron Curtain, even on a Washington main street, gives the visitor an eerie feeling. Up the steps of the large stone Embassy you walk. The lady is rare indeed who doesn't feel she should powder her nose for the FBI cameras which she is sure "must" be secluded across the street,

grinding off a recording of the visitors in hopes of getting the goods on some future Judy Caplan.

Once inside you see red, deep red plush carpets, heavy red velvet drapes that adorn gold leaf and white paneled walls. Up the circular stairway you go to the elaborate reception rooms which take up the entire second floor. A handsomely uniformed orchestra plays from a balcony which—you blink twice—features a hammer and sickle in the iron grill work.

Then one of the "masses" done up in gold braid asks your name and you are presented to Vishinsky, the powerful little man who looks, on social occasions anyway, like a jovial American banker.

"What about invading Mars?" one sarcastic reporter asked him in passing.

"Oh, no," he shot back through an interpreter, "Mars is on our side."

From behind a palm, the society reporters stood and counted noses to see not only who did show up, but who didn't.

Undersecretary of State James Webb was there in place of Secretary of State Acheson who was en route to Paris. But there were no other cabinet members. A great many of the guests were curious newspaper correspondents. Nearly all of the diplomatic corps showed up, except anyone from the Chinese Embassy, still in the hands of the Nationalist government and the Yugoslav Ambassador, who was not invited.

Past Vishinsky and into a large and crowded ballroom was a giant-sized picture of Stalin, backed by a mound of red carnations and chrysanthemums. From four bars vodka, champagne, and the best of American liquors flowed.

Two replicas of the Kremlin were used, one in ice, which seemed an appropriate material, the other a six-foot cake which centered the fifty-foot dining room table sagging with food. Mrs. Joseph Davies, wife of former Ambassador Davies, author of "Mission to Moscow," cut the cake as the greasy-haired, plump, and gold-toothed wives of the Russian Embassy clerks looked on. Mrs. Davies, at sixty, remains the most beautiful woman in the nation's capital. Her chic hat and dress were the picture of what the well-dressed American woman wears if she has a million dollars and reads the fashion magazines.

Another incongruous sight was the Russian Orthodox priest whose flowing robes and crosses told that he was head of the Russian church in this country. The great multitude of Senatorial and Congressional faces were missing. True, many of them are back in their districts. But others obviously don't want to be seen at the Russian Embassy this season.

A Russian buffet table is no place for dieters. Fish, turkeys, pork stared up at the hundreds of people who crowded the table even an hour and a half after the party was supposed to be over. At any other Embassy, there would have been greater restraint, greater respect for Emily Post. But here, where the food is billed as being the best in the Capitol [sic], dapper old gentlemen and ladies in fancy hats with well-manicured palms pushed and shoved to be sure they had heaped their plates high. Some of the bluest blood in America behaved like the starving masses.

Toward the end of the party, Vishinsky moved from room to room and talked with guests. It was an awkward procedure, for surrounding him as he walked were four or five stocky Russians who tried, unsuccessfully, to be inconspicuous as bodyguards. Suddenly he appeared in the smoky ballroom where I was standing. He was almost at my elbow. He looked at the one big window which had just been opened a bit for badly needed fresh air. Quickly he leaned over to a guard and whispered something. The guard moved immediately to the window, shut and bolted it. Could it be that this little man with the unrelenting voice that keeps America afraid is scared, too, by open windows and the darkness outside?

Then there were some of the more local parties given by lobbyists with the liquor business introducing all the things you can do with a bottle of bourbon besides drink it—namely, put it in pâté, stew, and so on—or the onion people running in bags of their finest produce from the Rio Grande Valley. You came to know the caterers and waiters better than the Congress because they ran for drinks, not for public office, and therefore never got defeated. Another night, another hors d'oeuvres tray!

Washington entertaining is the most democratic in the world. Betty Beale, the society columnist, once told me, "You are not chosen by family or money in a democracy, but by election or appointment. A Supreme Court justice may pick his teeth, but he will still be the lion of the party because of his position."

Because of the nature of the political game, there are more parties and mixes of people in Washington. Power is the name of the game. Conversation is confined to who's in and who's out and what's happening to take them in and out. For a reporter, parties were a marvelous place to pick up news. You met the attorney general, who was deciding whether to send troops into Little Rock during the school crisis, diplomatically reminding him you represented *The Arkansas Gazette* and needed to be alerted on any development, hopefully ahead of time. It paid off with a scoop.

In this "company town" news sources were often neighbors, but we never felt it comprised us in our reporting. There is a discreet distance you learn to keep, but this was pre-Watergate Washington, and we were a smaller, more personal colony of newsmakers and newswriters.

As the years passed and the press colony changed, we would find ourselves eating hot dogs at Art Buchwald's neighborhood Fourth of July picnics with the town's most powerful clad in designer blue jeans . . . or going to Walter Lippmann's cocktail parties, where drinks were served out of empty peanut-butter or jelly glasses. Everyone has a secret thrift . . . mine is cutting off lights; Lippmann's was not renting glasses. He must have eaten a lot of peanut butter and jelly, because the parties usually drew about 150 of the town's best-known headliners and byliners. His career spanned a long period of history, from the Treaty of Versailles to the Great Society, Woodrow Wilson through Lyndon Johnson. No wonder his hatred of the Vietnam War was so passionate. He had seen too many starts and stops in the peacemaking business.

Seeing newsmakers without the barriers of secretaries and press spokesmen was a big help. And it served their purposes, too. Hostesses who befriended presidents, such as Perle Mesta with Presidents Truman and Eisenhower, were often called upon to hold a party for the purpose of providing a meeting place for two factions at odds over a piece of legislation.

The Perle Mesta formula was to invite people who were used to going to parties. "They will make the party go if the other guests just stand around like sticks," she used to say. Music was a must. She also believed in having the music playing as you entered the room—not a band still tuning up when the guests were arriving. Round tables, but not too many. She had them stashed away to move in later and prove what a draw the party was. Empty tables are depressing. Perle found "occasions" to celebrate: a senator's birthday, the arrival of a new ambassador. She once gave a party for my husband because she didn't want him overlooked when I was press secretary at the White House and getting a lot of attention. Another time, Perle asked Lady Bird Johnson what she could do to help out during one of the weddings, and Mrs. Johnson said, "Have over the kinfolks from out of town. They'll be thrilled to be invited to one of your parties!" And so she did, and so they were!

Both Johnson daughters married during their father's presidency. Lynda Bird Johnson's wedding to Charles Robb was the first for a presidential daughter in the White House since Eleanor Wilson's fifty-three years before. The Johnson/Robb wedding and reception was one of the most memorable parties I've worked on or been to. The transformation of the East Room from wedding chapel, with an altar of green-and-white "bee" lights, to reception room in 15 1/2 minutes flat was a tribute to the capable and determined Bess Abell, Mrs. Johnson's social secretary, who believed that absolutely nothing was impossible and proved it repeatedly during her tenure—defying all odds and meeting all challenges! In the interim, guests danced in the hall or visited in the state rooms.

It was an early December military wedding. The brilliant color of the bridesmaids' Christmas-red dresses, the blue of the marine uniforms, and Lynda—classically beautiful in an ivory satin dress that complemented her coloring and stature—added to the pomp and history of the ceremony.

As Lynda descended the staircase on LBJ's arm, it made me think of other fathers and daughters who had descended that same staircase on their way to similar ceremonies. One of them, Alice Roosevelt Longworth, was present that day.

For weeks beforehand, we studied previous White House weddings and found that Ulysses S. Grant's daughter Nellie's marriage to Algernon Sartorial was by far the most brilliant and extreme White House wedding. Both bride and groom carried bouquets during the ceremony—his was orange blossoms, tuberoses and pink buds with a little silver banner that read "love." Two hundred of Washington's highest ranking were invited, but the names of the bride and groom were not mentioned on the invitation. The president was unhappy that his nineteen-year-old only daughter was marrying an Englishman and had only reluctantly consented to the union. The wedding was followed by a twenty-nine-course seated luncheon, and the menu was printed on satin. So opulent was the meal that halfway through it, guests were served sorbet and encouraged to stroll through the state rooms before returning to the feasting! Just imagine:

> Soft crabs on toast
> Gâteaux garnis de crabes and champignons, sauce à la crème
> Croquettes of chicken with green peas
> Côtelettes d'agneau, sauce à la tartare
> Aspic de langues de bœuf à la moderne
> Woodcocks and snipes on toast
> Broiled spring chickens
> Salade, sauce mayonnaise
> Strawberries with cream
> Bride's cake
> Charlottes russes
> Croquembouche
> Corbeils glaces à la jardinière
> Gâteaux de trois frères
> Epigraphe la fleur de Nelly Grant
> Pudding à la Nesselrode, sauce à la crème
> Corbeils d'oranges garnis de fraises
> Gelée, blancmangée à la Napoléon
> Plombières garnies de fruits et fleurs glacés

Ice cream of various flavors
Water ices of various flavors
Small fancy cakes
Punch à la Romaine
Coffee
Chocolate

I had already been broken in with presidential daughters' weddings by Luci Johnson's marriage to Patrick Nugent. That one was even more complicated because the marriage ceremony took place at the National Shrine of the Immaculate Conception, five miles from the White House reception that would follow. The event is now a jumble in my mind, but I do remember quite clearly two telephone calls from the father of the bride.

"Liz, Dave Dubinsky [head of the International Ladies Garment Workers Union] just called up and was crying. He has been my friend all his life, and he wants to know why my little girl is getting married in a nonunion gown. Does Luci's wedding gown have an ILGWU label in it? If not, get one. I don't want to make grown men cry."

Two days later another "disaster" occurred. Luci had chosen August 6 for her wedding day, which is, alas, the anniversary of the bombing of Hiroshima.

"Liz," LBJ barked, "if there is a mistake that hasn't been made in this wedding, it's because you haven't thought of it!"

Encounters like that build characters. By considerable plotting, the bride wore something borrowed, something blue, and a label from ILGWU. But the August 6 date stuck because, as I told the Japanese embassy, which had complained, American girls set their wedding dates for reasons quite apart from politics!

The top Washington social event is always a White House wedding, but another memorable White House party was the one given in Princess Margaret's honor. It was a glittery affair with diplomats, cabinet secretaries and ranking officers, movie stars, and society's "beautiful" people. I suppose what has immortalized the event was Christina Ford's bosoms popping out of her dress as she threw everything she had into a spirited rendition of the "frug"—much to the delight of her partner, the Honorable Robert McNamara, secretary of defense. In reflecting upon that moment, I don't believe it was Christina's bosoms that were particularly memorable so much as it was that they made their appearance in the hallowed and historical home of the president of the United States of America.

During the five years I was at the White House, I found out night after night about the planning that goes into such state occasions. We had parties in sweltering heat, hailstorms, blizzards, and on star-kissed nights. We had a carnival on the south lawn, dinners in the Rose Garden, a steak fry on the roof. Guests included heads of state, prominent Americans, and old Texas friends. I loved it the morning it was snowing—the first snow of the season—and the president looked out the White House window and, touched with the romance of the scene, said, "Let's have Congress over this afternoon."

All day we scurried around getting ready for a get-together of a *thousand* people. A reception with refreshments and music was held. Congress was charmed. LBJ was pleased. We were hysterical over the hilarious operation.

I helped plan another reception—in stark contrast to that one—with the president, who, during a visit to Pakistan, invited a camel driver over to America for a visit. Bashir, the camel driver, was accustomed to eating with his fingers, so we had a menu that made it possible for all of us to eat with our fingers, including fried chicken, stuffed celery, deviled eggs, and potato chips. I recall looking around the table and seeing the presidents of four banks and Neiman-Marcus all eating with their fingers to make the camel driver feel at home.

One of the touches of the Johnson years was naming food for the honoree, an idea of Bess Abell's. I do think she went a little far when we served chicken breasts à la Muriel Humphrey— but the concept is good.

Now, entertaining at my own house, I have adopted her idea. When my longtime friend Allen Drury came to town to promote his newest book about politics, I served political stew, corny copy cornbread, caucus salad, and party punch on the rocks.

Health—mental health—was the theme of a party I gave for a psychiatrist friend. Guests received an invitation that read: "To relieve depression (mental, not economic) you're invited to a non-stressful evening around a relaxing fire and piano."

We served chicken curry à la Thorazine, crazy mixed-up salad, strawberries with guilt-free whipped cream. And around the piano we sang semistressful songs: "Pack Up Your Troubles" and "Your Cheatin' Heart."

We never can get enough Mexican food in Texas—TexMex, that is. It's good, it's colorful, and it's great to serve at informal dinners or large parties, and we have an unending source of ingredients available in local stores.

Some of the caterers in town have started using little wooden carts as serving bars, but my dining room table looks right for a Mexican buffet with a blue rough-textured cloth, a basket of blue, orange, yellow, and red napkins, a huge sombrero with Mexican paper flowers spilling out or my three Mexican lady figurines with fresh flowers, wooden plates, and more straw baskets to hold warm tortillas and dishes.

For a gathering I called a "Mexican Fiasco," we served:

Chili con queso with chips
Chicken enchiladas
Guacamole on the half shell
Trays of fresh cherry tomatoes, carrots,
     celery, sweet red peppers and asparagus
Mango ice cream and Mexican cookies

Of course, frosty margaritas and Mexican beer are a must!

It gives me pleasure to use my house for good causes. The Jacuzzi, which seats eight, and the spectacular view of the city's skyline give the parties appeal, and local groups like the public broadcasting station and friends who are involved in Access for Youth like to auction them off: "A Champagne Jacuzzi Party for Eight at Liz Carpenter's—Bubbles, Bubbles, Bubbles!"

I supply the place, champagne, hors d'oeuvres, and sometimes a shapely friend in a mermaid outfit as my contribution. The committee does the work, and it helps the community. To my amazement, the parties have been auctioned for as little as $200 and as much as $2,500.

I also use the house as a place for fund-raisers for friends who are running for the state legislature, congress, or mayor, and particularly to help women candidates, who historically have a more difficult time raising funds—still. I have a marvelous old tree stump that is just right for stump speeches, as well as trees where campaign posters can be hung.

A children's Christmas party has become part of the season for me. My children adored them, and now my grandchildren do. When Texas keeps me for Christmas, I include all my small kith and kin. I have living nearby almost twenty great-nieces and nephews under the age of twelve. We still make candy houses— an idea that dates back to Scott and Christy's preschool days.

We begin by frosting cardboard box houses, covering roofs, and outlining doors and windows with a variety of festive candies. These are then placed on breadboards or flat pieces of very sturdy cardboard, which we cover with white frosting to look like snow. All kinds of candy walks and walls can be added, and it hardens and lasts through the season.

Lots of low tables, small bowls of gumdrops, candy canes, Life Savers, nonpareils, and colored sprinkles are set out in the workplace. Naturally, newspapers are needed to save the floor.

I prepare the basic structure of the house from boxes I've gathered from the grocery store, careful to select only those that will fit the breadboard pieces. Once set up, it's amazing how imaginative children can become, creating their own architecture and designs with the candies.

It's a messy party, but not as messy as Grandmother's Day, when my friend Betty Talmadge lets eight or ten kids hand-paint each other and then washes them off with the garden hose before she takes them home. I'm not brave enough for that! But my Christmas party is always a fantastic success, and after we've had hot chocolate, popcorn balls, and ice cream, each child takes his or her own candy house home for the holiday season. It goes into the trash can after New Year's, and my breadboards come back to be stored for the following year. It's my way of getting into the Christmas spirit and the delightful world of children.

Each summer my family gathers at a rugged camp in the Texas hill country. These reunion suppers have become historic family traditions. When you have been at it over campfire, open hearth, wood stove, gas, electricity, and microwave for over fifty years, recipes are handed around. As a child, I remember the dozens of cakes, pies, cookies, and homemade ice cream that followed a groaning board of picnic fare. Our family had so many favorite reunion picnic recipes that we urged my home economics–major niece, Cindy Sutherland Myer, to compile a family cookbook. She put together *Krazy Kousins Kooking*, and it includes a variety of picturesque recipes. Now, when we gather for Thanksgiving or in summer, we check the cookbook to see who the best family cooks are, and they're the first to be invited!

AUNT LUCILLE'S GREEN GRAPE COBBLER

Gather grapes while seed is still soft and grapes in green stage. Line pie pan with pie crust. Cook 2 cups green grapes with 4 cups sugar until grapes are just about to pop a little. Add rest of grapes, then another pie crust. Sprinkle with sugar, 1/2 pound of oleo—slice and spread. Bake in 325° oven.

FAIRES SUTHERLAND'S FRIED FISH
(*Biggest one was 75-pound catfish!*)

Catch the fish. Clean the fish.
Put a little soda in water and set the fish in it for 1 hour. This takes out the muddy taste.
Slice on each side of backbone. Salt, pepper, add garlic salt, then roll in lots of cornmeal.
Use iron skillet 2/3 full of hot lard.

Heat to boiling, then place in the fish.

When the fish rises, it is done.

(Serve with potatoes, black-eyed peas, sliced tomatoes, coleslaw, and cornbread.)

BOB LEE AND JOHN D. SUTHERLAND'S CABRITO

Slaughter and skin a 2- or 3-month-old goat. (Or buy one already prepared for cooking.)

Season with salt, black pepper, garlic salt, and onion (quartered).

Wrap carcass in foil. Bake in 300° oven for 15 minutes to the pound. Or, better still, dig a pit and build a fire at the side. As the fire turns to coals, place coals in pits. For a grown goat, double your cooking time.

Use barbecue sauce on the side.

SISTER ALICE'S BUTTERMILK CANDY

2 cups sugar

1 cup buttermilk

1 teaspoon soda

1 tablespoon white corn syrup

1/2 stick butter

1 teaspoon vanilla

2 cups pecans

Cook all but vanilla and nuts in three-quart or larger saucepan to the soft ball stage (240°). Add vanilla and pecans, and beat until mixture becomes opaque and starts thickening. Rapidly drop spoonfuls onto wax paper.

THIS MORNING the rental service is setting up tables on the lawn, much to the annoyance of the deer, who claim my yard as their own. The old piano is being tuned. That piano has rolled up lots of history. We bought it for $475 on the installment plan back in 1960, because Speaker Sam Rayburn was coming over and our female friend with the unusual name, Hank Fort, songwriter and performer, wanted to sing "Save Your Confederate Money Boys, the South Will Rise Again." She wrote that and "Put Your Shoes on, Lucy," as well as musical toasts to all her friends. It was quite a gathering—a backyard party with Senator Kenneth Keating playing Les and Hank Fort playing me in a corny, slapstick rendition of *This Is Your Life*. The occasion was my fortieth birthday. Someday that little piano, which has been moved indoors and outdoors in Washington, and now in Texas, is going to give up and fall apart. But hopefully not before I do.

The piano reminds me of the time that the famous pianist Van Cliburn arrived in Washington for a concert at Constitution Hall and the airline lost the clothes bag with his white tie and tails. It was Sunday and he couldn't get another outfit, so he phoned me to see if he could borrow my husband's. But while Les owned a number of tuxedos, he did not own tails, as they are rarely worn in Washington.

"I know someone who is just your height and does own a white tie and tails," I volunteered. "Let me call him and see if he won't help you out."

A quick call to LBJ. "Sure, he's welcome. Tell him to come over."

A major pin-in was needed since the president was many pounds heavier than the slender pianist, but it worked and Van Cliburn played the piano that night in the president's clothes.

Tonight, I have called my friend Louie Gusik, who owns a nearby restaurant, to help me move the piano, and he sent over four waiters to carry it from the living room to the outdoor deck perched over the city. A full moon is promised, and with two well-known Austin entertainers, pianist Jerry Earl and vocalist Barbara Amaral in front of the microphone, it is going to be a spectacular event. One hundred people are coming . . . give or take a dozen. I always add more people to my guest list the last few days before a party. It's my right, I tell my friend Shirley James, who wishes I would stick to the original game plan. My habits mess up her lists. Shirley has humor and ideas that flow with mine.

I've been checking with the weather service for a few days and feel confident that I won't have to move the party inside at the last moment to keep my guests from being drenched. Shirley always refuses to think about rain because she's convinced that makes it happen.

The food tonight will be "down home" with meat loaf, mashed potatoes, squash, black-eyed peas, cornbread, and banana pudding—and I've conned Shirley into cooking it. Party food doesn't have to be elegant to be good and appealing. My guests seem to savor the stews, cheese grits, honey-baked hams, peach cobblers, and other home fare I like to dish up.

MEAT LOAF

2 pounds very lean ground
  beef
2 eggs, slightly beaten
1 tablespoon prepared
  horseradish
3 tablespoons minced
  onion
1 tablespoon Worcester-
  shire sauce
1 cup soft bread crumbs

½ pound raw bacon,
  chopped except for 2
  strips
1 cup milk
½ cup catsup
1 teaspoon lemon juice
2 cloves garlic, minced fine
1 tablespoon salt
½ teaspoon pepper
Fresh parsley, minced

Mix beef and chopped bacon with eggs, milk, bread crumbs, and remaining ingredients. Shape in an 8 x 11 baking pan, and cover with sauce made from 1 cup catsup, 1 tablespoon Worcestershire sauce, and 1 teaspoon lemon juice. Place strips of bacon on top, and bake at 350° for about 1 hour.

It's nearly party time and I relax a few refreshing moments in the Jacuzzi before donning one of my "long-flowing caftans"—an attractive concealment for the overweight.

The guests are beginning to arrive—they're mostly old

friends with a few I've only recently met. It's the "bay at the moon" group. We get together on the night of the full moon each month and do just that! It's fun, a good way to get rid of tension and a great excuse for a party. A good "oooooo," owl-like "whooo," or periodic yelp—each to his own sound and ability— brings in other night sounds. Sometimes even the coyotes on nearby hills respond.

Our most erudite member, Coleen Hardin, studied up on moon lore and, as a result, named us the Ninnies . . . the Society of Nin, to be more proper. Since then we have bayed from the Davis Mountains, where we went to spot Halley's comet; from a boat on Lake Travis; from my front yard; from the Hardins' ranch; and from Henrietta's hill. Henrietta went us one better and combined poetry about the moon with the baying. She also invented a "moon" drink, an orange potion with *bay* leaves.

Moon baying can be psychologically helpful and revealing, too. You don't really know someone until you have bayed with them. For instance, Fred Ward, a darling of a man, informed us during a baying episode that he had composed a song back in the Depression. He was pumping gas as an all-night attendant and got so lonely he took to songwriting to while away the hours. He wrote about the "up" side of the Depression, and his hit number was called "The National Recovery Act for Love." He not only sang it for us, but danced it as well. It's an irresistible song, especially to anyone who grew up during that depressing time.

> *We need a National Recovery Act for love,*
> *And a department to consult the stars above*
> *So we can go to Washington,*
> *Marching one by one,*
> *Tell our troubles to the red, white, and blue,*
> *And hurry home marching two by two.*
>
> *We need a lobbyist to represent each state,*
> *To keep the home fires burning in the grate,*
> *To help a fella find a mate,*
> *I advocate to legislate*
> *A National Recovery Act for love.*

Fred went on to become executive director of the National Council on Crime and Delinquency and, in retirement, is a consultant on the subject.

We begin to sing songs to the moon: "Moon River," "Fly Me to the Moon," "Old Devil Moon"—and presently, as though on cue, the big orange moon slowly rises over the state capitol. It's a glorious sight, and one I never tire of. The moonrise is the signal for the baying to begin, and we do it with abandon! Just cup your hands to your mouth and let go with a sound like the hound of the Baskervilles. New friends are polite enough or game enough not to look horrified and soon join in the fun: "Ooh—ooh, ooh, ooh!"

A party like this always ends too soon. It's complete only if two or three favorites linger and relive the evening over the last of the champagne. It's great to have friends, great to be alive!

HEALTH
AND LEISURE

I HAVE BEEN BLESSED with high energy all my life and cursed with a lousy figure for most of it. I stand five feet one inch when I stretch and weigh in at anything between 160 and 195, which crowds a lot of flesh in that space. Lovably round, I say. Overweight, yes, but it's all me and I can't help feeling personally defensive about it. I shun friends who talk dieting all the time. I keep thinking that if science is smart enough to put a man on the moon, it could give us a pill that would simply regulate our weight to a nice 135 or thereabouts.

Occasionally I take a journey into the land of the spas and dieters. I like the massages and facials much better than the aerobics and exercise. In my opinion, these were devised primarily for suicidal types. I am really as much a misfit at these places as in the dressing rooms of most department stores. I wish I were as rich as Mary Lasker, who used to take her sister, Alice Fordyce, along to The Greenhouse, a fancy place for pruning down people instead of plants. Mary would lie abed, waiting for her appointments for facials and massages, and explain to the spa managers, "I brought Alice along to do my exercises." As a result, Alice lost weight and inches and Mary came home rested.

A magazine asked me to do a personal piece about some of the posher spas—The Greenhouse in Dallas, the Golden Door in San Diego, and any others that crossed my mind. I did, and it ended up being called "I Was a Fat Farm Dropout," which was appropriate enough. I can manage the routine three days only. After that I am sore, tearful, and angry that no one thought to declare that fat is beautiful early on and let it go at that.

I was thin once, long enough to get married in a size eight wedding gown, but having found hormonal happiness, I promptly began ripening out, cooking for my new husband with my new cookbook. He was crazy about the *Better Homes and Gardens* lemon cup. I wanted to please him, so our early marriage was heavily fortified with bridal forays into good eating. It exhausts me now to remember those days as newlyweds in Philadelphia, where Les was stationed in the navy. After giving two days to housework, I went to work for the United Press, deciding life had to be fuller than cooking and keeping the two-room flat clean. Les's office was five minutes from our tiny apartment in a big brownstone on Delancey Place—a cab's ride from the UP office. We were both hungry for sex as well as food but were short on cash, so we'd race home for an hour's lunch. I would beat him by ten minutes and mix up homemade biscuits to spice up leftovers from the night before or improve the doggie bags we brought home from restaurants. After lunch, we had for dessert . . . lovemaking. Imagine real, homemade biscuits and real homemade love all in an hour. That's when weight gains began . . . with blissful happiness. If it's true that making love burns up calories . . . I lost all of three hundred calories a day!

When we moved to Washington after V-E Day, we began newspapering and spent thirty-two years around the buffet tables of that wining and dining city. Les was six feet tall. But at five one, I had the handicap. It took no time at all for me to round out. I transformed golden caviar sent by the shah to his embassy into permanent bulges, not to mention chocolate-covered strawberries hung lovingly on a sculptured piece of driftwood by Perle Mesta herself; crepes made over the campfire by a retinue of woodsy-looking butlers during one of Marjorie Merriweather Post's "roughing it" cookouts in the Adirondacks; homemade peach ice cream at the LBJ ranch. These are among the souvenirs I carry with me on arms, legs, and middle. Having had the fun, is it really fair to all those marvelous hosts and hostesses to turn their culinary efforts into nothingness?

My doctors and friends are not so sentimental and say, "Off with it!" So I began my life of spas. I have been to most of them, writing or talking my way through because I cannot afford to pay their high price on beef removal. I have been to so many that I am, in fact, an overeducated spa dropout.

I can tolerate a spa once a year—for R and R. But something has to be done to liven them up mentally, and that is happening at some that cater not so much to the rich as to the working professional who is aware of the need to get rehabilitated periodically.

I found these oases of exercise and celery sticks even before jogging was a way of life and health food stores were in the hands of the hippies. I became such an expert on fat farms that a group of us started a do-it-yourself spa. For ten days, we ran our own cooperative at the country place of Patsy Steves in Comfort, Texas. We called it "the Think and Shrink Tank" and even had T-shirts made up proclaiming our thinking and shrinking. We hired a gourmet cook who weighed in at about 105, an aerobics teacher all of twenty-two years old with the heart of the Marquis de Sade, and a facial and massage woman. We did it all like the best— with flower arrangements, beautiful china to compensate for the shortage of calories, and inspirational signs around the pictur-esque walks: "If you want to be happy, be" and "Today I have grown taller with trees." Things like that. Best of all, we had eve-ning programs to keep our minds off *food:* an investment banker drove over from San Antonio to tell us how to invest our money; Scottie Fitzgerald Smith talked about her parents, Scott and Zelda, and their life and times of living well around France; and I told about riding the trail for the Equal Rights Amendment. One evening we saw an old movie, and another we listened to some great music. This made it all bearable. Best of all, the ten-day cost to each of us when all was divided up was five hundred dollars, about one-third the cost of a commercial spa.

About that time a new spa was born in Texas, the Phoenix Spa. I always thought a good motto would be, "Out of my flab, a sex object will rise," but they didn't go for it. The owners were nice enough, however, to ask me to conduct the evening think tanks at their place in a wooded section of downtown Houston. It was a breeze and allowed me to cut out the aerobics in the after-noon and plan for our nightly discussions.

By then the place was filling up with more professional women—young lawyers and real estate experts. There was one from Connecticut who had to keep leaving the jazzorama class to make million-dollar deals by telephone, which was within ear-shot. Another interesting addition was an aged and lonely widow from Wyoming whose ranch gate was fifty miles from her house. She had inherited thousands of acres, about the same number of sheep, and one Mexican cowboy who was good for running the place, but limited in conversational topics.

"You can only sing 'Alla en el rancho grande' so many times before it becomes old," she explained. "So, once a year I pay to come here and listen to what the rest of the world is saying. It's safe. I am well taken care of. I even lose a pound or two, but mainly it's company I want, and I am willing to pay for it."

Once in Washington, we organized a "Fat Cat Democrats" diet group. We met weekly on Capitol Hill at the office of Senator Abourezk of South Dakota. He kept the scales next to his desk, and when we arrived for the five-thirty meeting, he would make us weigh in right where he could read the scale. This was because he was the steadiest weight loser and he wanted to gloat. The leader of this group was Matt Reese, who described himself as a "yo-yo" because his weight went up and down. "I have more suits in my closet than Frank Sinatra," he would tell us, "but no more than two which fit me at the same time."

Matt was a political consultant and ate compulsively when he was out on the campaign trail, which was all the time. He returned from one of these forays and sheepishly explained what had happened one evening in a remote Ohio village. "Do you realize the lengths to which my dieting has driven me? John Glenn and I had been out all day looking for votes and making speeches, and we never found time to eat. Finally it got to be eleven o'clock at night and I started looking for a restaurant. All of them were closed, airtight. I panicked and started running around beating on the doors. Just then I spied a machine that had cheese and peanut-butter crackers, and I pulled out the quarters and started feeding it. The damn thing was broken. I shook it. I lifted the whole machine up. I beat on it, cussed it, and not a crumb. Let me advise all of you to carry a care package with you when you campaign. I could have been arrested for what I did!"

Like thousands of women, my bookshelves are lined with diet books, going back to the now discarded Mayo diet, which had you eating chicken and eggs until you cackled. Then came the all-fish diet. You didn't get hungry, but you had this terrible urge to spawn upstream. There are diets that specialize in carbohydrates, and others that leave it to fruit and cottage cheese; and then there's the old Weight Watchers, which keeps you chewing salads and bread. Our former mayor, Carole McClellan (now Carole Keeton Rylander), used to drink about fifteen Coca-Colas a day. Hard as she worked by day and played tennis by night, she ran up the scales to 195 pounds and wore a size eighteen. Then she discovered Lean Cuisine and cut out the Cokes. In the process of shopping for Lean Cuisines, she met the grocery store owner and wound up marrying him. She got down to a size six, appeared in Texas's most fashionable fashion shows, and turned Republican. I don't know whether her caloric-economic cutback had anything to do with her politics, but it all happened in the course of two years and improved the Lean Cuisine market in Austin as well as the Republican party! Some of us remain Democratic "fat cats" and can never quite forgive her for getting thin, marrying, and leaving us. I don't believe what she says—"Inside every fat cat Democrat there is a skinny Republican screaming to get out."

It is hard to decide how far to go for your health. Every time I really go on a diet, I start getting colds and all sorts of little niggling ailments. I don't know whether it is my mind rebelling or my body.

"I'm not going to give you another diet, Liz, or send you to the nutritionist another time," Dr. Dick Fleming of the Mayo Clinic told me on my last check-up there. "*You know* what you need to do. Get it down! Strangely enough, you are one of those few people who gain weight but keep a normal cholesterol count ... and your triglycerides are also in good shape. In fact, the pulse on your ankle is that of a twenty-year-old."

I could have told him my pulses are like that all over, but I restrained myself and went out and had a butter pecan ice-cream cone in celebration. My downfall is ice cream. Would the Lord have had Dolley Madison invent it if He hadn't wanted us to eat it?

I also really like to cook. What I can do on a rainy day with one turnip, a soup bone, and lots of vegetables is magic. In fact, the only really creative part of running a house is cooking, creating a table of joy, and having hot biscuits in the oven. I like that kind of world and hope it won't kill me.

A friend who is thin as a rail, Ellen Temple, tells me that her mother taught her from childhood: "Your body is your temple, your structure. You are the pope, maintenance foreman, the concierge for life. No one is as interested in that temple as you are since you are in charge. Treat it accordingly." She has and does. In fact, her name wasn't even Temple when her mother first told her this. She went right out and found a man named Temple and married him, which, in my opinion, makes her body also *his* Temple.

My doctor has told me that I should picture myself as an automobile, When you buy an automobile you can use it any way you want for the first two or three years. You can abuse it. You can take rough roads. But after that, it begins to break down. You need new tires. Parts have to be replaced. You begin to rust. So you learn that if you take better care of that machine, it will run a long time. I told him that is true of Volkswagens, maybe, but how about the Rolls-Royce that I envision myself to be?

You can get advice on handling your health from anyone, particularly those without a medical license.

"Learn to eat like a king at breakfast, a queen at lunch, and a pauper at dinner," someone suggested to me. I never tried it.

Chris Silkwood at the Phoenix Spa, who has a hard time keeping meat on her bones, suggests you enter a grocery store with a battle plan . . . the "big O" system. "Wheel your grocery cart around outer shelves only. That puts you in reach of the fresh vegetables and fruits, the meat counter, and the dairy products and the nutritious foods. Never, never go into the center with the baked goods and canned stuff!"

"Envision yourself as a pie," she also advises, which was her mistake, for she set my mouth watering and thinking Texas pecan, or Louisiana black bottom. "You divide your pie self up between the physical, the mental, and the emotional. Make the pieces even. Divide your time accordingly."

People have been given advice on food for centuries. The more you read, the less you trust. Strange how rapidly doctors change their minds about what is good for you. I was thirty-five when I had my first bout with diverticulitis. The doctor put me on puréed spinach and applesauce and warned me against ever taking another mouthful of popcorn, cashews, or grapenuts. Now the cure is the opposite: roughage. The more shredded wheat, whole grains, and cactus roots you can shove through your gut, the better. Fickle, that's what they are. I am still torn between Equal, Sweet'n Low, and real sugar. There's something said against all of them.

If you want to have some real laughs, look for a manual on ailments, particularly women's ailments. Henrietta brought me a copy of the cookbook *Bull Cook and Authentic Historical Recipes and Practices.* On page 156 it describes "How to Make Authentic Mayonnaise." Incidentally, the book was given to her by Frank McBee, chairman of the board of TRACOR, a worldwide business headquartered in our own Austin. Frank had given Henrietta a goose. (I don't mean *that* kind of goose, but a real goose that he shot.) She didn't know how to cook it, so he supplied her with the cookbook and even marked it for her. He particularly marked the section on making mayonnaise, which contains this warning: "If you are a woman, do not attempt to make mayonnaise during menstruation time, as the mayonnaise will simply not blend together at all well. This is not a superstition but a well-established fact well known to all women." I certainly hope it is known to Hellman's and Kraft's, or they're going to blow their business right off the map! Actually, as far as Henrietta was concerned, it was sheer flattery on Frank's part to mark that section. But he is the kind of courteous man who would have marked it even for Grandma Moses.

The book also has a timely cure for radiation and upset stomachs: red pepper! "Many believe that eating foods with red pepper is bad in general for your health. This is not true. Our modern-day scientists now have proven that people who eat food seasoned with hot pepper resist atomic radiation much better than people who do not eat it. In fact, people who use considerable hot red pepper in their foods are almost immune to atomic radiation except in severe form." Three Mile Island could have learned a lot from Henrietta's cookbook. There is also a folk prevention for pregnancy:

"Catherine de Medici, to gain political power, would gather a group of two hundred beautiful young girls and carefully train them to entertain men. Her group was called the *Escadron Volant*, and she would send them out singly or in groups to gain favor and entertain political rivals. The girls were all taught to eat green apples and drink a cup of vinegar to keep them from getting pregnant."

It's the little juicy tidbits you find in old books, including a sure cure for horse wounds: human urine. Such morsels boggle the mind!

Another friend, Terry Hershey, says her mother would always warn her "not to stand in overdrafts," as it was overstimulating to girls. Terry has avoided overdrafts but remained stimulated to age sixty-five—the last time I saw her—still the sultry-eyed vamp she was back in college. Speaking of stimulation in the lower parts, I have met a wide variety of gynecologists who have various approaches to diverting attention from the humiliation that comes to every woman as she mounts the examining table and places her feet in the stirrups for a Pap smear. What do you talk about? My Washington doctor, knowing that I was a friend of Art Buchwald, always started talking about a recent Buchwald column just as he was in up to his elbow and I was in no position to laugh. "Did you read Wednesday's column on White House books? It was a real howl."

His system worked for diversion, but it damn near ruined my friendship with Art. Every time I would see him in the press gallery, I'd blush like a schoolgirl and disappear as soon as possible.

I confessed this to my friend Martha Keating, and she promptly told me about her gynecologist back home in Atlanta. "He was harelipped, and the funniest man I've ever known. He became a gynecologist in spite of himself. Back in medical school, he thought that absolutely *no one* would ever want to go to a harelipped gynecologist. So he set out to be one. Everyone in Atlanta went to him. And you know why? On the ceiling of his office he would tape large posters. One time you would be flattened out, look up, and see a grizzly sailor making a face at you. Another time, it was Clark Gable. He made a game of it, and everyone forgot about his harelip as a result."

Southern women are accused of liking to talk about their parts, and I believe it. If you want to get into a real conversation on D&Cs or boob sizes, I recommend you go south of the Mason-Dixon line.

My friend Dr. Ferrol Sams is most fond of a patient he calls Miss Cleo, who has worn nothing but lavender and gray since her husband, Mr. Arthur Lee, passed on. Miss Cleo delicately refers to everything below the waist as "down there." Says Dr. Sams: "In this day of openness and frankness, I really miss 'down there.' I get offended at all of the corrections humans try to make on what God Almighty gave them. It would never occur to Miss Cleo to have a breast augmentation, a process which is more ridiculous than its recipients imagine. If women knew what plastic surgeons make their breasts look like in the supine position, they would never submit to what they call a 'boob job.' The boobs look good from a distance when a woman is standing up, but when she is lying flat on her back on the examination table, they shift around like so many saucers of clabber. They are never lined up correctly. I have a whole covey of operated ladies to whom I refer as the girls with the cross-eyed nipples."

PART OF HEALTH, I'm convinced, is to ignore it if possible. I really can't remember much about menopause. I was working for Lyndon Johnson at the time, and he kept me too busy to experience a hot flash. Of course, I sometimes saved them for weekends when I had sympathetic attention and listeners. I think being active and busy as well as reasonably happy are all good rules for health.

I like eighty-year-old Millicent Fenwick's philosophy of life. The strong-spoken, beloved former congresswoman from New

Jersey told me from her desk in Rome, where she ran a U.S. food program, "Don't stop! Keep at it! Don't give up! Not for a moment!"

Practicing good health habits can be financially rewarding. Iphigene Sulzberger, ninety-three-year-old grand dame of *The New York Times*, likes to tell the story of a New York woman who would take her constitutionals daily, plotting her path past Madison and Eighty-first, the Frank Campbell Funeral Home, so she could use the handy powder room. Each day she signed the book at the door as a matter of courtesy. Once, to her surprise, she received a phone call from a lawyer informing her she had inherited $25,000 from an old gentleman whose will bequeathed his money to whoever came to his funeral. She was it.

Norman Cousins believed that laughter was the best medicine, and he also thought it had healing powers. Confined to a hospital bed with a serious illness that didn't seem to be getting any better, Cousins persuaded the doctors to let him check out of the hospital and into a nearby hotel. He made the switch, taking along a nurse who liked to laugh and an arsenal of funny books and old movies, including those of Groucho Marx and Abbott and Costello. For a month, Cousins simply indulged himself in laughter . . . and it worked. Not only did he heal himself, but he went on to write and speak on the subject all around the country.

Whenever I'm feeling blue, I find that laugh-giving friends are a marvelous antidote to depression. People who feel sorry for themselves can be a real drag on the healthy, and it's best to avoid them unless you can find a way to give them a little joy so you will get some in return. Once when I was lecturing in Atlanta on "Humor as Therapy," a woman came up to me after the speech and said, "How can you be funny if you're just naturally melancholy?" This woman is very funny, in a droll sort of way. But to answer her question: You read humor, you don't dwell on the morose or the darker side of human nature, you force yourself to see the funny side of a situation.

Larry Markes, my old gag-writing friend in Hollywood, is rarely home, but his telephone recordings are hilarious for those

TOM LANKES

Now come the joys of aging and freedom and determination to enjoy friends, like my energetic tennis-playing sister widow, Henrietta Jacobsen (above), and to visit with my children Scott and Christy (right, above), and grandchildren, Bonnie and Les. One-on-one with Les took me to Knotts Berry Farm, and to Disneyland with my daughter-in-law, Jean Carpenter.

TOM LANKES

who listen, and for him in creating them. I often call Larry just to hear his recorded voice—knowing I will laugh and be cheered up—and also knowing I'll have the fun of repeating his message to everyone I talk to, thus spreading a little laughter around . . . courtesy of Larry.

When California was in the national news after weeks of hard rain and mud slides, Larry's recording began with a singing line, "Raindrops keep falling on my head . . . Oh, hello there, I'm up on the house mending a leaky roof, but as soon as I come down and get these soaking clothes off, I'll call you back if you leave your name and number."

Then he has a sexy message that begins in a sultry whisper, "Oh, it's you. I'm dying to talk to you, but I can't right now . . . for reasons you'll understand. Leave your name and I'll call the minute sheeeee leaves."

I like people like that. They add spice to life, which tends to be too bland most of the time.

Most presidents I have known were looking for a laugh. Throughout history, they have often had the equivalent of a "court jester." Ike had George Allen as a golfing partner; Harry Truman kept his old army buddy Harry Vaughan on hand; Jack Kennedy delighted in the company and Irish wit of Dave Powers.

FDR created his own circle of humor by giving funny names to his closest associates. "Tommy the Cork" (Thomas Corcoran) and "Henry the Morgue" (Henry Morgenthau). Roosevelt had every reason to feel sorry for himself: his personal handicap, polio, kept him confined to a wheelchair. But he didn't. Instead, he brought laughter to the White House. Once, when humorist Will Rogers visited the White House and Eleanor Roosevelt received him, he asked, "Where is the president?" She replied, "Wherever you hear the laughter, that's where you'll find him." The presidents who fared the best were those who, even in the darkest hours of our country's history, could find humor.

THERE IS A THEORY that worry can cause cancer. Any number of cases can be cited of women, greatly depressed because of a mate's infidelity, who develop cancer. Depressed people seem to develop headaches, allergies, and backaches, as well as other health problems, along with feeling sorry for themselves.

The last few years women have heard a lot about stress, a recurrent word with the increasing success of women in the professional world. In my opinion, stress beats boredom. And even though I know I'm overweight, I also know I'm healthy. So I am simply not going to add to the "stress" of my life because a lot of advertisers spend millions of dollars trying to tell women what they should look like. The Lord didn't decree us all to be Twiggy or Brooke Shields. I never will be, and as long as I exercise some each day, sleep well, and have energy, I'm not going to wear myself out trying to be something I can't be. I've made peace with my weight, and I wish everyone else would.

I am sorry no one told me about calcium at an earlier age, or I'd have started popping the necessary 1,500 mgs. a day at age thirty-five. Women have just started paying attention to their health and going after research money for it. I enjoy being kept abreast of these developments as an advisory committee member for the Women's Fund for Research and Education, which does its good deeds with grants for health research into women's ailments. It makes grants and provides educational booklets to women of all ages. The "Healthy Woman" chapter in its publication *A Primer on Women's Health* states:

> The "secrets" of optimal health of vigorous older people around the world include combinations of habits and behaviors.
> These people:
>
> • are active and busy, often performing physical work and walking every day;
> • do not smoke;
> • drink alcohol not at all or in moderation;
> • get up and go to bed early;
> • are slender and erect;
> • eat a simple diet which is low in fat, cholesterol and

red meat, and includes lots of fresh fruits and vegetables, cereals and grains.

The benefits derived from good habits far exceed their perceived inconvenience. Once you incorporate healthy habits into your life, you are apt to become addicted to them.

I WOULD ADD one more recommendation: Do something new each week!

The biggest turnaround in our national habits has been in smoking. Knowing the tobacco lobby, composed of a great many charmers and southern storytellers and a large contingent from Sir Walter Raleigh's economic program for Virginia and North Carolina, I could never have guessed how quickly tobacco would become a no-no. Speaker Sam Rayburn smoked two packs a day to his grave at a late age. His health formula for a long lifespan: "Every morning, a little bit of bourbon and a little bit of honey." I have friends who are downright rude about smoking, with signs over their mantels reading, "Thank you for not smoking." I also have a rebel smoking friend whose pillow on her living room couch proclaims, "Thank you for holding your breath until I finish this cigarette." The tobacco ban hasn't affected my own habits, but then, I never smoked. Of course, I tried it when I was about fifteen and first learning how to be a news reporter. But I could never master it; the cigarettes kept rolling off the typewriter. I had to give them up, and it was easy, since they kept getting in the way. I must confess, some of the best times of my life have been spent in smoke-filled rooms.

YOU CAN GO crazy listening to everyone's plans for good health. Life is a gamble, and if you want to stack the cards in your favor, you must spend some time at it. But not too much. Once when I was feeling poorly and sorry for myself, my doctor whipped out a prescription pad and scribbled on it: "You need to get excited about something." I did and felt better instantly. (The butter pecan ice cream in the refrigerator helped!)

Someone sent me a verse that says a lot about aging and health:

I'M FINE

*There's nothing whatever the matter with me, I'm just
    as healthy as I can be.
I have arthritis in both my knees, and when I talk I talk
    with a wheeze;
My pulse is weak and my blood is thin, but I'm awfully
    well for the shape I'm in.
I think my liver is out of whack, and I have a terrible
    pain in my back;
My hearing's poor, and my sight is dim, most every-
    thing seems to be out of trim, but I'm awfully well
    for the shape I'm in.*

*My doctor says my days are few, for every week there's
    something new.
The way I stagger is sure a crime, I'm likely to drop off
    any time;
I jump like mad at the drop of a pin, but I'm awfully
    well for the shape I'm in.*

*My teeth eventually will have to come out, and my diet
    I hate to think about;
I'm overweight and I can't get thin, my appetite's such
    it's bound to win, but I'm awfully well for the
    shape I'm in.*

*Arch supports I have for my feet, or I wouldn't be able
    to walk on the street;
Sleep is denied me night after night, and every morning
    I look a fright;
My memory's failing, my head's in a spin, but I'm aw-
    fully well for the shape I'm in.
My moral is, as this talk I unfold—that for you and me
    who are growing old,
It's better to say "I'm fine" with a grin, than to let
    others know the shape we're in.*

I'M FINE, and I ought to shout about it.

I wonder what would happen if I took out an ad, not in *The Wall Street Journal* as my brother Tommy suggested, but in one of those singles magazines: "AVAILABLE: one aging female who does not like an all-feminine world, an ERA advocate who doesn't mind fixing dinner or, better still, breakfast for someone who'll clear the table and carry out the trash. Likes to read, swim, walk, cook, nurture, sing, dance, laugh."

Like thousands of singles everywhere, I have lived long enough and experienced enough of life to be realistic and infinitely more interesting because I am older, wiser, and, yes, plumper. So how do I use my new leisure? With no man in my life, I need to create a world of men and women around me. And it can be done. I often need a more interesting world when I am alone.

Leisure, a wise person once told me, can be an Achilles' heel. I think it was Laurance Rockefeller who said it: he was a man who could afford leisure but never indulged in it. He would go out and chop wood at the JY Ranch in Wyoming just to allay his conscience, if he'd sat around too long. But he planned leisure for others—the Jackson Hole, Wyoming, development for mountain climbers, the Caneel Bay plantation in the Virgin Islands for snorklers, and the Woodstock resort in Vermont for skiers. He even helped boost short skis for those who couldn't master the long ones.

Since I have Rockefeller tastes on a Liz Carpenter income, I have to tone them down considerably. So for leisure I have a formula: splurge and starve, some of both, which accommodates my financial seesaw. The trick is to find a way to make time a pleasure for myself and others while staying within my budget.

Back on my sixtieth birthday, I was reminded that "we pass this way but once," so then and there I decided: Never say no. That sounds more dangerous than it has turned out to be. I haven't broken any commandments knowingly, but I have allied myself with people and events that provide me sometimes with relaxation and sometimes with exhilaration. My leisure planning is styled to offer opportunities for quiet moments, for pampering, for doing something that gives me life and a sense of well-being. It can be as simple as what to do in an hour when you are really, really lonely or as involved as preparing for a well-planned week or month.

For short-term leisure, a bubble bath can be the perfect ticket. Put on your favorite music, take the phone off the hook, line up the lotions and Christmas bath powder, and lay out your thickest towels and a favorite nightgown so everything will be at hand when you emerge. Fill the tub with pleasant-scented foaming gel and sink in. You can simply drift and daydream or get comfortable with a plastic pillow behind your head and read a novel. What luxury!

Books are another answer. I have a friend who says her favorite moment is when she has a clean house and a dirty book. I never find enough time for all the books I want to read. Usually there are three or four on the nightstand that I'm in the process of reading, but the joy of spending a whole evening with a book I'm dying to read—that's living!

Massages are available and worth the $35 or so an hour as a special treat to myself on Mother's Day or even Ash Wednesday. They're relaxing and good for circulation. Long ago I discovered how therapeutic they can be in times of stress and overwork. Occasionally when a friend is facing problems or having a particularly low period, I'll invite her over for dinner, a soak in the Jacuzzi, and a massage. It doesn't make her problems go away— nor mine—but it physically restores you to face them. And my friends feel pampered and loved because they know I care about them.

Movies are also a good leisure-time activity. The funny ones are my favorites—especially if the dialogue is clever—and I like to go with a friend who will "hash over" the plot with me afterward. This, for me, can also bridge the years between an aging aunt or a darling grandson.

What are other enjoyable leisure activities? Go browsing at a farmer's market, then bring your selections home and cook them

with a friend or two. A special camaraderie can develop over a
chopping block, and you have the bonus of good conversation
around the dinner table. Or take something you've cooked to
someone. Cooking brings out creative and nurturing instincts,
and there's the satisfaction of doing something for someone else.

Walk a mile at dawn or sunset—it's good for the body, better for the soul. Study the wildflowers, listen to nature's symphony, look around and discover something different that you
haven't noticed before. This requires no special equipment, nor
do you need a team or a partner. It's a good time to meditate or
simply clear your mind completely, making it receptive to whatever comes. It can be a splendid adventure.

Jean and David—the sixty-two- and seventy-two-year-old
newlyweds—have put in a new tennis court nestled in the woods
behind their home. It puts exercise close at hand and is an adven-
turous device to draw young friends into their daily orbit.

Maggie Cousins found adventure of a different sort. Weary
of coping with snowy streets and hailing elusive cabs to get
around Manhattan—her home for thirty-eight years—the then-
fiction editor of *Ladies' Home Journal* and former Doubleday
editor went south to San Antonio. She took a flat on the west
bank of the San Antonio River, right above a bar and a coin shop,
turning her back on her Sixty-third Street apartment, which had
been the gathering place for interesting people. The established
and the striving young alike had come there to exchange ideas,
talk of books and authors, and feast on Maggie's Texas-fried
chicken. How could she leave all that behind? She simply took a
deep breath, packed her books, and headed south.

"It's marvelous to be old if you have your health and a little
bit of money. It doesn't take much, but you have to have a little
to belong to things," she said. "You must give up things as you
get older, like driving a car, but you must also put in something
new. I'm interested in things now I never had time for when I was
working—like city politics and civic affairs. I'm on the San Antonio Arts Commission," she added proudly.

Maggie did what uprooted people sometimes forget to do—

jump into the life of a new town. She soon heard about Fiesta—a colorful celebration of Mexican culture with lighted river parades of flower-decked barges, music, food, and events taking place in the little Mexican village near the river. She signed up as a volunteer to man one of the many booths.

"I sold piñatas, and it was the most fun I ever had," Maggie said, and laughed. "One man bought five on his way to the airport—a big bull, some donkeys, and clowns. I'll bet his wife could have killed him!"

Occasionally, extra time lets you think about the problems a busy schedule just doesn't allow. What do you do when you're blue, depressed, or feeling simply rotten? One woman keeps a package of bittersweet chocolate bits in the refrigerator and eats the whole thing . . . slowly. Others seek some form of physical activity to redirect their dispositions—tennis, jogging, bike riding, handball. Dress designer Mollie Parnis employs an old Jewish adage: "When you have troubles, hang them out like wash on a clothesline and compare them with everyone else's; then you'll gather them in and forget about them."

I once knew a public relations executive who was on the verge of a nervous breakdown. His doctor prescribed, among other things, baking bread. It's the kneading that's so therapeutic. My friend went out and bought a book on baking bread and went through it alphabetically. "I'm only in the K's," he reported, "and I've already used eight hundred pounds of flour. I'm driving my neighbors wild with the smell of baking bread, and that makes me feel wonderful!"

Gardening can also lift your spirits. It's Bess Abell's release, and she says, "When I'm blue, I plant flowers. It gets my mind off whatever is worrying me, and I guess it's the sort of thing our grandmothers did when they went out and bought a new hat."

Follow Maggie Cousins's lead—get involved. Churches offer Bible classes, choirs, and singles groups; there are bridge and poker clubs, civic clubs, alumni activities. Volunteer your time as a docent at a local museum; make recordings for the blind; sign up with a wonderful group called Meals on Wheels that delivers hot meals to the elderly and needy; support a candidate, not only with your vote, but by actively spending a few hours a week in the campaign office. It's hectic, and you'll meet all kinds of interesting people who are working toward the same goal you are. This builds friendships and certainly chases the "lonelies" away.

When I told friends I was headed for a graveyard cleaning in deep east Texas several years ago, the response was, "You must be short of things to do!"

Not at all! Annual graveyard cleanings, all-day picnics, and singing-on-the-grounds have been a major social event in rural parts of Texas since people first started getting buried there in the 1800s. Then the families did the cleaning themselves. Today it is a get-together to raise money for the caretaking. The scene was the Ebenezer Cemetery in Arp, which is near Troup, Omen, Overton, and Tyler. My fellow "cleaner" was Bob Waldron, well-known Washington interior designer who hails from Arp. He wouldn't miss going home to this June event for anything!

"In the old days when the crops were laid by—about watermelon time—the men in the community would come and rake, hoe, and burn the trash, and the women would bring the food. The custom went on until we finally hired a caretaker," he explained to me. "Now it's gotten to be more a reunion of old friends and descendants. Most of us in Arp know more people in the cemetery than in town. We pay our respects, visit with each other, and collect funds. And we look forward to it all year."

At the cemetery there was a welcome breeze blowing across the five acres of tombstones, and the peaceful silence was broken only by the call of a bobwhite or the whistle of the Missouri Pacific, which still stops in Arp for freight. Stately old cedars, magnolias, oak trees, and soft pink crepe myrtle embraced the gray granite tombstones that mark the families there: Jarvis, Woolf, Bradford, Lewis . . . most of them kinfolk. There were familiar lambs for the infants and, of course, clasped hands and vivid quotations: "Her end was peace" and "Earth has no sorrow that Heaven cannot heal."

There were Confederate graves, and as one gentle lady informed me with a smile, "We even have two blue-bellied Yankees who married southern girls, came to live here, and loved the town."

Under a grove of trees, hampers were unloaded and table-cloths spread over a long E-shaped table. Then the delicacies were put out: dishpan chicken pie, fried chicken heaped high, hams, bowls of potato salad, watermelon, chocolate and pine-apple cakes, chess pies, and huge jugs of iced tea. Soon, the pitch was set for the hymns: "Love Lifted Me," "When We All Get to Heaven," and "He Keeps Me Singing." Next June, I *have* to go back again!

But my leisure specialty is planning vacation house parties, and I have done this for four-day weekends, a week in Martha's Vineyard, or a month in Spain. I like to fill them with unexpected adventures and ingenious happenings. I enjoy renting or borrow-ing the house and going there a day or so before with a helpful friend to get it ready. This is part of the fun. You can transform a drab summer rental with fifty dollars' worth of geraniums, a rented piano, and humorous signs of instructions for your awaited guests. This whets my imagination and utilizes the experience I accumulated during my political years as an "advance woman."

I invite guests via funny memos. One rental house was made more inviting by labeling the tiny rooms: White House East Room, Lincoln Room, Queen's Bedroom, West Room, Red Room. Humorous signs on the doors help guests remember which room they're in and compensate for the size or sparseness. A few dollars for fancy soap, good reading light bulbs, the latest magazines, and a bulletin board offering meal times, movies to be shown, sign-up lists for tennis or early-morning walks keeps things running smoothly.

Vacation house parties have become times I savor. I apply all I learned from the big-time party givers in Washington and taper it down to the size of my pocketbook. Sometimes you have a friend who will be a financial partner in your enterprise. Then, with your favorite guests, four or six or eight, you can have a lark instead of taking customary tours and reading markers. It suits my preferences and energies better than the packing and unpacking of extended trips.

I have spent a month in Santa Fe taking in the operas and lunching leisurely around the town's picturesque square. I have exchanged my Texas house with someone for theirs on the coast of Spain. I have engineered an apartment on Grand Cayman Island. And I have planned long weekend think tanks at several ranches within an hour's drive of Austin.

All of these have been delicious moments, fulfilling my need for people. I simply can't bear to vacation alone, and this is my alternative. My recipe for a house party includes some basic ingredients: a special setting for the right ambience; a servant or two; and enough space for six or eight. Share the rent with your guests, if necessary, or let them chip in on food, a rented car, wine, entertainment. Invite the kind of people who know enough to do this.

The guests must be genial people who bring some special qualities: laughter, philosophy, good cooks, singers, talkers. Don't try to even up men and women—that's impossible. But two interesting women are preferable to one boring male leech. I don't mix small children and adult friends. Both need undivided attention. I get fragmented if I try to mix them. I like to divide chores in a way that doesn't make them seem like work. Once on Martha's Vineyard there were five couples sharing a house for a week. Each couple picked a night to "do their thing" in the kitchen, and we dined lavishly with work at a minimum, sharing the expense of a local college student who came in to clean up!

Entertainment at a vacation house party can be varied. Pack a picnic hamper and a blanket and take everyone off to an outdoor concert or theater. Play charades. Sing, even if it means renting a piano and hiring a pianist for a couple of hours. Have an evening of reading aloud, with each guest presenting his or her favorite piece of literature or poetry. You don't have to be a writer to enjoy wordsmithing. To vary conversation and avoid stagnation, I like to include local people.

Dispositions are likely to stay compatible if you can find a masseuse who makes house calls. I once turned a Ping-Pong table and sunbathing pad into a massage table, and we lured a German "magician" who handled five massages in an afternoon at $10 per body. Good for her and great for the guests!

I am a real nut about local fresh-produce markets, so I seek them out and gather in a supply of fruits and herbs and vegetables just to make the place look homier and offer the taste of the country. Often I come upon a new variety of fruit or vegetable I have never seen before.

Thoughtful, cheerful guests can really make the difference. I have come to appreciate the guest who was ingenious enough to organize everyone into a bucket brigade to pass buckets of water from the swimming pool to the house so we could flush and wash when a water shortage cut off our supply for two days in Spain. She also poked around the pantry and found champagne to serve our bucket line, making the chore festive. And I will never forget one couple who hired a van so all eight of us could enjoy each other's company and hear a hired guide as we toured Mexico. On that same trip, my children hired a mariachi band to surprise us at dinner one evening.

Each trip offers new opportunities, and sometimes even a "do-nothing" afternoon spaced in the midst of other activities is most welcome.

It gives me such pleasure to share my life that I can't imagine not doing it. It is the world's greatest insurance against isolation and loneliness. I can never offer a Marjorie Post kind of vacation house party, but in memory I can still relish the ones Les and I were fortunate enough to attend at Marjorie's elegant homes.

In taking trips that cover more geography, I like to catch up with old friends while enjoying their hospitality. Here you have to observe some of the "good houseguest" rules. A visit will be met with more enthusiasm if you make your plans known well in advance with exact arrival and departure dates. If you have to change plans or cancel them altogether, let your prospective host know as soon as possible—this will leave a more favorable impression for the next time.

Arrive with a case of wine or champagne, a roast or ham, or some other usable contribution to the household. Plan an evening out that is your treat—dinner or a play, or both. A sure way to kill off future invitations is to be late for a group excursion. Be creative. One friend always takes along a camera and, after the visit, sends a small album filled with the photos and appropriate captions to her hosts. Be willing to pick up after yourself or help out—the extent of this, of course, depends on the particular circumstances of the household.

One of the best house party hosts I know is Gore Vidal, who owns a villa overlooking the Amalfi Drive in Italy and runs it like a Roman emperor . . . well, a faded-blue-jeaned Roman emperor. The villa was my destination one summer when I was writing my way around Europe and had told Gore I would be in the neighborhood. He quickly said, "Come and stay a few days," and it took me all of sixty seconds to accept. We are longtime friends from Washington, and I have the added "in" of having known his grandfather, the late Senator Thomas Gore of Oklahoma, one of the few people Gore admired completely.

La Rondinaia—the Swallow—sits amid olive trees and flowering oleander about two thousand feet above the blue Mediterranean. Here Gore writes his novels and sees friends who happen to be in the neighborhood, like me, Clare Luce, Imelda Marcos, Paul Newman and Joanne Woodward, Mick Jagger, Andy Warhol, Johnny Carson—and, oh yes, Princess Margaret.

His key to writing and entertaining simultaneously is his good friend Howard Austin, who relieves him of guests, takes them sailing or swimming and lunches them until about four each day while Gore writes. By twilight, when his work is done, Gore settles down on a big pillow by his coffee table and is ready to hold court. He makes it all seem so effortless, but it is Howard who has overseen the dinner planning. Usually it's a two-course meal, soup or fruit, then a meat and pasta and salad, and sometimes ice for dessert. The food is superb but is not the main offering: that is conversation itself. There is something refreshing about being around someone who is totally uninhibited about whose toes he steps on. Not for a steady course, but two thousand feet above the Mediterranean, where no one else is listening, it's not a bad way to spend several evenings.

ONE OF MY ANNUAL leisure-time favorites comes each January when some good friends, Lottie and Arthur Temple, gather their friends together to literally "cook a ton of chili." They have the good fortune of living in the East Texas Big Thicket, a retreat that is wooded and hidden from the world and whose central headquarters is in a town called Diboll, pronounced Die-ball. It is from his office in Diboll that Arthur Temple deals in magazine stocks and most of the timber that leaves Texas.

Arthur, who is now sixty-five, likes to spend his leisure hours with the longtime Big Thicket friends in his company who have helped make it what it is today: rich and prosperous. And he likes to spend that time in his own habitat. So, when the deer hunting season begins each November first in Texas, he and his friends kill their quota in a place called Boggy Slough. The meat is stored and frozen until January, when he holds his annual chili-cookin' weekend. This I never want to miss. I was invited to join the SOBS, the Sportsmen of Boggy Slough, an organization of a few people who are willing to stand for two days and cook chili over giant tin drums in a shed behind Arthur's camp, located in Scrappin' Valley, amid pine trees and lakes. Warm fires by night, guitar pickin' by Buddy and Shotsie, Arthur's kids, and singin' by all are the evening's entertainment. By day, you pick the gristle out of the cooking chili and help package it, and on Sunday you go home with a share for the rest of the chili-eating season, which, in Texas, ought to end in May but for real fanciers lasts all year round. Most of the people present are over sixty and look forward to this treat all year. In fact, one of them, Jim Shepley, who was president at *Time*, scripts the initiation skit each year. A lot of leisure hours go into that weekend, and I wouldn't trade it for any other; it embodies characters that I like. And it isn't everyone who has the chance to help cook a ton of chili!

Men are becoming ingenious at creating adventures in their single senior citizenship. Sid Freidberg, a friend in Washington, went through a painful divorce and now at seventy-two has found a strange and chauvinistic formula to make things livelier.

"Yes, I am lonely many times," he told me. "I would like to have a companion and be able to just pick up and go to a movie with someone . . . but I am having a good time by getting out of my own skin and playing a part with different women. Depending on the woman's own interest, I take on the role of gardener, theater critic, traveler, or what have you. It sounds crazy, but it helps me overcome my inhibitions.

"It turned out that my role playing is often with someone who is about thirty," he continued with zest. "I found to my surprise coming back from Europe recently that I was bringing trinkets to nine different women, all in their thirties. I realized what had happened to me. I have been collecting young women companions, and in one or two cases for a more intimate relationship. I began in a grocery store with a can of tomato soup. I stood at that shelf until I spied a nice-looking young woman, and as she passed me, I asked her, 'Do you know how to make this for one?' She began to tell me . . . and we became good friends and never did make the soup. I have used that more than once . . . and it generally works.

"The thirty-year-olds make me feel young. They are mostly independent young professional women who do not have any idea of marrying me. It does bother me occasionally, conversationally, that they don't remember who Donald Nelson was. You and I know that he headed the War Production Board and was an important man in this country during World War II. But they add to my companionship.

"It's not always the most flattering kind of experience." He laughed. "I asked one student after class, 'Would you like to go punting?' 'I'd love to,' she answered. Later I asked her how she felt about being with a seventy-two-year-old man, and she said brightly, 'I've always had a good relationship with my grandfather.' "

I have never been so timid that I have to pretend I am playing a role. But I have found that my resolution—Never say no—doesn't always pan out to be fun. Example:

One of the most popular columnists in Austin, John Kelso, who writes about "Bubba land"—translated "good 'ol boy land"—invited me to judge the "Ugliest Pickup Truck in Texas Contest." His newspaper, *The Austin American Statesman*, gives John a budget of $25 to stage this annual event. It's held on a partially vacant lot next to the Hog Eye Bait Shop, and the ambition of all "bubbas" with ugly pickups is to win. John said he needed to add a little style to this year's event and asked me to be the "celebrity" judge. The invitation was irresistible. This was something I'd never done before, so naturally I said yes. And I went into it with zest.

Henrietta helped me convert some old glasses into a lorgnette for close, snooty inspection. To this I added a white parasol, large flowered hat, and white gloves for "the white glove test"—if a truck failed to leave dirt, grease, rust, or worse on my gloves, it didn't qualify. It all went well enough, except I had forgotten how hot it could get in "Bubba land." The temperature topped one hundred degrees, and there was no shade on the lot. The parasol saved my life, along with the ginseng iced tea and cold ice packs that John's wife made available when the judges looked faint. I wasn't the only one who couldn't take the blistering sun for very long as we looked over the eighty-five entries, which included a pickup with a load of manure and two pink, plastic flamingos; one all rusted out with a hood cover that didn't fit; and one with side panels riddled with bulletholes, à la Bonnie and Clyde. One of my co-judges was a roofer from Houston who had recently roofed the entire fourteen acres of the Astrodome. "I've known heat and hellish weather," he said, swigging an ice-cold beer and mopping his face with the ice pack, "but I have never been through anything like this day."

The contest winner was a twenty-five-year-old "bubba"

whose wife told spectators, "I wouldn't ride in this thing for any reason."

"She hates it," he said, smiling. "She hates it with a passion. But the truck will be here when I die."

"That will be shortly!" she told the crowd.

One of the entrants told me that the composite pickup truck owner is "short of cash, drinks brake fluid instead of Shiner Bock beer, and whenever possible lives by the bumper sticker motto 'Do It with a Rented Tool.' "

That was a day with no silver lining, except to have met some interesting characters, but it taught me there is virtue and a lot of good sense in sometimes saying no!

There are a few other things *not* to do with leisure. Worrying, for instance, is a waste unless you put a time limit on it. If you can't find a solution after worrying about your problem an hour, then shelve it or send it to someone else, like through one of those chain letters.

Joining a local singles club is recommended by those of my friends who have done this in the wake of a divorce or death. They claim it is like group therapy and everyone is there to make friends. I have one male friend who belongs to two such groups: one a very conservative sort of waltz-every-Thursday dance club, the other a full-schedule club with jogging each morning and cooking, playing cards, sailing, or pairing off in smaller groups each evening. I get tired just hearing the schedule, but it works for him.

If grandchildren are within reach, a favorite leisure activity is one-on-one time with them—a special outing, reading aloud, or letting them choose what they want to do with an afternoon. I have friends who draft a list of alternatives and let the child do the selecting. What is a leisure activity for the grandparent can be a lifesaver for the parent.

Leisure pastimes after sixty can be grand ideas for grandchildren. My own mother was a godsend when my children were born. She was the one who pulled herself out of a warm bed to walk and rock the new addition to our household so we could sleep. Little did we know how much we were going to need her. Mama would somehow manage to settle the baby down. Sometimes I would get up early in the morning and find little Scott snuggled in the arms of his grandmother as she rocked and read to him to keep him quiet for as long as possible. I have a snapshot of her reading "Poison, Poker and Pistols," an incongruous title for a grandmotherly lady with a sweet face and white hair holding a sleeping baby. In Scott's baby book, I found a poem she used to sing softly to him as she rocked him to sleep. She had written it for her own first son and repeated it to each successive child. She called it "The Rocker with the Sleepy Little Creak."

> Full well do I remember when a very little boy,
>   And I'd had all of the playing that a child could
>   well enjoy,
> I'd climb up in my mother's arms, so tired I couldn't
>   speak,
>   And she'd rock me in the rocker with the sleepy
>   little creak.
>
> I'd cuddle down and listen while she softly hummed a
>   tune,
>   Which the rocking chair kept time to with a
>   drowsy little croon,
> And like angel wings a-fanning was her breath upon my
>   cheek,
>   When she rocked me in the rocker with the sleepy
>   little creak.
>
> It was not so very handsome, it was old and brown and
>   worn,
>   But had carried me to slumberland since ever I
>   was born,
> And I'd not change seats with any of the mighty or the
>   meek,
>   When she rocked me in the rocker with the sleepy
>   little creak.

But now I'm many, many miles away from all that
pleasant scene,
And many full and busy years stretch out their
length between,
But I'd give all that I've gathered could I rest me for a
week
While she rocked me in the rocker with the sleepy
little creak.

There is a vital connection between grandparent and grandchildren that allows you to be role model, nurturer, historian, mentor, and wizard—someone who makes things happen for them. If our life expectancy is going to be as long as scientists claim and the world is going to be as mechanical as the technicians foretell, then we can make a big difference in keeping it human and life-size for the small members of our family. I can hardly wait to be unleashed on them full-time.

AGING:
Growing Old with Grace and Humor

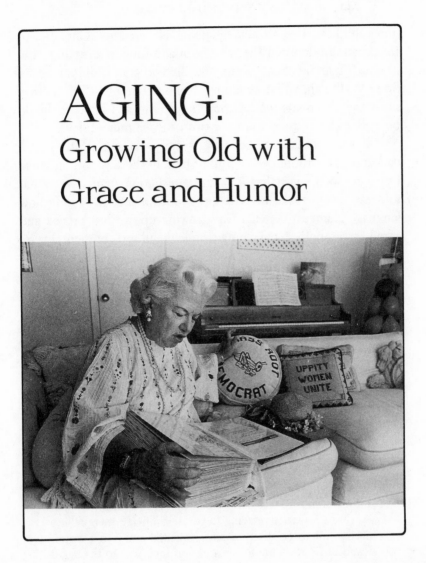

Aging is mind over matter. If you don't mind, it doesn't matter.

TODAY IS MOTHER'S DAY, and I woke at three-thirty as though I were needed to fix a baby bottle. I couldn't go back to sleep. I lay there an hour or more thinking about my distant children and

grandchildren. I've already opened their presents. Christy sent
the geranium doormat that I've been admiring in a catalog. And
my Seattle family, Scott, Jean, and the two grandchildren, sent a
Sony Walkman, which made me feel au courant—"in," as they
say—and also made me feel that they know, as I know, I should
be walking more than I am . . . two or three miles a day.

It was too early to get up. At 3:30 A.M. everything is still
dark outside without even a hint of pink in the sky. So I lay there
trying to do the visualizations and affirmations that Christy has
told me would make my energies work for me. It's funny how
language changes. When I was growing up, we just prayed and
asked for strength. Now young people do all sorts of mental gym-
nastics with gurus and mantras. Christy was a precocious medita-
tor. At sixteen she was exploring her "outer mental" by staring at
three pieces of fruit and a flower. I have a hard time remembering
all the rules, so I made notes when she gave me a lesson in visual-
ization at her New York apartment. I had put the notes in my
billfold. I was glad they were there this morning.

How to Tap into Creativity

Meditation is critically important. Set aside five to thirty
minutes a day. Get comfortable, in bed or on the floor, with
your spine straight.

Be at peace—experience peace—channel yourself to
higher power. Put your thoughts on a shelf and tap into the
universal mind. We are all part of one bigger spirit. When
you meditate, you are part of that universal spirit.

Do affirmations, saying to yourself, Divine energy flows
through me as creativity. I am a talented and gifted writer.
Beautiful words come to me and find their way to the pages
of the book I want most to do.

Thoughts have power and cause things to happen. Visu-
alize yourself in a bookstore, signing, selling, smiling as people want to learn what you know.

Pretend it is now and treat it as happening.

When you are into it, put your thoughts in a pink net or
light bubble and toss them in the air.

"I know this sounds nutty, Mom, but do it, play mental basketball with your thoughts, tossing them about in a light balloon. I make mine pink," Christy said.

She was right. I do feel nutty. But I also feel relaxed. I made my "thought ball" lavender.

"As you meditate each day, and you must meditate each day, you will feel something better manifesting itself in you in totally satisfying ways for the higher good of all concerned. So be it. So it is. It really works, Mom, but don't infuse the practice with desperation or hurry. I just conclude at the end of each session, Let go. Let God."

I like that part the best. I lay there and tried Christy's routine. I went back to sleep for thirty minutes. When I woke the deer were at the feeding cans, knocking them about, so I got up to tend to them . . . like hungry babies. *Don't they know this is Mother's Day!*

What a difference time makes on our demands! Thirty-five years ago I was feeding a baby, today I am into deer feeding. I opened the door on the morning, felt a soft cool breeze, and heard the loveliest sound—the cooing of a dove. A whole covey has settled in the honeysuckle vines. They come up mornings and evenings to eat the leftovers dropped from the bird feeder. I think Christy's advice on meditating worked because the world came alive for me, and I felt propelled to go to early church. Even by myself.

I did and was rewarded. There was only a small crowd, but part of the service was the baptism of a three-month-old baby girl, Carla, looking darling in her father's arms. As the minister took her into the family of God and placed the water on her head, she made—I swear—the same cooing sound of the dove, so soft, but distinct throughout the church. It was a dear and refreshing moment, and it brought back memories of the baptisms of my own children.

I got home early from church, and the phone was ringing. First, a call from my Seattle family, then from Christy in New

York, wishing me a happy Mother's Day. Both before ten o'clock. I couldn't help smiling about that. When Scott and Christy were in college, they were likely to sleep late and then let their social life delay their Mother's Day calls and gifts until late Sunday. Meanwhile I would fume and wonder if they had forgotten me completely on my once-a-year day.

Finally, I made a rule: If you haven't remembered me by ten A.M., you're out of the will. Which really is laughable, because my worldly goods are limited to this house, whatever it holds, and what little is at the bank. I'm not worried about leaving much more. I want to live it up a little myself. I have never believed that worldly goods are as precious an inheritance as the legacy of values: a zest for living, a love of learning, faith in oneself. I love the bumper sticker I am seeing more and more: "Yes, we are spending our children's inheritance."

Aging has become very stylish. All the best people are into it—doing all kinds of jazzy things. Ever since I started writing about it, I hear from hundreds of people wanting copies of a magazine article I have done on the subject or sending me their own thoughts.

"Age is opportunity," someone wrote:

At 100, Grandma Moses was still painting.
At 94, Bertrand Russell was active in international peace drives.
At 93, George Bernard Shaw wrote the play *Farfetched Fables*.
At 90, Pablo Picasso was producing drawings and engravings.
At 88, Michelangelo did architectural plans for the church of Santa Maria degli Angeli.
At 85, Coco Chanel was head of a fashion design firm.
At 84, W. Somerset Maugham wrote *Points of View*.
At 82, Winston Churchill wrote *A History of the English-Speaking Peoples*.
At 82, Leo Tolstoy wrote "I Cannot Be Silent."
At 81, Benjamin Franklin effected the compromise that led to the adoption of the U.S. Constitution.

All of these are famous people, but it is not unusual nowadays for anyone to know a group of people who are aging and active. You have only to look around or answer the phone, and there they are. Across the road from my house is an Austin lawyer, Emmett Shelton, who at eighty-two is still a real estate developer after sixty years in the business. Emmett walked off most of the property lines that now exist in West Lake Hills when it was still undeveloped country. Some claim he did it after a slug or two of whiskey, which he is known to enjoy, because the property lines are wavery. Emmett knew the early pioneers in these parts, the cedar choppers who were the only inhabitants until the 1950s. They chopped cedar in fall and winter and made moonshine during Prohibition. He did well with them, perhaps because he was a good customer. It paid off, and now, in his old age, he has fun giving his land and money away to colleges and universities in the area.

"Why, I remember when your acre was offered to me for four dollars," he said as I grimaced. "That was a long, long time ago!"

Emmett is active in other areas as well. He is a member of the symphony, and with Joyce, his energetic second wife, he takes all the widows on the hill to concerts.

Up the road is Mary Koock, who founded the best restaurant in town, Green Pastures, as a way to feed her family. She is seventy-six now, trim and active. Too active when driving! You risk your life if you accept her offer to drive you somewhere. Once she got four tickets in one encounter with a police officer. When she went before the judge he asked her if she knew about the defensive driving course. "Do you want me to teach it or take it?" she quipped. A fantastic sense of humor has seen her through nine children and fourteen grandchildren, as well as running the family restaurant business from their hospitable home. There were some very hard financial times for her family.

Once, when the gas bill was overdue and the man from the gas company was coming to cut it off, Mary whipped up a cake and brought out party hats. When he arrived, she was standing at the front door waving him in. "We wanted to celebrate your coming," she told him. The gas bill was delayed another few months.

The house was known as the Faulk house, Mary's maiden name, and it was a place that drew friends from all over town to enjoy homemade ice cream on Sunday afternoons during the Depression. I wonder if this kind of scene exists anywhere anymore. It was only fifty-five years ago, but urbanization and the mobile society in which we now live make it seem like a tableau vivant in a museum.

At eight years of age I was one of those guests, because my older brother and sister were friends of Mary's brother, John Henry Faulk. There on the Faulk back porch, someone would bring out the ice-cream custard—twelve eggs, one pound of sugar and two quarts of cream—all within mooing sound of the source. We would pour it all into a gallon holder, and the teenagers would beat the block ice in a tow sack with the flat side of an axe. Rock salt and ice were added alternately, then the process began in earnest. The tow sack was carefully folded, and we children fought to take our turns sitting on the freezer until our bottoms got cold. When the handle would turn no more, the water was drained, the salt carefully wiped away with a well-worn cup towel, the dasher gently removed and placed in a large bowl so we could take turns licking it. Then we waited impatiently while the freezer sat under a shady tree for two hours. Sometimes we couldn't wait. My mouth waters at the memory—the best ice cream I've ever had!

In the evening we were likely to go see the cook—Annie May Finney—in a performance at the nearby Friendly Will Baptist Church in the black neighborhood. One evening we were treated to *The Life of Jesus Christ* in eleven acts. Because the performers had come to the church from their jobs, the audience arrived before rehearsals were finished. So we sat and listened in awe to the voices from the other side of the white sheet curtain, strung along a clothesline. After an hour or so the performers were ready. The curtain was drawn back by two youngsters to reveal the set. One side of the stage was labeled "Hell," the other "Heaven." Jesus Christ was powdered up to make a white face, just like all the pictures in the Sunday-school books. His role was to persuade sinners to believe in him and thereby move across the stage to heaven.

"Leave the cities of sin," he intoned in a deep voice, "the cities of Jerusalem, Dallas, San Antonio, and Manchaca—leave wherever you are and come to me."

When a sinner moved over, we all applauded vigorously. We even saw him perform one of the miracles: turning water into wine before our wide eyes, a ceremony that consisted of adding water to a mason jar that contained red Jell-O. Again we applauded enthusiastically.

In today's vocabulary, I guess one could say that south Austin around the Faulk house and the Friendly Will Baptist Church was one of Austin's first integrated neighborhoods. But that sounds too clinical. The Faulk house was one of the few in the area occupied by a white family. We just thought of everyone as friends and neighbors out there.

Judge Henry Faulk, patriarch of the large family, was an early and open Austin Socialist who read *The Milwaukee Leader* and was an admirer of Eugene V. Debs, once a guest in the Faulk home.

I always think of the judge as being very like Atticus in *To Kill a Mockingbird*. He was the champion of the underdog, who was quite frequently black. The powerless took all their troubles to him. He did what he could and collected little for it. A divorce from Judge Faulk cost five dollars and included some extras: the papers got a red, white, and blue ribbon pasted on them with a gold gum seal—suitable for framing. When Judge Faulk died, his funeral brought the biggest turnout Austin had ever seen from the black community. They had lost a real friend.

The only thing missing from Judge Faulk's funeral was that it couldn't be handled by King Tears Funeral Home, where Annie May had always advised him to go because "they do so well by the survivors. They fan 'em and give 'em ice water whether or not they are kin to the corpse."

Another old friend, I don't quite know *how* old, but she's been around long enough to have played with Tallulah Bankhead in *The Little Foxes*, is Eugenia Rawls. A deeply southern woman, she is still out on the road giving various one-woman performances: *Fanny Kemble, Women of the West,* and *Tallulah.*

Poetry and regional nostalgia are our ties. Recently she came through Austin, and I gathered poetry-loving friends to read aloud some of their favorite verse. Eugenia's was best, something she had written on trains and planes between engagements that was reminiscent of her childhood in the South.

> *Where are the ladies who rocked on porches in*
> *green summer evenings,*
> *Chattering in their soft southern voices,*
> *Wearing dresses of cool voile or dotted swiss with*
> *lace-edged collars,*
> *Pinned with a brooch of cameo.*
> *Delicate faces like crumpled tissue.*
> *Miss Mamie or Miss Mattie*
> *Telling stories of some distant cousin in a distant*
> *time*
> *While a child crawls up onto a lap,*
> *Nestles into a sweetly powdered throat,*
> *Is comforted, made much of,*
> *Petted and praised,*
> *Is lulled to sleep in*
> *Green summer evenings.*

Eugenia is following the advice I got from an eighty-year-old ranchwoman friend, Lavinia Griffith, who drives her well-worn cattle truck to town sporting designer clothes and family diamonds. Lavinia says: "Never give up. Never give up, Liz." She is the best example of why you shouldn't: movement and circulation energize her.

•

SOMEONE ONCE ASKED General Charles de Gaulle, "General, isn't there anything you fear?"

De Gaulle thought a minute and said, "I fear the shipwreck of old age."

That was quite an admission from a man who was proud and seemed immortal, probably even to himself.

I fear loss of memory and experience it every day. "Your mind is full of so many things," I am told. Yet something does happen as one grows older that makes it harder to remember a date, a name, an event. I read that lying on a slant board helps tremendously. But I think dancing, getting angry about something, and speaking up for your beliefs are all circulation boosters.

So is using your brain. The brain is like a muscle; if you don't use it regularly, it will become flabby and useless. An inspiring example of someone who never stopped thinking can be found in Cato the Elder, whose life spanned the third and second centuries B.C. At eighty-four he was writing treatises and studying a new language. Every evening he repeated the events of the day so that he might keep his memory in order. He had to do this, according to psychiatrist Francis J. Braceland, because "anyone living in the midst of such studies must keep his mind in full stretch like a bow and never allow it to go into old age by becoming slack."

Eileen Shanahan wrote me about an interview she had done for The New York Times with Dr. Morris Lewi when he was ninety-seven and still dean of the Long Island School of Podiatry.

"When I asked the inevitable question, 'To what, Dr. Lewi, do you attribute your longevity?' he replied, 'I never wasted time resisting temptation.' "

I find that aging is not just a biological process, but a psychological attitude that is within our ability to control to some extent. Money helps. Even a little, enough to pay for membership in an interesting group or a vacation trip. Most people waste too much time debating whether or not to do something. If you have the slightest urge and the bare means, do it. For instance, the right time to travel is when you have the chance—not when the weather is right or it is convenient for a lot of others, but when *you* have the chance. The older I get, the fewer suitcases I carry. I buy things along the way. I book fewer engagements and stay in each spot longer. I would rather sit on a plaza and sip a cool drink, taking in the flavor of the country, than try to see every museum or redwood. What I really savor is getting the feel of the place.

One of the best trips I ever took was to Spain, where I had a room with a view shaded by an olive tree, a pool, and a copy of James Michener's *Iberia.* Before I got there I planned to make the most of my money with lots of excursions, but I discovered that all the sites in Spain are five hours apart. So I let my fingers do the walking and lay in a hammock under the olive tree and read. I saw Spain from that hammock and the Michener book, but what a good place to absorb it! I would never have read *Iberia* with as much insight if I hadn't been in Spain. But I would never have made it through the heat and dust of that country or come home as relaxed and informed had I not done so under those circumstances. Being allowed to break your own rules is an advantage of aging. I make the most of it.

"Miss Lillian," mother of then-Governor Jimmy Carter of Georgia, once told me, her eyes twinkling devilishly, how she had joined the Peace Corps when she was well over sixty. Our conversation occurred in an upstairs bedroom of the governor's mansion in Atlanta, where she was temporarily out of action. She had been turning somersaults, practicing yoga, or doing something equally surprising, and had broken her shoulder blade.

"Shortly after my husband died, I went down and signed up for the Peace Corps, thinking my children would talk me out of it. They didn't even try. 'Go ahead, Mama, that's wonderful,' they said. So, of course, I had to go."

She ended up working in a hospital that sounded like the black hole of Calcutta. I somehow pictured this southern lady being assigned to desk work. Not at all. It was the operating room for Miss Lillian. And what did she do?

"Why, I helped do vasectomies, honey, to Indian men, and they were so grateful it would make you cry!"

After listening with rapt attention to her description of vasectomies in Calcutta, I asked, "Wasn't the experience repelling in some ways?"

"Oh, no," she replied with zest. "I loved it!"

Miss Lillian returned and traveled through Georgia talking to garden clubs, United Daughters of the Confederacy chapters, and other such groups that rarely hear about either the problems of a country of 800 million or vasectomies. Later she wrote a charming book called *Away from Home*, which includes letters to her children from India.

I once attended a party in the townhouse of the late J. Foley Covington, publisher's representative of Simon & Schuster. Cov was one of the last of a breed of courtly southern gentlemen. He scouted manuscripts for New York publishers. It was sheer enchantment to browse through Cov's library, perhaps the best collection of first editions of southern writers anywhere.

The party was very Atlanta-ish—Miss Lillian standing to receive guests in a soft blue silk dress, her white hair brushed back smoothly, smiling graciously and laughing with the well-wishers. Family surrounded her: "Ruth the faith healer," as someone put it, and Gloria, her coauthor, were standing next to her.

"Are you the motorcycle rider?" a guest asked of Gloria.

"I once was," said Gloria gaily.

I can never be surrounded by Georgians without seeing them all as characters right out of *Gone with the Wind*. Miss Lillian was a twentieth-century avant-garde Aunt Pitty Pat. Judy Carter, something of a Melanie with a gardenia in her hair, but with Scarlett's firm chin and good aim, which could shoot down a Yankee soldier on the stairway if necessary.

Somewhere in that room, I kept feeling, was surely a guest who had been present for Margaret Mitchell's autograph party. Celestine Sibley, *The Atlanta Constitution* columnist who knows everyone and all their family skeletons, introduced me to Yolande Gwin, for years the society writer on the Atlanta papers.

Yolande looks like a veteran southern society writer ought to look: plump from eating thousands of watercress and cucumber sandwiches. Slightly overpowdered and wearing a white organdy embroidered dress, she was ladylike, even as she hiked her dress up to sit down beside me on the Victorian sofa. "I made this dress myself, and I made it too tight," she explained.

"Of course I knew Peggy Mitchell. We were all in the Atlanta Newspaperwomen's Club, and we met once a month at different houses. Peggy had an apartment, and she always had a lot of 'throws.' You know what a throw is, honey—t-h-r-o-w. That's something we use to cover up things when company comes. Peggy had these throws over stacks of stuff, and not for years did we realize that all those evenings we had been sitting on her manuscript. Yes, sitting on *Gone with the Wind*.

"Of course we all knew Peggy was writing the great American novel, and we'd ask her about it from time to time, never really expecting it to show up. Then I got hired by *The Washington Times Herald* to write their lovelorn column, and I had to get caught up with unfinished stories before leaving Atlanta. I called up Peggy and asked, 'What about the book?'

" 'Yolande, I have today sold it to Macmillan and Company!'

"You'd think that would be great news in Atlanta, but it really wasn't at the time. I wrote a rather prosaic announcement to the world, saying, 'Another Atlantan has joined the ranks of distinguished authors.' "

Miss Lillian's book was no *Gone with the Wind*, but its words reflect a woman with a great deal of courage who inspires commitment to humanity in the letters she wrote home to her children about her experiences in that hospital with lepers, starving people, and sick children covered with boils. Some of them died in her arms because she could not bear to have them die alone.

There are many poignant passages, one written on December 2, 1967:

I had a strange experience today. One of the patients is a tall young man who has TB. He went to Bombay to have a lung operation. Before he left, he came by and asked me if I would pray to my God for him. He said he was also going to pray to his God, but he believed that mine might be a little kinder than his. I am convinced that it was really intended for me to come to India. In fact, I believe it so strongly, I don't think I could have *not* come!

As we age, we realize more and more what an important role fortune has played in our lives: chance meetings, opportunities, and luck. Averell Harriman, who was over ninety years old when he died, had spent more than sixty years in public life, probably longer than any man in American history. He once told me the story of a decision, which goes to show by how slender a thread our fate hangs:

"I had just entered Yale and been chosen for coxswain because I was too frail to be a rowing member. Yale had not beaten Harvard in the crew races in years. My father sent me to Cambridge University in England for the summer to learn their winning techniques—an extra beat and a half had made them the top team. I spent several weeks making notes and eating alone in the big dining room, never invited to join the crew. The time for me to go back to Yale arrived—just before their first big race occurred. They warmed up to me: 'You can't possibly go now just before the first race. Can't you delay your departure?' Suddenly they were inviting me to sit at table.

"I went down and canceled my ticket home on the *Titanic*," he said with a smile, anticipating my wide-eyed reaction. Then he added, "That did make a difference in my life."

He kept his options open. He didn't say no. He was as "fluid" as a very impromptu president wanted him to be. At seventy-five, he was virtually picked up by the ears and put on a mission of vast importance, an around-the-world trip "to listen for peace feelers" over the Christmas holidays. That was the expression, although it had a ring of irony because Harriman, while highly accomplished, was already wearing two hearing aids. He tells the story in his own words:

"It was December 1965, shortly before New Year's, and President Johnson called me on the phone and said, 'Averell, have you got your bag packed?'

"I said, 'Well, it's always packed, Mr. President.'

"He said, 'Bob McNamara is here with me. [McNamara was secretary of defense.] He's got an airplane waiting to take you to Europe.'

" 'Where do you want me to go?' I asked.

"He said, 'That's for you to decide.'

"Then he explained that he was going to continue the Christmas pause in bombing the north, and he wanted to get support for his peace move. He wanted to get peace negotiations started, and that was what I was to do. I left that evening at eight o'clock. I had no orders except the general instructions he gave me. So I headed first for Poland."

A month of cease-fire—thirty-seven days, to be exact—was utilized by Harriman on stops at various countries, but Hanoi never lessened its grip. Another effort at looking for peacemakers had failed. But to be still on tap for a president and turn his experience to the call of the country within a few hours' notice was an act of patriotism and revitalized our peace efforts as well as Harriman. What if he had let age stand in his way? Ambassador Harriman died at ninety-four, still eager about life, people, and new ideas.

Public service, such as living outside your own personal needs, is life giving. My mind turns to Rose Kennedy, who at ninety-six still encourages her grandchildren to enter public life, run for office, although her own family has suffered in tragedy and public embarrassment. Her conviction came early as the daughter of Boston's colorful Mayor "Honey Fitz," and she stuck to it. Mrs. Kennedy went out on the hustings herself for Jack, Bobby, and Teddy, believing fervently in the contribution her family could make to the national good.

We aging are increasing by the thousands, role models for

other aging. George Burns won't give Caesar's Palace a ten-year contract because "they might not last that long." Helen Hayes, eighty-six, and Dorothy Kirsten, seventy, hold center stage at Galveston's recently renovated opera house. Horton Foote, who has just won an Oscar at seventy, is master of ceremonies. They are there to help raise money for Lady Bird Johnson's National Wildflower Research Center. She is seventy-four. The audience is filled with friends from across Texas who can afford $500 a seat. Hearing aids, canes, a wheelchair or two, are in good supply. Foote skips a page of his script and introduces Miss Hayes before her turn. Someone backstage whispers his mistake. "Oh, I'm so sorry," he says. "I'll back up." No one minds. The show goes on, and they are all—Dorothy Kirsten's voice, Helen Hayes's Victoria Regina—just as we remembered. Before the final curtain, when Victoria's Diamond Jubilee is over and Helen Hayes is alone on stage in her taffeta gown and her lace hat remembering the day out loud, she says, "As we rounded the corner coming back to the palace, a group of rough-looking men broke through and ran alongside the carriage shouting, 'Go it, old girl, you've done it well.' And, oh, I hope it's true. It is very gratifying—very—to find, after all these years, that they do appreciate all that I have tried to do for them, for their good and for this great country of ours. . . . Hark, they are still cheering, Albert. Oh, if only you had been here."

There wasn't a dry eye in the house. Everyone, the audience as well as the performer, knew what it was like to want to share a moment with someone who was no longer there.

I WENT TO Washington to help raise money for the journalism school at the University of Texas. Walter Cronkite was the star of the benefit. He's our prize alumnus. It was a roast, so quite different from the tone of the Galveston performance.

Walter's mother, now ninety-four, was at his table and warning all the roasters not to say anything bad about her son. How could they? As Dick Cavett pointed out, "Roast Walter? I'll just use the jokes I used at the Mother Teresa roast."

Actually, they should have asked Walter's mother and wife to speak. Both are blessed with a marvelously quick repartee. Walter's mother, Helen, told me that she had a hot romance going. "But the other night I had to slap his face." I asked if he had gotten fresh with her. "No," she replied, enjoying getting the best of me, "I had to wake him up."

Betsy, Walter's wife, can match her mother-in-law. Recently they went to Mexico on their fortieth wedding anniversary and took a room at the same hotel they'd stayed in on their honeymoon. "The last time we were there, I sat in the bathroom and cried," Betsy said. "This time, Walter did."

Having two irreverently funny women in his life has undoubtedly kept Walter young. And, of course, Walter can be funny, too.

On this occasion, he was king for the evening, seated on a giant royal chair with a lighted halo over his head. Age was a theme of his response: "I was there covering the hot news through the Salem witch trials, and the Gettysburg Address, and the scuttling of the *Graf Spee* . . . all the up-to-the-century news. Your generous accolades this evening, with buzz words like venerated, time-honored, revered, kindly, made me feel as though I were at either a wake for George Burns or the opening of Al Capone's secret vaults. You see, I am standing before you as somewhat of a graying fraud. I am not the most trustworthy voice in the land. I am not the most reliable expert on growing old gracefully. I am not really your uncle Walter, and being avuncular does not mean I have the offshore drilling rights to history. I have been in news when it was old, I have been in today when it was tomorrow, in tonight when it was this afternoon. Thank God for the digital watch; otherwise I'd be lost in the sands of time."

Naturally, Walter's mother, Helen, thought his presentation was the best. Helen spends all her birthdays, which come in August, with Walter and Betsy in Edgartown at Martha's Vineyard. On her ninetieth, they honored her with a street dance. Everyone turned out for it; Helen showed up with a broken leg and, of course, a beau in tow. That was one of the few times she was ever willing to sit something out.

Aging inevitably brings a harvest of bad news, friends in trouble with the complexities of life and friends dying. We can listen. We can help. We can be a loyal friend when it's most needed.

WITNESSING HUMAN TROUBLES and yes, tragedies in the lives of friends, is one of the legacies of aging. This year has brought me a bumper crop: a sordid news story about a friend, tying him to charges dug up from old court records by a reporter who uses blood in his ink: a young couple, for whom I have equal affection, at the breaking point of marriage. The tearful wife calls and says her husband beat her up. It is hard to believe. Do I really know someone who beats his wife? I listen for an hour—sometimes listening is the best you can do—and call her mother long distance to tell her that if it were my daughter, I would want someone to call me. I urge her to come and be with her daughter as she decides whether a divorce is right. Is this butting in? I don't care, someone needs to make things better.

Human needs. We can reach out a hand, make a cheerful phone call, drop by with a flower or plant, find a funny movie to take them to, use our own inventiveness, give something of ourselves, be a friend. We "old folks" have known loneliness, isolation, injustice. We should have more empathy than the young. That is a major advantage of age. We have learned to accept people without passing judgment. "Who ever told you life is necessarily fair?" someone once told me. It isn't, but if we can't turn the world around, we can at least bolster the victims.

I can practice that quotation someone sent me for Christmas: "A friend is one to whom one may pour out all the contents of one's heart, chaff and grain together, knowing that the gentlest of hands will take and sift it, keep what is worth keeping and, with a breath of kindness, blow the rest away."

Just this morning I read about a Mrs. Buchter of Manhattan

who wrote the following as her last will and testament: "I leave my best wishes to members of my family (including Morris's family) and want them to get exactly what they gave me—nothing." She bequeathed money to "my closest friends, whom I love, not only because they were interested in my welfare, but because they took me out for drives, had me as their houseguest, and remembered me on every holiday in their homes."

No one had known that she was wealthy, but she divided $2 million among her friends. She knew exactly who her real friends were, and no one was nice to her simply because she was rich . . . because they didn't know it.

The young haven't suffered enough to be tolerant. I have a young relative who suggests that I should drop the friend who's having some problems that are being aired in the newspapers. "Don't get involved," she says.

That reminds me of the time I went to work for the government in the Carter administration. Since the Watergate scandal, the government requires high officials to fill out lots of forms. One said, "Do you know of any relative who might have been arrested or done anything to embarrass the administration?" I simply wrote, "Thousands." I got the job anyway.

"Don't get involved"? My whole life as a reporter, in politics, in life, has involved me in things. Why change now? I am really out of sorts with uninvolved people. The classic case is the story of a crazed man in the Museum of Modern Art who started spraying red paint on Picasso's great painting *Guernica*. The newspaper said that someone in the crowd tried to stop him, and another sightseer shouted, "Don't get involved."

Imagine that! I have neither the time nor the inclination to pass judgment. But I do know I can make things easier for friends while they are walking through the fire. It is my duty, and it is my pleasure. As is so often the case, the giver is the receiver. There is great therapy in giving. My Jacuzzi has become a wailing wall for my friends, young and old. They come up to talk about their careers, their job loss, their husband loss, their defeats. Sometimes they come to celebrate a triumph. I would be lonely indeed if no one needed me.

THERE IS NOTHING more liberating than age. The family is raised and the responsibilities done. There is no boss to please, no school principal to answer to, no husband to nurture. So what can we do with this new freedom?

We don't have to create or establish who we are. We have our identity. We can underline who we have become. We can make more of ourselves. Even the children's writer Dr. Seuss, who is now eighty-two, is into advising "obsolete children" in a new book, *You're Only Old Once*. We have the freedom to be innovative.

Instead of looking at life as a narrowing funnel, we can see it ever-widening to choose the things we want to do, to take the wisdoms we've learned and create something. The world needs creative thinking to find solutions to new problems. Just look at Hands Across America. There it was, an old problem—hunger—and someone was smart enough to provide a new approach.

So, free at last, we look at our own situation and try to shape it to serve our pleasure, our income.

For Katharine Hepburn, it is just doing more of what she has been doing, but using her talent while suffering a life-threatening disease. I watched her in the TV special *Mrs. Canfield Wants to Get Married* and realized how liberated she had made the industry by her own talent. An old person was not being played by a young woman with aging makeup, but by the real thing, someone who had experienced it. She gave television validity.

Luvie Pearson, widow of the columnist Drew Pearson, has never tried to be more than an interesting companion and homemaker. She uses her time teaching bridge to people in a nearby retirement home. It is her talent, and she makes it available to shut-ins. She told me about a woman accountant who has already moved into the retirement home though she is only semiretired.

She works at her accounting firm downtown and is available to the retirees to do their income taxes for a small fee or nothing. What a break to have an in-house accountant.

An old schoolmate wrote, "Older persons should engage in a certain amount of planned selfishness. They have spent many years doing for children, mates, family, and friends. They did untold hours of rituals simply because it was expected by business, family, and society. I say rewrite these rules to give yourself a new independence. Perform a few cartwheels just to show them and yourself. Above all, be gentle with yourself."

We have two qualities that are acquired by age: patience and passion. We have the patience that comes with wrestling with problems through life. Most of us know what it is to suffer, what it is to lose, what it is to be conscious of death. With that comes an understanding that can be shared with all.

We have undoubtedly been passionate about some cause, and that passion can breathe new life into our oldest ills. We can help a confused society find its way back to clarity of purpose. We've been there. My cause is equality of women. I know how much I am needed to remind women if they have any doubts about fighting for their equality. I've been there, I can help them reaffirm their faith in themselves. I know a macho man when I see one, and I can tell these women how to beat him at his game. It's one of my greatest pleasures. I can help good women get elected, and good men, too. Lady Bird Johnson tells me she thinks my white hair lets me get by with a lot. I wouldn't color it for anything.

I think before retirement, or as soon after as possible, you should take stock of your talents and use them. Maybe you're burned out on the old job, but an old hobby opens up a business opportunity. When a friend of mine who was in shipping got recycled out, he took some capital and started a ski resort, something he had always wanted to do.

When another friend, Douglass Cater, now president of Washington College, but philosopher, reporter, and colleague in our White House years, found he had to have bypass surgery, he decided to use the hospital time listening to music he'd never had time to enjoy before. He spent days selecting the cassettes and in the odd waking hours put on his earphones and conquered feeling sorry for himself. In fact, he even wrote a story about it—"How to Have a Heart Operation and Enjoy It"—and sold it to *The New York Times* to help pay for the operation. I spoke to him yesterday and found he's about to have yet another operation, this time on his knees. He says they are worn out from begging for money for the college. "This time I'm going to write a book called *Parts*, for as we live longer, we keep getting pieces here and there replaced." I must remember to call Libby, his wife, the day of the operation. They are a lucky pair but have spent lots of hours in hospitals. Fortunately they have each other to stand by and a sense of humor to keep their spirits high.

I TOOK A QUICK look at the calendar beside my bed to see what tomorrow, Monday, holds. It is June 9. That's a day I never forget. Mama would have been ninety-nine years old. She was born in 1887. I've been thinking about her a lot this last weekend and how much she would have enjoyed the lives of her children and grandchildren. I wish I could have taken her to see Salado's sesquicentennial when I rode in the parade with "Sam Houston." She gave me Salado, all the Salados of my mind that to me are synonymous with "roots, continuity, and values." I wish I had had her around longer, to learn, absorb, ask.

Among the letters I have saved are those my mother wrote to me as I started on my career, which she very much wanted me to pursue. In them I read her constant guidance, her subtle warnings, and her unconditional love. When I informed her about my first job, she wrote:

July 18, 1942

Dearest Child,
    I can't begin to tell you how perfectly, absolutely thrilled I am over your success, which I feel you have created yourself by your industry and ability. I feel, too, that you have made a very substantial contribution to save our country

from those whose "pocketbooks are their principles." You have heard that famous quotation, haven't you? It was made before I was married, when there was a campaign on to abolish the saloon. Jim Ferguson, who was a banker in Temple, took the stump against it and in a speech he made in Temple in his customary eloquent manner, he reared back on his heels and shouted, "Some say the saloon is against their principles," with a resounding slap over the side pocket where the pocketbook was supposed to be. And hasn't he lived up to that? But the more publicity that is given to the findings of the committee, the more the Senate will have to heed them, or explain to the people back home why they didn't.

Now that Creekmore Fath [the general counsel of the committee and a friend from back home] has the first co-ed to ever be vice-president [me], why, look out, Standard Oil, General Electric, & all saboteurs, and remember, "The Eyes of Texas are upon you." It is the Texans who are distinguishing themselves in this war and it is the Texans in Washington who will save our country in governmental affairs, and I wouldn't give anything for the part my children are playing in it. I phoned Sue and asked her to call Leslie and Elgin and she said she'd be thrilled. Then I saw Mrs. Shelley watering her yard and went over to give her the news. She and Mr. Shelley were most interested and enthusiastic and Mr. Shelley said to tell you to put him on your mailing list. Nearly everyone has asked if this job would change your plans to go to Northwestern University next year, which Aunt Alice and Jim have so generously offered to send you. Apparently not,
  Much love, darling, Mama

I was almost twenty-two at the time; my mother was fifty-three. I count the latter young now, but then I always thought of her as one age: old, with masses of white hair done up softly, smiling through deep brown eyes. She was wise, loving, full of news, humor, and encouragement that came across the miles week after week. In a letter to her one of my cousins wrote, "Mary E., you grasp the entirety of life and are philosophical about it." As I grow older, I look more like her—short and plump—and there are even some pictures of my grandson Les and me which at a quick glance look as though they could be of Mama and one of her children. Rereading her letters, I see how much mine meant to her by her slight reprimand when I missed a week of writing home: "Please do write, Mary Elizabeth, for we read and reread your letters and picture ourselves in those places with you. They are like a fresh breeze."

What a lot we lost when we stopped writing letters! You can't reread a telephone call. I am chagrined that my letters to my children and grandchildren are limited to special occasions, while the phone bills are high. I call once a week to check up in snatched messages, relate quick anecdotes, and tell them I love them. But it is not the same as a cherished letter.

The loving parental hand reflected in bold, brave scrawl followed my every footstep. I wrote home with girlish enthusiasm about my visits with Maury Maverick, the unorthodox Texas Democrat who was head of the Small Business Administration of the New Deal. His son, Maury junior, was an old friend . . . well, really, a serious boyfriend from university days. Then in marine boot camp at Quantico, he was back and forth on weekends to his parents' home in Washington, one of those handsome red-stone houses on Jefferson Square near the Mayflower Hotel. One time I wrote my mother, "I think I will marry Maury, Jr." Back came the letter of warning:

> In regard to your last letter, don't be precipitate in any decisions you make. I've found it a good idea never to make final decisions till you are at home and in normal surroundings. When one is away, one's judgment is apt to be influenced by the excitement of strange environments and associations. The Mavericks may be all right, but they have been termed by conservatives "extremists" and by those more outspoken "crackpots," and I want you to think long and hard before you align yourself with anything but the best. The qualifications you mention of an old Texas name and being a Southern gentleman are fine and much to be considered, but I have known people with both of those who were about as congenial to live with as a Bengal tiger with a tin can tied to his tail. Don't think I disassociate background for a minute, but

consider individual characteristics as well. However, you
should be a fairly good judge of character by now, only keep
your eyes open, and not in a credulous baby-like stare either.
And remember, the acid test is a house party or pack trip over
the mountains. I don't want you to miss your years in college
[Northwestern graduate school in journalism] next year, and
I imagine you would rather go into it with no entangle-
ments. . . .

I was annoyed because I knew that my mother was not generally one to label people. I sent an impudent reply.

Mrs. Sutherland, for your information, the Mavericks are not
crackpots, they are very nice refined people. Mr. Maverick is
a character. Besides, the only people who call them that are
Tories. And my campus political experience taught me one
thing and that is not to give a darn what people called you, as
long as you know you're right.

What a goddess of wisdom she was, and how much her enthusiasm for my life and my work meant. She was always supportive. I was unconscious of her influence at the time. Washington
held me spellbound, still does in many ways, though I think of it
now as the place where I lived from my springtime to autumn
years.

The letters written in those first days of 1942 were prophetic:

My first day in Washington has been a success. I have only
been hit by two cars and one ten-ton truck. Just kidding! I
created a sensation when I offered my place on the bus to an
elderly lady, and I deserve all my merit badges for hiking
around the White House. I've decided to live in that house
someday so get that Latin-American block of votes on the
line pronto.

I go to work Monday writing stories. If I'm any good at
it, Senators Bone and La Follette will get me an appropria-
tion.

I'm really enthusiastic since no publicity work has been
done so far and it is an opportunity for me to make the job
what it can be. Investigation of the Sterling Products begins

Monday. They probably have the blackest record of any chemical company in the world so things will be popping. Particularly since their retainer lawyer [the famous Tommy Corcoran] arrived, had lunch with Creekmore and offered him a job at $25,000. Creekmore refused, of course, and Mr. Corcoran has been hopping ever since. He is perhaps the most powerful lawyer in the country, rode into every Washington department on the Roosevelt bandwagon, and has a hold in every bureau. In fact, he may win the fight but he's probably more scared over this University-of-Texas-ex Fath than anyone else. [Fath was earning the top Senate salary of $7,500 a year. But these were the days when U.S. senators were making $10,000.]

I do hope that I can make a success in Washington. It will be the only way to repay you for your sacrifices and them for their generosity. Don't worry about me. I'm having a wonderful time. Use the money for something useful like some clothes for yourself. They certainly give you a new outlook on life.

All my love, Liz

She didn't use the money for herself, of course, but kept offering it to me by mail and sending along $50 or $25 here and there so I could make little trips to Boston and New York. She helped make that summer an unforgettable one of spreading my wings, of being free from exams and studying, of having that bachelor of journalism and the wide world in my hand. And oh, how I relished every moment.

Rereading these letters, I am surprised at how conscious I was of history, and how it still lingers in all my travels, making me want to know who walked there first, whose footsteps brought that ancient soil to now. I must have sensed that my homebound mother, tied to family responsibility, lived vicariously through my letters.

Letters from back home remind me of the draft boards and ration books of the time. Ever present was my mother's encouragement for me to make the most of my time in Washington, never a note of nagging to come home and help out. My father had had a stroke. Money was short. While she wanted me to know of it, she was encouraging my discovery of life in the big cities.

> When I was interviewing the Travis County Sugar Rationing Board, the girl who handled my application for sugar to make preserves with asked me if I was your mother. She said she knew you in high school. She said she wished now she had gone to the University but she went to business school instead. That's the reason I want you to make use of all opportunities you can. If you don't, you will wish in a few years you did. Let me know when you wish me to send you the extra money you need when and if you go to New York.

And to New York I went for my first visit in 1942. I wrote her every detail. As I reread the letter, I suspect many other young women and men have written about their first visit to New York. It's a classic experience.

I was with an old *Daily Texan* friend from university days, Elgin Williams. It was a friendship without romance, maybe the best kind for a discovery of New York.

> The sidewalks of New York have been worn down an inch after this past weekend when two Texans wandered New York with $20 worth of change and a lot more gall. Even O. Henry who starved in Greenwich Village for three years never saw as much of New York on as little money as we did. But let me tell you about it from the beginning.
>
> We got into Penn Station and took the escalators up while Elgin made a few bitter remarks, "If you're fighting for equal rights for women, then why in hell don't you carry your own suitcase?" all of which I ignored. People were hurrying everywhere, loudspeakers calling about trains, every corner filled with a soldier saying goodbye to a sweetheart or a wife. When we walked out, Elgin had to lead me along while I gazed heavenward at all those skyscrapers. New York has never seen a more complete tourist. Those buildings just keep going up and up and up. We took a bus over to Elgin's friend where he was staying. All the way I hung out of the bus window looking at real, live pawnshops with the three

balls and listening to the new hit tunes that came blaring out of the little music shops.

Elgin had talked about a little spot that would be the perfect place to eat, different and cheap, and as we were worried about funds, "cheap" sounded good to me. We hopped on the subway and were whisked to Greenwich Village, and pushed back through the crust of the earth to the surface in that wonderful New York way.

Well, "cheap" was right. In fact, the meal was free. Do you know where we had supper? At the Salvation Army Center down there. I had read about the famous center where you sit in a little church and listen to a minister preach for awhile and then they give you a bowl of soup, but I never thought I'd have dinner there. Now, Mama, don't worry because it was wonderful fun. There weren't but three other people there and the preacher knew we were just making a sociological study because he came back and talked to us a lot about saving souls in the Village.

Then, back to Broadway by subway which is all dimmed out because of the war. We went to several theaters to try to get in but all were sold out. Finally, we got the last two tickets for standing room at *The Eve of St. Mark,* a new Maxwell Anderson play with Aline McMahon [sic] which is one of the best plays of his I've ever seen, I'll say. It's the only play of his I've ever seen. It had been raining and we stood like drips in the back until the curtain went up and we made a bee-line for the only two seats left—$5.50 seats for the measly $1.65 paid to get in. Everytime the usher would pass we'd just know the people who belonged in those seats had come and we would sink a notch lower. I wish I could describe the awful feeling you get when you see the little flashlight flickering toward you. However, we kept them until the second act when the capitalists arrived and out we went back to standing room. After the lights went out again, I spied two buckets of sand handy in case of an air-raid so we each grabbed a bucket, plonked them in the aisle right by the people who'd just turned us out and saw the rest of the show from the buckets of sand. Thank God for the Sahara!

We hopped on one of those two-decker buses and rode up to Central Park. I kept feeling like I was going to topple over. Then we tried to bargain at Central Park with one of the drivers who takes you around in a horse and buggy. He wouldn't yield from his $3.00 for one-half hour's ride. So we nailed Elgin's heel back on his shoe and walked through the park—huge with large lakes, swans, benches and statues.

Finally, we walked over to Columbus Circle where all the radicals make speeches but it was too late so we bought hot chocolate at a little garden stand and called it a day—a great, wonderful day.

Sunday the rain had stopped. We ate breakfast at an automat where you put a nickel or dime in a slot and a fried egg comes out all salted and peppered for you. During breakfast, we had a good intellectual discussion on what technology is doing for America. We caught another double-decker bus down Fifth Avenue and loved seeing store after store bearing the names of famous trademarks I've seen advertised in *Mademoiselle:* Saks, Lord and Taylor, Yardley, Bonwit Teller, Chase National Bank. Elgin boomed forth with Easter Parade all the way, much to the delight of the driver since we were the only ones on the bus. The park at the entrance of Greenwich Village was filled with children playing on slides and see-saws (far too many kids for the number of slides) and perambulators. I wonder why it is you see so many more in New York. The day was clear and the artists were hanging out their paintings for Sunday tourists. Most of the paintings were pretty bad, too many loud colors, but the artists were the best picture themselves. They wore berets and some had paint dabbed on their clothes. The haircuts were something. You could tell they were done with scissors hastily on Sunday morning before going out to sell their wares. Newspaper notices, which they live for, were torn ragged-edged out of the paper and pinned by their displays even if the artist was barely mentioned.

Looking down the long narrow streets you see every piece of clothing hanging from windows, women shaking their brooms and mops out of third story windows to the street, vendors with little wagons selling wares. And how the place smells of garlic and red pepper!

Walking into the heart of the village which most tourists miss you see a portrait of the Dead End Kids unfold before your eyes. It was heartbreaking—gangs of boys playing football in those crowded streets, shouting and hollering, dropping the ball in the gutter. On one corner were four little boys much younger than Billy [my youngest brother] sitting on the corner playing poker and betting with pennies. There were little girls (they start wearing lipstick at age 8) who jabbered back and forth on the steps or shouted to their mothers two stories up. It wasn't a very pretty kind of world and seemed to me right off the pages of *What Makes Sammy Run.* Little wonder the arsenals of democracy have to be tested every twenty years when they have a weak link like this one.

Back on the artists' sidewalk exhibit was one little lady with a water color of the Ark and the plaza which I bought. She was 90 years old and has lived all her life in the Village. Then we ran into a wonderful character, a man standing in front of a painting of footsteps in the sand and saying with all the gestures of an actor, "And footsteps are left like scented rain." Elgin said it stunk but you know me, I grabbed Elgin by the hand and held him there while we got in a conversation with him. He is a poet but can't sell anything so he teaches ballet to two or three little Italian girls each Sunday morning. This keeps him up for a week. He said he used to live next door to Thomas Wolfe when Wolfe lived in the Village and that got Elgin interested so we sat down on a bench and talked. He talked with gestures and poetic words. While we were there the church bells rang and he put one hand to his ear and said, "Hark the angelus!" The poet told us about being in a show with Grace Moore before she was famous. Now he says that when she saw him two years ago, she told him he looked like seven miles of bad road.

We headed to the top of the Empire State and the view is worth every cent of the $1.80 it cost. On one side the East River, Brooklyn Bridge and Wall Street. On the other, the Hudson, New Jersey, and to the southeast the Statue of Liberty. You can't imagine the feeling you get seeing the tops of skyscrapers for miles and miles and realizing that here, set on this little island of Manhattan, are the same number of people as in all of Texas.

In the afternoon we went to the famous Metropolitan Opera House and bought tickets for the Ballet Russe. We got the cheapest ones at $1.56 and entered the hall where famous singers of the world have sung for half a century. It was like a bit of the old world with giant candelabras, four stories of boxes, red velvet rugs, and we began our climb to our seats at the top of the top balcony. I needed a mountain goat usher and Elgin swore an eagle was sitting in the seat next to him. I'm sure the people who save their money and hunger all week to buy a ticket to the ballet appreciate the art more than the ones in the boxes. The ballet was wonderful, two famous ballets, a Chinese legend, the other a Russian legend, and the last number a ballet of the southwest. Somehow I hadn't pictured cowboys in ballets shoes but they did a good job of portraying the west. I think when an art, like ballet, can interpret 20th century life equally well with the 11th and 12th century life, it will always survive.

I checked out of the hotel so I wouldn't have to pay for two nights and we took our bags to a locker in Penn Station, then a bus over to Battery and Wall Street, but it was too dark to see much. We bought a couple of hot dogs and munched them back to the subway and went to the theater in Rockefeller Center. Sonja Henie's "Stars on Ice" extravaganza was playing. She wasn't in it but the show was great. Our seats were so close to the stage, I thought one of the skaters would land in my lap. Elgin said he wished we could compromise and get seats in the middle of a theater sometime so we could see the stage. First, on the rafters at the ballet, and practically under the stage at the ice follies. Twinkle Watts, the six-year-old star of ice-skating, had two numbers. She's a darling little girl. After that we took the bus to Penn Station and boarded the 12:30 A.M. train, slept to Washington. I've never been so exhausted but it was a wonderful week-end and I'll never forget it. Oh, yes, I forgot to tell you that on Saturday night we passed the back of *The New York Times* where the papers were coming down the shoots and pitched into trucks. We stood there in child-like admiration and awe of one of the world's greatest newspapers. Elgin said, "It won't be long until we'll live upstairs." I don't doubt it about him. He has a brilliant mind and will probably be very famous someday. I really enjoyed seeing New York with him. He has that nonchalance that doesn't gripe if his feet are wet, or if we get shuffled in the crowd, and he has the intelligence and interest to try to see New York from every angle, not just Broadway and Fifth Avenue. It was great to see New York for the first time this way, on a shoe-string, and still see the bright lights. I can appreciate all the trials of the young writers who remain obscure in a Greenwich Village garret, the wonderful exultation of the motorman and his wife who sit close to the ceiling of the Opera House to see the ballet, and thousands of other feelings that go through you in New York. I didn't have time to see Grant's Tomb but that doesn't worry me a little bit.

All my love to you and keep writing. Your letters really brighten up my day,

Liz

WHAT FUN IT WAS to write of my experience to my mother—she was always enthusiastic about all I was doing. My mother died at sixty-three. I doubt her death was necessary, if only medicine had been more advanced.

That is a bounty that this generation will have, and I hope they think of it as a bounty. Their parents, aunts, and older relatives are going to be on hand a lot longer. I hope they make the most of them. They have a lot to learn from them. It's an attitudinal thing, and what I have been witnessing in print and in conventions I attend foretells a big change . . . for the better.

Once when I was feeling sorry for myself I decided it would be healthy to outline my fears of aging. There were five:

1. Not feeling needed
2. Not feeling a sense of purpose
3. Losing control over my destiny
4. Not feeling loved
5. Not being touched

This year has taught me I can correct, almost wipe out, those fears. I can

1. help meet human needs;
2. reestablish my identity with my family and my community;
3. use new freedoms and new time to give joy and to take it;

4. renew myself by exposing my brain to new ideas, thoughts, and active people;
5. give love.

I went out to the American Association of Retired Persons' national convention, which drew twenty-two thousand people from fifty to ninety-four years of age. What I discovered was they looked thirty to one hundred. But no one was there to nurse complaints. All were looking for ideas on living their lives more fully.

AARP is the fastest growing organization in the nation with nearly 25 million members. Its director, Cyril Brickfield, asked the question: "Who are these people?" And he answered it, "They are our fathers and mothers, grandparents, aunts and uncles, and friends. They've seen this country through the flu epidemic of 1918, the Depression, the wars, and the lindy hop, the conquest of polio, and the economic progress of the 1950s. They've worked hard, to earn a living and for the sense of joy that comes from giving of themselves without expecting anything in return. They personify the work ethic and the volunteer spirit that built this country."

Aging does bring serious problems: health concerns, diminished financial resources, and isolation. So, what can we do about it?

There were seminars on how to handle money, how to plan a new career, how to be an effective volunteer, how to laugh, how to love.

George Burns at ninety provided an evening that proved the old vaudevillian's sense of timing, gags, and songs had not diminished because his body was more shrunken and frail. For an hour he stood, danced a bit, sang, and delivered his jokes without a note, without a break, without a chair. "I'm older than most countries," he said. "I still like the girls. Some of them are younger than my tuxedos."

Dr. Ruth, the advice giver on sex, told a spellbound audience how to indulge as prowess fades. She didn't mince words.

She addressed the issue directly, facing the need for sex and how to achieve it. "Use it or lose it," was her advice.

There were a lot of people there who are doing just that. They were the gray heads who often gathered in the four Jacuzzis to talk after the meetings. I was at first shocked, then pleased, that so many were attending with a "friend" who had become a companion. I found myself envying them.

After the convention I met my grandson in Anaheim, and he was a marvelous companion. We did Disneyland, Knotts Berry Farm, and the beach. We went to a movie, which he picked. Living two thousand miles from Seattle, I am going to do more of that kind of thing: having a rendezvous with my grandchild halfway across the country instead of waiting, waiting, waiting for an annual visit at Christmas or birthdays. I think he enjoyed it, too, and learned. He kept hearing me talk about senior citizens, since I was fresh out of the AARP convention, and asking bus and taxi drivers if they had a senior citizen discount. One taxi driver asked, "Where you folks from?"

"Seattle and Texas," I replied.

My grandson piped up in explanation, "The senior citizen is from Texas."

When we said good-bye to return to our homes, I told him, "We've got to keep meeting like this. Where would you like to meet next time?"

He bowled me over with his answer, which came with a mischievous gleam in his eye after a long pause. "Well, I've always wanted to see Korea."

I think I'll try to talk him into Yellowstone National Park.

As I LOOK BACK on all that has gone into the aging of Liz Carpenter, I wonder how much of life is planned for us. How much just happens? I always felt that life just unfolds as you go along and that luck has a great deal to do with it, being in the right place at the right time. Now I see it with wiser eyes, and I wonder if there isn't something more. Almost two decades have passed since I lived those intense years at the White House, and as I ex-

amine the family records in old trunks and other archives, I begin
to see myself as part of the subconscious continuum of voices that
have spoken from the people of this republic, this democracy,
since its beginning. I am a temporary heir of past learning.

What did it all teach me—the years I worked in Washington, as reporter and public official? To get the facts, search for
truth, check bases, pick brains, sort out what is valid and what is
false while juggling deadlines. Persuade the reluctant. Rally a
constituency. I learned all this as part of my daily work. And
then, the small lessons: how to write a speech for presidents and
cabinet members, how to handle tough questions from reporters,
how to make things happen, how to utilize government to
achieve the ends of the people, how to plan a presidential trip,
how to sidestep wrong suggestions with an alternative instead of a
"no." These were the quick skills I acquired by necessity. I
watched the Great Society as it emerged. I thrilled to it and
espoused it. And I am convinced that a democracy is not to be
operated to do the least, but to help the most. I learned in my
four decades in Washington that one person can make a difference.

From FDR's thirties we learned that government can be
mobilized to lift a people's hope and spirit, to use government as
the tool to provide jobs and security.

From Truman's forties we learned that in adversity we could
become a united people with a strong faith in ourselves.

From Ike's fifties we realized there are periods when it is
helpful—even necessary—to mark time, digesting what has gone
before while waiting for the next surge of activity.

In the sixties, when that surge came, we learned that even in
a time of affluence—unlike the thirties—government can be used
as an influence to attack the old entrenched evils that threaten to
corrode a society: bigotry, injustice, poverty, and illiteracy.

The seventies brought a confusion of images we are still trying to sort out. But we did learn from a national trauma—Watergate—how secure our national institutions are.

In the eighties we are still watching the events pile up from which the lessons of this decade will be learned. For myself, I do not like the eighties so far. I see a return to the worship of materialism that I thought had disappeared. But as an incurable optimist, I do not think this present climate of pandering to the worst of our national spirit will long survive.

The pendulum keeps swinging, and each forward thrust moves us on. We are a better nation now than we were in 1936 . . . and hopefully one hundred years from now we'll be better still.

THE NEXT ADVENTURE

TODAY I AM SIXTY-SIX years old. Another September first! It's been a year since I first sat down to relate what I know of life as I have seen it, lived it, and learned from it.

Here at my window and my word processor I have run the fullness of seasons since last September when I began this book. Never have I been so conscious of weather: the glory of the sun-

276

rise, the fall mists that hover over the river as November comes, the crisp cold of winter, the thunderheads and slashes of lightning, and the marvelous fragrance of grass after a spring rain. Even the summer heat has its own charm with the steady sound of the katydids. I have loved this year of discovering me, thinking about life as I have never concentrated on it before.

Even as I struggled to remember and write it down, I have felt a gratification that comes from doing something you are likely to put off forever. Now—free at last! It is done, far from perfect, but done as well as I can. It was good to wrap it up in a year because I hope a lot of carefree days and years are in front of me. Now I can be more creative in filling them. It is a matter of pacing, walking hand in hand with your own conditions.

A new crop of baby deer have been born, fed daily by their "mamas," Henrietta up the hill and me, here in my last-lap house—the house for the happy hour of my life. To my delight I have had a year with them now, feeding them, talking to them, and they have learned to come when I play the soundtrack music from *Out of Africa.*

"You have created your own Serengeti," Lady Bird says from the Jacuzzi as she looks toward my "herd" of fourteen. I started out with just a few, and now, almost every day, there are twelve or more.

It has been a year of staying in one place, unusual for me. I liked it better than I thought I would. I've made peace with being at home, peace even in living alone. It's very relaxing not to be packing all the time, not to care about papers being stacked around on tables or having a perfect house. There is a beautiful cobweb an energetic spider has spun across the alcove in the living room. It can wait.

Writing the book has also been an excuse to keep phone calls from fragmenting my day. The answering machine takes the number, and I return the calls in late afternoon. This isn't the former me. My old instincts as a reporter kept me from letting a phone ring more than twice. I was eager to know what the world was bringing me in terms of news or conversation. President

Johnson was worse about ringing phones than I was. Even in the Oval Office he would answer it before his staff could, often with the curt salutation, "This is Jack Valenti's secretary."

This year has taught me I can live without constant phone calls. Silence is restful. And I have learned that people will come to me if I ask, instead of my rushing off to meet them for lunch downtown. A couple of spunky friends arrived for an appointment one day with a basket of food, saucily announcing, "Meals on Wheels."

It was Alice Roosevelt Longworth who taught me the lesson of letting people come to me. Once she confided to me at a Washington cocktail party, "Just sit down and see who turns up. The most interesting people will."

I couldn't do it then; I am better at it now. And it pays off in conserving my energy, giving myself time to fill up my senses with the beauty of nature, tastes, and fragrances. I like to feel the wind, drink in the moon, smell the honeysuckle, hear the violins, revel in the dance of life.

Time—I have a whole new understanding of it. When I was young, time was a clock signaling me to class or to deadlines. Someone defined time as an hour that seemed like a minute in a kiss, a minute that seemed like an hour when touching something red hot.

For me, time is milestones, and I am finishing this year with a sense of new freedom to use the last golden grains of the hourglass for my happiness. For me, time is running out. It may be days, months, or years. But there will be the final departure.

I find myself writing more last letters, sending more flowers, attending more memorials. Here on this hill, I live daily with life and death. In this year alone, the widow population has increased by one. My back doctor and friend, Dr. John Buckley, died after a tragic and rapid bout with cancer, leaving Suzanne and their little girl. I've lost my accountant and neighbor, Carl Kraus. He died at forty-five of a heart attack, a special loss to his family as well as to the high school his twins graduated from just two weeks after his funeral. He had been an enthusiastic PTA member and fund-raiser for the band.

On the brighter side, my young neighbors, the Barbees, just had their first child. The whole street was filled with construction trucks during the building of the nursery. Seeing life and death so close makes me treasure more the moments with friends, with this home—my fifth—where I have lived now ten years, where I can come to find relaxation and peace of mind and spirit. I believe that if life is worth doing well, so is dying.

I think of Scottie Fitzgerald Smith, daughter of F. Scott and Zelda Fitzgerald, who died this June in Montgomery, Alabama. Her death came after a year of cancer and treatment that didn't work. She went home, started her "archaeological digs," and mailed all her friends clippings that she had saved about them and thought they might like to have. Our mutual friend, Marie Jemison, wrote me, "Scottie is checking out. She is throwing out the stacks of newspapers she has saved all her life. She told me, 'I don't want anybody to come in here and find all this stuff.' Her children came last week to choose from Zelda's paintings."

I remember those delightful pixie paintings done during the Fitzgeralds' days in France in the Roaring Twenties, which Scott and Zelda epitomized and captured in books as well as life.

Scottie sent me several batches of old Washington clippings of my husband and me in those days we all shared. In one we were dancing at the Indian embassy. In another, Les was doing the "frug" with Mrs. Nehru. The clippings were full of the kind of chitchat about parties that Washington thrives on. They brought a flood of memories. I used the clippings as an excuse to call her once more.

"We must be in communication," I said, "because I was just beginning to write my chapter about Washington entertaining, so your clippings will be helpful."

"Well, you can't believe how much stuff you can get rid of as long as the stamps hold out," she said with a tiny laugh.

She was weak, her voice soft as chiffon, placid as a night under the stars of Alabama or the Riviera, both home to her.

We chatted about old days in Washington and on the campaign trail. Finally, we got around to the inevitable, "How are you?"

"Not so good," she replied. "So this is a farewell call."

"It can't be. We all need you, me especially," I replied.

"I would love to read your book," she said, and being Scottie, always generous, she added, "You've been spectacular."

I rushed on with words and memories about traveling on the *Grassroots Grasshopper* when she and I went campaigning for the Democratic ticket. *She* had been spectacular, and unforgettable, too. I could remember how appealing she'd been standing on the stage in Birmingham and saying, "I am Scottie Fitzgerald Smith in Washington, but in Alabama I am Zelda's daughter." You could sense the ripple of pride in the audience. Her speech was written like the fairy tale "The Emperor's New Clothes"—a different kind of political speech, but there was no way to miss her point. She was telling her Alabama homefolks not to vote for Nixon. They cheered her. She was one of their own with the same gutsy forthrightness they knew in Zelda. Finally we ended the memories and said our good-byes.

I hadn't foreseen how very soon the phone call would come. Only two days later, I was awakened in the early morning with the call that Scottie had died peacefully in the night. She would be buried in Maryland with her mother and father, Scott and Zelda. They were—the three of them—all remarkable people whose talents and style set them apart from the crowd. For me, they will ever be American cameos set in time waltzing in the moonlight on a southern veranda. Too many good people leave our midst long before we have finished talking with them. The next day the final batch of clippings came.

THIS HAS BEEN a reflective year. I've thought more about living and dying than ever before. My goal—to write down my thoughts so my grandchildren can know me after I have departed this world—has propelled me to think about my times, my family, my friends, and my philosophy.

It's a generational thing, I believe, taking time to think "me." My generation was so hell-bent to get out into the world, make a living, and do it in a romantic and interesting way that we didn't stop to analyze ourselves the way our children do. We were, without knowing it, the "we" generation, in contrast with the "me" generation we gave birth to and raised in more affluent days than our own.

I feel as if I have been on my own psychiatrist's couch, and it has been revealing. It has forced me to pull out old letters, read through old scrapbooks, and organize clutter and loose papers that I've saved without really knowing why.

What was I thinking of so many years ago when I clipped these lines from Yeats's "When You Are Old":

> When you are old and grey and full of sleep,
> And nodding by the fire, take down this book,
> And slowly read, and dream of the soft look
> Your eyes had once, and of their shadows deep;
>
> How many loved your moments of glad grace,
> And loved your beauty with love false or true,
> But one man loved the pilgrim soul in you,
> And loved the sorrows of your changing face. . . .

Whatever I might have been thinking then, I find it a reassuring message now.

I have always found it hard to throw anything away. I treasure old school pictures, graduation certificates, and mementos of all sorts. I wonder if anyone else will ever have time to pack and move them or even look at them. I have wondered what I should do with them. They could go to library collections. My children can have a go at them first. But where do these things really belong? I can help out by making some decisions now, while memories are fresh in my mind.

Lately, I've caught myself thinking quite a lot about what to do with my possessions. I'll be walking through the house and suddenly remember that the Salinas painting of bluebonnets goes to Scott, the other Salinas with the yellow flowers and live oak trees goes to little Les, along with the picture in my bedroom of the little boys climbing the tree. I bought it because it made me think of him. Christy has greatly admired the painting of an avenue of trees from Luxembourg that President Johnson gave her father, and she should have it. I know my daughter-in-law, Jean, who has her own silver and china from old friends in Mississippi, will understand that I want my daughter to have my silver and china, the Lenox with the roses that Les chose when we married and the Portuguese pottery with the geraniums, most of which Christy gave me. Jean is into great art, so the painting I commissioned Fleur Cowles-Meyer to do for this house, and which is one of the most impressive items in it, will go to Jean and Scott. The slate nautical coffee table, which Les had in his office, will go to Scott and eventually to my grandson. All my phonograph records and stereo equipment, old and new, will be just right for my step-granddaughter, Bonnie, who has several sets of grandparents to Les's two.

Am I just doing my lawyer out of an addendum to my will?

My children will be imaginative about friends and family members who get various mementos: my gigantic cookbook collection, special pictures, or personal items. So many people have been close to my life, and I'd love each of them to have a reminder of a moment shared, friends as well as family.

What shall I do with all the thousands of photographs I've accumulated? For instance, I have one of "the Duchess"—my first boss, Esther Van Wagoner Tufty—posing with Wallis Warfield Simpson, the duchess of Windsor, in 1942. Strange how I came upon it after all these years in a drawer the day before the duchess of Windsor died. It was the timing that struck me. I had even forgotten I had it. Then a week later, "my" duchess, Esther Tufty, died. It's spooky how these "messages" seem to be timed. But I have lived long enough to know that one does receive signs: "There are more things in heaven and earth, Horatio, Than are dreamt of in your philosophy."

Who will treasure as I have this letter of admission to Eleanor Roosevelt's press conferences?

June 15, 1943
Dear Miss Sutherland: The Standing Committee of Mrs. Roosevelt's Press Conference Association has accepted your application for membership in this group. Thank you for sending the dues so promptly. Cordially,
Mary Mason, Secretary-Treasurer

I'll never forget the day this very green reporter with the brand-new press pass climbed the majestic stairway to the second floor of the White House to attend, with thirty other newswomen, Mrs. R's press conference. My first one! She was there, standing at the head of the stairs, slightly stooped, smiling, greeting each of us individually. Like thousands of others, I felt her personal warmth.

Mrs. Roosevelt greeted me, and I moved to the chairs around the tea table and the largest silver service I had ever seen. I watched her as the rest of the women reporters arrived.

"Oh, hello, Martha," Mrs. R said with an affectionate giggle. "Whenever I see you I think of bad housing."

Martha was Martha Strayer, who had just finished a series of stories about the slums of Washington. Actually Martha looked like bad housing. She wore the sturdy flat heels and black suit that was the customary dress of women reporters in Washington at that time.

Can you imagine thirty newswomen in hats and white gloves? But that was the dress of the day. There were no microphones and no cameras at the press conference. TV coverage was years away, and radio programs for women were confined to, as "the Duchess" told me, "what to do with a tired piece of lettuce." We were all pad-and-pencil reporters, wishing every first lady was just like "Mrs. R.," who made news and lifted our copy off the society pages.

Every newswoman in this country should be forever grateful to her for being news and allowing only women to cover her press conferences. There had been few newswomen before, only the ones who covered parties for the society pages of Washington. By creating something in our behalf, she forced the AP, the UP, and *The New York Times* to put a woman on their staffs. She opened doors for women that would never close.

Mrs. Roosevelt did not let herself be the whole story. She had two or three women from the women's bureau, Ellen Woodward, Mary Keyserling, and Secretary of Labor Frances Perkins—those remarkable women who authored so much of the New Deal. She turned to them as we sipped tea from the fragile White House china and made notes. "Frances, tell them what you are doing about Social Security and wage and hour laws," she would say.

She was always inclusive, always concerned. Finally, a social writer had to ask the inevitable question: "At the state dinner on Tuesday, Mrs. R., what will you wear?" Mrs. Roosevelt looked to her secretary, Melvina Thompson. "Oh, dear, Tommy, what shall I wear, the black chiffon or the blue lace?"

Such was my introduction to Mrs. R, press conferences, and the national social conscience.

THERE ARE CURSES as well as blessings in having saved everything, carrying it with me from house to house, fearful of losing a part of my life. Why did I save all this stuff to cart around? I found out why in putting together the jigsaw of my life while writing this book.

Maybe it represents what my life has meant—my "persona," which I carry with me all the time as a snail carries its shell. One friend says that in her mind's eye my shell is a hymnal, a unique piece of jewelry, my white hair, a question mark that travels with me, the reporter, and some very worn shoes. I do wear out shoes quickly. I think now, as I contemplate the last house, that the ultimate home of the inner "me" will eventually have traveled from Salado to . . . well . . . heaven.

"In my father's house are many mansions. If it were not so, I would have told you." That line from the Bible, John 14:2, keeps going through my head as I think about the next house, my final and ultimate home.

This present happy hour house is the perfect setting for exploring that inner me. I hope I'm lucky enough to be here to enjoy the beautiful view, my own bed, and a sense of peace and comfort until the golden moment of departure. When that moment comes, I want a good exit line. It would be hard to top Vice-President Alben Barkley's. When he died, he had just preached a sermon at a church in Virginia and ended with "I would rather be a servant in the house of the Lord than sit in the seat of the mighty." Then he dropped dead. I think Barkley, who loved the thundering roll of words in the United States Senate, would have been most pleased with his final performance.

General Arthur MacArthur, Douglas's father, provided the best drama. He was attending a reunion of his old comrades in arms and opened his remarks with, "This is the last speech I'll ever make." It was. He dropped dead at the end of it. His orderly walked forward to the flagstaff at the podium, took down the flag and spread it tenderly over the body, and then fell dead beside the general. Not bad! So much better than needles and tubes and gasping one's way out of this world.

General Sam Houston must have relished his death scene. Houston, the subject of many legendary stories, was always under attack by the Texas newspapers. At the end, he summoned in two reporters who had been sitting out his death under a tree in front of his home near Huntsville. He motioned one to sit on one side, the other on the opposite. In a death-rattling voice, he said, "Boys, I want it recorded that I died like Jesus Christ, between two thieves." It's really too good a story to be true, but I like it enough to repeat it, and I hope he had such satisfaction.

Tallulah Bankhead used a single word in her parting: "Bourbon." And Oscar Wilde's last words were, "Either that wallpaper goes or I do."

I could do worse than simply repeat my grandson's wisdom: "All you have to do is believe in yourself and things start happening." If I believe in myself, in the way I have lived, and am relaxed about the next stop, my final home, heaven, will be there for me, even more joyous than this life.

Most of my life has been joyous. I was reminded of that this year rereading letters from my mother, who died in 1950, filled as they were with laughter, memories, and gentle advice. It was like a warm, long visit with her. I know I will see her again. My brother Tommy wrote the words on her tombstone:

> She was the best evidence of an almighty, loving spirit, for nothing else could have created her.

As usual, Tommy hit the mark. Her letters of encouragement, family news, humor, and admonitions to "see the brighter side of life" are a reminder of how wonderful she was. I hope my life has the impact on my children that hers did on me.

Tommy is a superb tombstone writer. He composed my father's, also, in tune with the business he spent so much of his life doing—building roads.

> *Full heart, swift hand,*
> *Long road, high land.*

Tommy has composed an epitaph for me, too: "Some gal." I'm not sure about that. I feel like Laertes at Ophelia's grave, asking the priest: "Must there no more be done?"

WHEN I LIFTED the curtain that I had pulled down after Les's death in 1974 and allowed myself to think about him, and us, I was overwhelmed by a rushing torrent of affection, a confirmation of how good was our love and our life together, especially the planning and joy of our family. My children and grandchildren need to know our love created them. They need to remember occasionally how much they were wanted and how life for us would have been so much less without them.

I wrote Les's tombstone myself because I think epitaphs must contain more than facts. I want to know the kind of person who rests there, and I am not all that interested in the statistics.

What seemed appropriate for Les, a reporter, a marvelous gardener, and loving husband and father, was:

> *Everything grew in his garden,*
> *His family with his love,*
> *His readers with his words.*

I really don't know where—or if—I want to be buried. Given the choice, I'd prefer to be bronzed and seated in my Jacuzzi to spout water like a glorious fountain over the city. There are so many rules these days, it's hard to die according to one's choice. But my ashes could be mixed into the molten metal, and I could serve a good purpose in death. (Note to whoever handles these arrangements: If you *do* bronze me, be sure I am clothed or at least draped in something attractive—and smiling, too—and I don't mind a few pounds being left off, for the sake of economy as well as beauty.)

Actually, I wouldn't mind being located down on the hike and bike trail near Cactus Pryor's bench. Cactus, Texas's famed humorist, is still thriving, but a few years ago the Headliners Club wanted to honor him with a big dinner. I talked them out of giving him the customary bronze plaque and into substituting a park bench down by the river. We did it up right, planting cactuses around it and calling it "the Cactus Patch" with a small inscription on a nearby rock: "To Cactus Pryor, who has given laughter to this town for more than thirty years." I wouldn't mind sitting nearby in a fountain, and I don't mind being a deer if they would prefer that.

RECOLLECTIONS FROM the letters and scrapbooks, baby pictures, boxes, and albums are often painful because those times are over, gone from life to the memory bank. Life rushed by, sweeping away the days and the moments much too quickly. Recalling them gave me the warmth of love again and made me more willing to accept the next home and experience that my faith has always told me existed. I hope my life passes muster.

Why do the traumas of life—the wrenching moments—surface so often, years after they have passed? I still get chills thinking of that day in Dallas—November 22, 1963. I was part of that motorcade. I agonized through the hours as we waited at Parkland Hospital. After Kennedy's death was announced, we raced across Dallas in a police car, only vaguely aware that while we had come with the vice-president, we were returning to Washington with the president. LBJ would have to say something to the nation on arrival in Washington. I was one of the few writers on hand. In my purse were some gold-edged cards with small embossed birds I had carried to have handy for Lady Bird for autographing. It was all I had, and on one card, I scrawled the most important piece of prose I ever wrote—the fifty-eight words LBJ used a few hours later when Air Force One arrived at Andrews Air Force Base: "This is a sad time for all people. We have suffered a loss that cannot be weighed. For me, it is a deep personal tragedy. I know that the world shares the sorrow that Mrs. Kennedy and her family bear. I will do my best. That is all I can do. I ask for your help—and God's." How did those words come in that awful moment, words I truly believe were handed to me by an unseen hand? But they came. And they were right. Most of us aboard the plane walked about as in a trance. Bill Moyers tells me that LBJ looked at me and said, "Write something for me to say, Liz." LBJ and I had both anticipated what was needed.

I went back to my seat and printed the words out on another card from the barely legible scrawl on the one in my purse, then handed them to Bill. Either he or the president changed the order of two words. I had written "God's help and yours," and one of them changed it.

I still remember the ride home, so silent, so tension-filled, everyone trying to do the right thing under such dreadful circumstances. The president was sworn in. I backed into the plane's cabin, having no desire to crowd up front, ashamed of my country, ashamed of Dallas. I remember having arranged it so the White House photographer, Cecil Stoughton, could take the historic picture. Like me, like so many on that plane, he moved automatically to do what his job required him to do.

"He isn't going to like this," Cecil said to me quietly, nodding toward LBJ, "but if there is a swearing-in on this plane, it is my job to photograph it for history."

I went to LBJ. He nodded, and the photograph was taken. It seemed that we were there so suddenly, on a new stage, in a new role, and, finally, in the helicopter on the way to the White House lawn that November night.

"Stay with Lady Bird and help her all you can," LBJ said. He went into session with the cabinet and congressional leaders he had summoned by phone from the plane. Lady Bird and I rode in the vice-presidential limousine to their home in Spring Valley, a dozen blocks from my own Woodway Lane house. A million thoughts raced through my mind. Both of us were well aware of the difficult days ahead—made even more difficult because this tragedy had occurred in our home state. Finally, in the silence of the limousine, we talked.

"It seems a terrible thing to say, but the salvation of Texas is that the governor was hit," I said.

She replied: "Don't think I haven't thought of that. I only wish it could have been me."

It did not occur to me then, though I think of it now as I look back on the span of presidents from FDR to JFK, but we live every moment with uncertainty when a single second can change everything: our role, our country. One person can make a difference.

These are lessons to which our ancestors—the "ancients" in this relatively young America—speak.

I COME FROM A long line of strong women and men of democratic values. Did I, in some unseen way, "remember who I was" that day in Dallas? Draw on strengths never before tested? Have I, in my public life of commitment to causes—many of them difficult—been speaking not only for me, but echoing the voices of my legacy? Have they spoken to me in the dozen or so times in my life when tests of strength were before me?

I read an old obituary of my great-grandfather: "He entered

the political arena with all the enthusiasm of his nature and stood up for the rights of the people against every form of opposition . . . yielding in his demand for the largest liberty to the citizen consistent to laws for the general good." Aunt Birdie was described as "one of the best women orators in the state." Aunt Luella was a leader for education reform. Perhaps it is in the genes.

I am trying honestly to appraise what I have been, the bad along with the good. I find I was always more confident than I remembered, arrogant at times, pushing forward too much to the next deadline. I see no gaps in the whole sixty-six years. I like it that way. I was a better daughter than I remembered in the flush of guilt at the times of my parents' death. I shared my life with them while I was away. My letter-writing mother and I were good companions, at home with one another on paper. It is deeply comforting to me to rediscover this.

But I also find a Machiavellian streak in myself, exaggerated, perhaps, by the natural fervor of youth and that Machiavellian city, Washington. Through the letters I see in myself a tendency to herd people to my way, using my enthusiasm to persuade them to come to Washington and relish it as I did. I reached out, urged, argued, rallied, nurtured, loved, influenced, and sometimes shoved and overpowered.

This is not your all-purpose good person, but I never yearned to be Pollyanna. My brother says I am a "stomach" person, not a "skin" person. I make the mistake of thinking everyone else is like me—open, energetic, outgoing, needful of action and people. I organize for myself and others. I give praise, and I need praise. Praise energizes me.

I discovered that this is an American trait during my first trip through Europe. I kept asking, because it always seemed to be part of the story, "Do you like America?"

A Dutch reporter turned on me abruptly. "Why is it so important to be liked?" he asked.

I do want to be liked. Like America, I probably try to cloak my friends in my own garments of emotion.

Life has taught me that my ultimate house—hopefully, heaven, the hereafter, the final stop—must have certain ingredients: warmth, love, affection, growth, and work. I need these things. Work is not normally what we think of as heaven, but I think it would be empty without it. I don't want to just sit around on a throne. I want to flap my wings and continue to fly, to be used. I hope my heaven isn't too restful.

Heaven has been very much on my mind and in my conversations lately, as I've approached the winding up of these reflections. Always the reporter, I've interviewed everyone, called up old friends, and asked strangers at parties what they think heaven is like. Everyone has some idea. Actually, there's more thinking about this matter going on than I had imagined.

My friend Erma Bombeck was at the head of my list. I know she'll go to heaven, and I knew she wouldn't laugh at my question. When I called, I found her at her typewriter, polishing off her first play. Her desk is virtually sitting in heaven, in an orderly room with a spectacular view on top of one of the Paradise Mountains near Scottsdale, Arizona. She can gaze into the valley below and across the rugged terrain of desert plants for miles and miles. Next to her office is a large kitchen, a dream kitchen, where Erma reigns supreme, cooking for returning children and visiting friends. The girl who started out writing obituaries on the Dayton, Ohio, paper, and has brought so much laughter to the world through her down-to-earth motherliness, deserves the beautiful place she has built where she writes her daily syndicated column.

"What does heaven look like?" she repeated. "I am almost childlike in my attitude about heaven. I see it as a place where there are billowing clouds, where you walk through a sort of Who's Who. There is Mozart, who died at about thirty-three, playing the greatest music he's ever played. We are all thirty-three years old. At least, that's how I feel, and in heaven we expand on what's been our life. I'm going to be funnier than I've ever been. We are going to be on a roll, productive. Yes, ERA will be ratified."

I got another gem breakfasting with Diane Sawyer, who had

once asked the same question of our mutual friend, Art Buchwald. "Art says he doesn't know what heaven looks like, but he wants the room with the best view."

James Beard, the late gourmet cook and culinary author, told me he didn't care what his view was like, but he wanted room service with caviar and toast—'very, very good toast. . . .' "

While I was in New York, I ran into one of my favorite people, Shana Alexander, who has spent much of her time recently trying to get Jean Harris out of jail. Jean, imprisoned for the fatal shooting of the creator of the Scarsdale diet, is the former headmistress of Madeira School and has used her time in prison to form a day school for the children of prisoners. It was difficult for me, knowing Shana's compassion for all life, to believe she meant what she said about death and heaven.

"You must remember, I grew up in a family of agnostics and atheists, so I feel that an afterlife is not necessary or real. When the time comes, a light bulb switches off." That philosophy seemed unsatisfying to me, and I asked Shana if she were content with it. "No," she replied, "I'm not, but I seem to be stuck with it. I wouldn't mind being converted."

I searched out my friend, Ernie Cuneo, living now with diabetes, which has resulted in the amputation of one leg. Discouraged? Not a bit. He has a cart and whisks himself around Washington to champagne lunches.

The last time I had such a lunch with Ernie, ever the lawyer, he said, "I want to meet my Maker face to face, if only to start cross-examining him."

"Since you are exploring heaven and death," Ernie said, "ask yourself, Liz, Why life itself?

"Think on what wise people have said, like Mark Twain: 'Whoever has lived long enough to find out what life is, knows how deep a debt of gratitude we owe to Adam, the first great benefactor of our race. He brought death into the world.' Or, if you prefer Browning: 'Ah, but a man's reach should exceed his grasp, Or what's a heaven for?' " Ernie is a rotund living volume of Bartlett's quotations. When his daughter was in college, she had the advantage of simply calling Daddy long distance instead of looking things up.

At a recent dinner party I was seated next to my favorite Rockefeller, Laurance, who had just given a commencement address at Princeton. Not content with the various drafts written by his staff, he finally wrote his own speech. "There is a line I am pretty proud of," he said. "I think it's good advice to graduates because it seems to say it all: 'Consider the sailors at sea, who are undismayed by the fact that they never reach the stars by which they sail.' " He wrote it down for me, slowly, tediously, on the back of his place card. I brought it home and put it on the mirror to read each day.

ELISABETH KÜBLER-ROSS came to Salado, of all places, for our country think tank to talk about life, death, and transition. I wangled an hour with her to explore this mind-boggling subject to which she had devoted her life, won prizes, and organized a worldwide networking system to help people live through illness, grief, and loss. Quiet, totally unadorned by makeup, jewelry, or fancy clothes, she preaches unconditional love. In her Shenandoah Valley Kübler-Ross Center, she urges people to view life as a series of challenging experiences from birth through death, rather than as a threatening and painful ordeal.

Death, she said, is a human experience identical with birth in that all human beings are born basically the same way and have to go through the same tunnel to come to the light. Once you know that death is not the end, but a transformation into a different form of life, you create the transition within your own psychic energy, something that's culturally determined. It can be a gate or a bridge or a tunnel. But behind this tunnel is an incredible light. In the near death experience, you can see a glimpse of that light. This is the spiritual energy and comes from God, and the closer you get to it, the more you are literally wrapped in love and peace. This is the silver lining.

"If you have had a glimpse of this light," she continued with the assurance that thousands of testimonies have given her, "it's absolutely and utterly impossible to be afraid of death."

We are beginning to hear more and more about near death experiences, the light and the tunnel, the return. Perhaps there are more people willing to talk about them. My brother George, lying in his hospital bed after having undergone a serious operation, had such an experience.

"I was absolutely awake," he said. "It was no dream, and I heard voices which sounded like they were coming from the hall. As I listened, I knew they were the voices of people praying for me. I felt I was in heaven, and suddenly there was such an overpowering sense of well-being in me that I knew it was God. Even though it was the middle of the night, I simply couldn't keep that experience to myself and I woke up Jean, who was sleeping on a cot near me."

George will never be afraid of dying.

One of the delights of my life has been to know Mari and James Michener during their time in Austin while he was writing his book about Texas. He is an easy man to know, and we have come to appreciate sharing book anxieties and just generally philosophizing during our joint efforts to get a writers' center going at the University of Texas. Jim, now seventy-nine, recently underwent bypass surgery. He has been a good person with whom to discuss religion and the future of life. He is poetic about it. He doesn't dwell on finding answers about the future because he decided at age nineteen he was never going to know any answers. But he has had some remarkable experiences.

"If I were a theologian, I would probably consider them signs," he told me. "I have come close to death five times or, more accurately, been spared death after very close calls. There were three air crashes. Then once, I was in a Saigon hotel room when revolutionaries broke in, brandishing guns. I quickly said, pointing to my typewriter, 'Press, Press.' They left. I also had a heart attack about as major as a person can have and survive.

"I remember a midnight in New Caledonia in the South Pacific. I saw my life with absolute clarity. I was walking down an airfield soon after my team had all died in a crash. I was left to wonder, For what reason was I spared? In that moment, alone, it was absolutely clear to me that I wasn't going to fool around anymore. I was going to behave in a certain way. I was going to do things a certain way. It was as clear as if it had been printed out on a TelePrompter. In the old pattern, you would say someone had spoken to me, but no one had. Or God had appeared to me. He didn't. I didn't see anything, but it was the turning point. After that I began getting serious about my life, and I began writing.

"I try to live like a Christian. I contribute to churches. I think they do very useful work. Theology I have no interest in, though I am a close friend of many theologians and a personal friend of the pope, who sends me messages from time to time. I am not an atheist. I just don't know the answers, and I have no interest in spending time seeking them."

ON A TRIP with Lady Bird to Mayo Brothers in Rochester, Minnesota, I spent a long time with Dr. James Cain, consultant emeritus and a man who has witnessed life and death as closely as anyone I know for forty years. He is now in his seventies. We talked at length about health and what I might expect at the time of death. It was a marvelous talk with a wise man about how to live and how to die.

"How can I die with the right attitude, a happy attitude, when that time comes? How can it be pleasant for me and easier on those around me?" I asked him directly.

"To me, death is one of the most exciting things you can think of," he answered. "I do have great faith. I am deeply religious, so I don't know what my answer would be if I were not.

"Most people, right before they die, are not worried. It's the family that worries. I have been impressed with something I have noticed about death: most patients do not have a painful death. I don't care what it is they are dying of. The good Lord prepares them. They are unconscious. The brain is not feeling the things that are going on. I am really quite convinced of that. There is a sort of built-in anesthetic. There is some medical evidence to support this view.

"I don't know what's out there. It's going to be unknown. Unknown to me is exciting. I know there is going to be an opportunity to find out how this world was created. I'll find the answers to some of the questions I've had about medicine. You, Liz, will go on asking questions and writing. Many things will become very clear."

One of the most down-to-earth people I know is Barbara Jordan, eloquent in expressing simple basics. She did just that when we discussed whether or not her personal code of religion allowed a hereafter.

"I believe, Liz, that I have a spirit that is not going to disappear. My body will die and disintegrate, but there is the basic law of physics, that matter is neither created nor destroyed. Now the skin and bones will go back to dust, but the spirit of that individual, the presence or 'is-ness' of me, will live. In what state, in what sense, I don't know. I haven't died yet. But I do believe that those of us who have lived well and tried to do things in a Christian and thoughtful and loving way will have a constructive role for that spirit, which will remain after the flesh is gone."

In my family are a hundred stories of faith and, yes, that awkward word for most of us, salvation. I find myself thinking of them now.

One ancestor was John Rogers, the first Protestant martyr of England, burned at the stake in 1555 because he refused to recant his newfound faith. At family reunions we often read his history. At the time of death he reached out his hands to the fire to prove to his followers that his faith was deep. A descendant of his, John Rogers, was fifth president of Harvard College. They lived up to the Rogers family motto: "We and Ours to God."

They must have had a profound effect on those of their descendants who lived on the frontier of Texas in the 1800s. My great-grandfather Samuel A. Rogers, who lived from 1810 to

1891 and wrote his recollections not too long before his death, bemoaned that "the fond associates of my early life have all crossed the River. Oh, a loneliness I hope none else will feel, and oh, how sad would I feel if it were not for the hope of meeting them again in a better world."

Isn't hope what makes the thought of death bearable? How else would life have meaning?

That faith was reflected again in my grandmother's life. Lizzie Laura Rogers Sutherland sensed something spiritual about her five-year-old son, George. In a letter of condolence written to Bell in 1896 on the death of their other sister, she wrote:

> I had read the telegram aloud to the family. Georgie said, "Mama, what is the matter?" I said, "Georgie, Aunt Frankie is dead and we will never see her again in this world." He replied, "But, Mama, we will see her in Heaven."
>
> Georgie is a strange child. I don't think he would care if he should die. Very often in having prayers in the mornings, I talk to them about the Bible and the precious promises therein and he remarked to me the other morning, "Mama, why don't God take us to Heaven? We have been here long enough." Then, he added, "Whenever I am bad, you read me that Book," meaning the Bible, and he told me he loved Jesus.

Young George didn't wait long. While he was riding horseback in 1904 to a July Fourth celebration, his horse suddenly shied as he raced it along a path, causing him to strike his head against a tree. He died instantly.

He was buried right away, for there were no funeral parlors or embalming procedures in faraway Nueces Canyon. My grandmother sat on the porch of their ranch house and rocked and sang hymns of faith for three days.

I HAVE NEVER BEEN with anyone at the moment of death, but I was with Uncle John a few days before he died at a hospital in San Marcos. He had studied to be a teacher there in that small

Texas town. He spent his long life as a principal and then as superintendent of schools for fifty years in so many small towns in Texas that a list of them looks like a bus timetable: Vernon, Texas City, Anderson, Rockport, Gonzales, Floresville.

He exited from this world as spirited and mellow as he lived his life, reciting Latin and quoting poetry.

A few nights before he died, the nurse found him awake at two A.M. "What are you doing?" she asked.

Cheerfully, he replied, "Why, I'm conjugating Latin verbs and declining Latin nouns."

At the hospital where I went to see him, he was a combination Father Time and Mr. Chips lying there with a crocheted brown cap to keep the air conditioning off his bald head.

He greeted me with a smile and kiss. "This morning I've been quoting Portia's famous plea for justice," he said, and I asked him to quote it to me.

In an unhesitating voice, he proceeded, in prayerlike cadence:

> *The quality of mercy is not strain'd,*
> *It droppeth as the gentle rain from heaven*
> *Upon the place beneath: it is twice bless'd;*
> *It blesseth him that gives and him that takes....*

A few days later we laid him to rest on the live oak-shaded hillside in San Marcos near the college where he and so many other early Texans collected their knowledge and went forth to teach among the schoolchildren of Texas. He left no children, except for the thousands he had taught to respect Latin verbs, nouns, and root stems, along with the words of immortal English poets.

Ruth Gordon died this year in her sleep; she was eighty-eight. I read her lengthy and joyful obituary with the memory of how I had last seen her, walking into a living room at Martha's Vineyard with her husband, Garson Kanin. She sailed into the room, took center stage, and never relinquished it. It was the way she had always lived, bursting with enthusiasm. *The New York*

Times said, "Miss Gordon was known as a woman of fearsome will and an insatiable hunger for new things."

When she made her Broadway debut in 1915, she got withering reviews. Heywood Broun, a top New York critic, said: "Anyone who looks like that and acts like that must get off the stage."

Ruth got the last laugh. She not only outlived him, she outdid him and won stardom. At age seventy-two, she won an Oscar. Her philosophy, as stated in her book, *My Side*, was, "Pan me, don't give me the part, publish everybody's book but this one, and I will still make it! Why? Because I believe I will. If you believe, it means you've got imagination. You don't need stuff thrown out for you in a blueprint. You don't face facts. What can stop you? If I don't make it today, I'll come in tomorrow."

IS IT POSSIBLE to live as well and die as peacefully as my uncle John, Ruth Gordon, Alben Barkley, and others whose stories we hear about and think about more as we approach death?

I have come to think of the hereafter as the last and ultimate home, where we become part of a universal soul and understand all we have striven to know before. This move requires no packing. We leave all the baggage behind. Now it is you and your inner home, the accumulation of love, knowledge, and wisdom that your earthly life has brought you and which you have shared. And you have reached the ultimate destination.

I was a lover of hymns as a child, and I learned the words of so many from the Cokesbury hymnal. I am struck by how many refer to heaven as home: "Jesus Is Tenderly Calling Me Home," "The Way of the Cross Leads Home." And consider these lines from the familiar "Amazing Grace": "Through many dangers, toils and snares, I have already come; 'Tis grace hath brought me safe thus far, And grace will lead me home."

I hope for a place of singing and laughter in a circle of all those I've loved who have gone before me. I hope there will be plenty of things left to do. It will be hard for someone like me just to lie around on billowing clouds, shining up my halo and preening my wings. I want to keep on learning and being part of things, entering the minds of those I've left behind with an answer, some guidance, or a kiss when they need it. I have experienced that comfort from heaven in my earthly homes—a warm, gentle touch, soft as an angel's wing, that brings with it a welcome feeling of well-being, a new thought, an expanded creativity, understanding the answer to the ever-present questions: Why am I here? What *do* I mean in the infinite scheme of things?

There is something healing about this confrontation with death. I don't dread it. I don't hurry it. I am confident there are many mansions, new doors in life's eternal quest for spiritual development, for everlasting love. If the mission of life is to become more like God, then on this planet we have only just begun. I want to continue to work and grow as the rest of my days unfold. Then, I would like to die as day ends, spent, used up, having given all I have to give to this earth. At home on my hill, I will reach for the evening star with joy in my heart . . . ready for the next adventure.

BUT NOT YET, not yet. . . . I took a look at my calendar for 1987, and I don't have *time* to die. I'm booked up. I have even greedily signed a contract for a speech in 1988 in Oklahoma where one thousand people want to pay me $5,000 to tell them about life. Such speaking fees send my brothers into gales of laughter. They can't believe anyone would pay me to talk since they've been listening free all their lives.

I recently joined a nearby fitness center; the membership is good for twenty-five years, and I hope I am, too. The fitness center is five minutes from my house. Why haven't I been taking advantage of it before? Damn. I wouldn't have gotten so stiff in the joints while I sat here all year with my Big Mac word processor. A new friend told me about it and took me to see it for myself. I go before daylight at six-thirty A.M., driving through the dark in my red exercise suit with the Mighty Mouse T-shirt my grandson bought me at Disneyland. This is an hour when you can think no one else is awake. You open the fitness center door, and bam!

there's a whole roomful of men and women of all shapes and sizes on treadmills, bicycles, exercise mats, or stretch machines. I haven't heard so much heavy breathing since I was a bride. A whole roomful of men and a lot of shapely females with all their makeup on were using these machines. Five days after I joined, I felt better and more energized. I also discovered that I can reward myself after exercise class with a "smoothie" (a delightful blend of fruit juices) or coffee. I sit and read the paper and let someone else make *me* coffee.

I have Christmas in New York all planned with my children and *grandchildren*. I've already ordered tickets for the *Nutcracker* ballet and two plays. Next spring I promised my grandson I would be there for Grandparents' Day at his school. I wrote it in red ink. April 27, Seattle, Bush School with Les. I can't miss that. My granddaughter is dating now, and I want to meet her beau. Forgive me, Bonnie, I mean your friend. "People don't say beau anymore," she tells me.

I have another project under way, helping line up Carol Channing, Liz Smith, Nora Ephron, Florence King, and Fannie Flagg for a Conference on Funny Women. They have said they will come in March, and we will provide an audience of students to learn how to write and perform humor. I love putting things like this together, and this one promises to be delightfully wacky.

By that time, the elections will be heating up. Texas State Treasurer Ann Richards may be running for something like governor. Lawyer Sarah Weddington, former assistant to President Carter, ought to jump in and run if there is a vacancy worthy of her. In order to see more good women in politics, I will help with contacts and occasional checks. This may be dreaming, but maybe, in the two-hundredth-anniversary year of our U.S. Constitution, we can celebrate by putting women in it—the Equal Rights Amendment. What a way for the country to celebrate! It just might play. Politicians do change their minds. I can keep reminding them, writing them letters, speaking out publicly, needling them, and shaming them into this long overdue action.

The Bay at the Moon Society wants to help me sell my book. They say we can rent a camper, paint it up with the name of the book, and put on an Indian medicine–type show, singing and selling in the towns that don't have bookstores. We'll sell it right off the back end, like a whistlestop. It would be hilarious!

Last night I produced a party that was sheer magic, and I want to keep doing that for special occasions. Bill Moyers came down to get the Distinguished Alumnus Award from the University of Texas. I've known him since he was a student journalist visiting Washington. In fact, I took him to his first White House press conference when Ike was president. For my party, I sent out invitations to forty-five people we both knew "to come and sing about it." And I went all out—pale blue tablecloths, big bright coral-colored daisies, lots of candles, tables of eight. And a special menu, which we put on a sign board labeled Soul Food à la Marshall in Honor of Bill's East Texas Hometown. People were delighted to get something new in party fare. The Jacuzzi was converted into Caddo Lake, and I attached a fishing pole to one side and hooked on it a silver fish I had bought long ago at a souvenir shop in Greece. It was also the perfect place to cook appetizers of fried-catfish morsels. We followed with filet of pork, baked yams, mustard greens, Texas caviar (which is really pickled black-eyed peas), cornbread muffins, and lots of sliced tomatoes.

The weather was with us—an Indian-summer sky and a big, round full moon out there, hanging like a proud banner over the main building of the university. Bill's university. My university. We've both traveled lots of miles since we left it. Bill was just back from the near miss summit meeting between President Reagan and Soviet leader Gorbachev in Iceland. Bill was on my right, and on my left I put Admiral Bob Inman, who knows the inside as only a respected intelligence man can. With dessert—Texas pecan tassies—I called on Bill and Admiral Inman to analyze the Iceland meeting. It was both chilling and thrilling to hear about it from experts. We listened spellbound to Bill's perceptive word pictures of the meeting, what took place and what didn't, the meeting's disappointments, the danger of closing any dialogue about arms control. That was the chilling part. But it was also thrilling to know that right here at my home in Austin we were listening to real firsthand experts on such a vital issue.

We also sang—and my kingdom, what voices! Maybe the discussion revitalized us, maybe it was because I had printed out the words to the songs in large type so we could all read them, maybe it was because Barbara Jordan, with her strong, commanding voice, led us in singing, often "lining" out the words in the old-fashioned way we used to do in church. As much as my old piano has wrung out voices, last night topped them all. We were "bringing in the sheaves" and finding "that old-time religion" and "marching in with the saints" all evening. Barbara even did a solo of that marvelous throaty blues number "Nobody Knows You When You're Down and Out" and, for an encore, "I Went Down to the St. James Infirmary." Fantastic!

This morning the phone rang off the hook. Everyone was thanking me for such a special evening. Well, if I can spend a little money and imagination and give people that much pleasure, as well as mental stimulation, I ought to keep doing it. Interesting people are coming through Austin all the time, old friends and new ones who should be honored for this and that. Besides, it gives me pleasure to plan a party and play off my imagination producing it.

Yes, dear children of mine. I *am* spending your inheritance, but I worked for it and I want to enjoy it. The door's open. The beds are made. Come on down and sing along with Mom any time you can. There isn't anyone I'd rather have at my house than you. I would give up anything to have that happen—except my independence. So life goes on, and this old girl and this old world just keep on turning.

I want to stay spirited, just like the lady at my party. She used to be dean of women when I was in school, and she knew Bill and his wife, Judith. When she arrived, she looked so frail, I found myself saying, "May I get you a glass of orange juice, Dorothy?"

She smiled at me and said, "Do you have anything stronger?"

I could have bitten my tongue for such a put-down. So of course I rallied her a Scotch and water. "I'm only ninety-three," she told me.

"You'll live to be a hundred," I returned.

"Yes," she said matter-of-factly, "I think I might."

Well, I may, too.

I savor moments like these, being with friends who have loved you sometimes in spite of yourself. And I want more of these times.

I guess what I want to say to you, God, is frankly, at this time, I've got a lot of things going. I'm busy and you're busy, so if it's all the same to you, I'll take a raincheck. But I want you to know that, as a result of this book and this year, I feel closer to you. I feel closer to your good earth, the glory of the fall leaves, the majesty of the ocean, the bursting of life all around me. Down the trail sometime I look forward to meeting you face to face. But I wouldn't want you to rush into anything.